Prt 1080

W9-BCR-638

TWAYNE'S WORLD AUTHORS SERIES

A Survey of the World's Literature

CHINA

William R. Schultz, University of Arizona

EDITOR

Kuan Yün–Shih

TWAS 562

Calligraphy of Hsiao-yün-shih Khaya

KUAN YÜN-SHIH

By RICHARD JOHN LYNN

Macquarie University,
Sydney, Australia

TWAYNE PUBLISHERS
A DIVISION OF G.K. HALL & CO., BOSTON

895.1
K95L
1980

Published in 1980 by Twayne Publishers,
A Division of G. K. Hall & Co.
All Rights Reserved

Printed on permanent/durable acid-free paper and bound
in the United States of America

First Printing

Library of Congress Cataloging in Publication Data

Lynn, Richard John.
Kuan Yün–Shih.

(Twayne's world authors series ; TWAS 562 : China)
Bibliography: p. 223–225
Includes index.
1. Kuan,Yün–Shih, 1286–1324.
2. Poets, Chinese—
Biography. I. Title
PL2694.K783Z78   895.1'1'4   79-21767
ISBN 0-8057-6404-6

For Anne and Joseph

Contents

About the Author

Born in Binghamton, New York, Richard John Lynn received his B.A. in Art and Archaeology at Princeton University, where he also began his study of Chinese. His M.A. in Chinese was completed at the University of Washington, and his work for the Ph.D. was undertaken at the University of Chicago, Stanford University and the Humanistic Sciences Research Center of Kyōto University; it was awarded in 1971 at Stanford. He held a Foreign Area Fellowship for doctoral research in Taiwan and Japan during 1968–69.

Mr. Lynn has taught Chinese Language and Literature at the University of Auckland in New Zealand during 1970–72, Chinese Language and Comparative Literature at the University of Massachusetts, Amherst, during 1972–75 and at Indiana University during 1975–77. He has also been a visiting Assistant Professor of Chinese History at Mount Holyoke College in 1974 and has taught Chinese as a visiting faculty member at Stanford during the summers of 1975–77. Currently he is Senior Lecturer and Head, Department of Chinese, at Macquarie University, Sydney, Australia.

Mr. Lynn's articles and reviews have appeared in *Literature East and West, The Unfolding of Neo-Confucianism*, W.T. de Bary, ed. (New York, 1975), *Harvard Journal of Asiatic Studies, Journal of Asian Studies, Journal of Asian History, Journal of Oriental Studies, T'oung Pao, Papers on Far Eastern History*, and *Journal of the Chinese Language Teachers Association*. He is also a contributor to *Sunflower Splendor: Three Thousand Years of Chinese Poetry*, Wu-chi Liu and Irving Yucheng Lo, ed. (New York, 1975).

Preface

This is a study of one of the major literary figures of the period of Mongol rule in China, the Yüan dynasty (1260–1368). During his own day, the sinicized Uighur Kuan Yün-shih (1286–1324) enjoyed the highest of reputations as a writer of both classical verse and prose (*shih-wen*) and the new popular form of lyric poetry, the *san-ch'ü*. Later ages have tended to ignore Kuan's accomplishments in classical letters, but his fame as a writer of lyrics has persisted throughout the rest of the traditional era and into modern times. Although the *san-ch'ü* as a genre is usually grouped with Yüan drama (*tsa-chü*), with whose lyrics it shares a common prosody, and with vernacular fiction (*pai-hua hsiao-shuo*) as a "popular" form of literature, it nevertheless retained close links with the grand tradition of "polite letters" and with literati culture in general. The sharp distinction made in many modern studies between so-called "popular" and so-called "elite" culture and literature in traditional China is in many respects a misleading oversimplification, since there were many individuals in later imperial China who seem to have moved freely between the two. Kuan was such a figure. Because of the antitraditional polemics of May Fourth reformers and their heirs and Marxist revolutionaries alike, the role of the literati in the development of popular literature during the Yüan, Ming, and the Ch'ing has been underplayed if not ignored in modern studies by native Chinese literary historians, whose views have tended to shape the way Japanese and Western scholars have looked at the subject. The time has come to take a new look at the later imperial era, to cast the polemics aside, and to try to determine the actual role the literati played in the development of popular lyrics, drama, and fiction. This present study, with all its shortcomings, should be regarded in part as just such an undertaking, at least as far as the lyric is concerned.

However, the continuing tradition of classical verse and prose during the later imperial era is not regarded here as a mere context or backdrop for developments in the popular genres. Readings in classical verse (*shih*) and in poetry criticism (*shih-hua*) of the Yüan, Ming, and the Ch'ing have convinced me that there is a great deal of intrinsic literary value here which deserves to be brought to light for its own sake, in spite of the general tendency of modern scholarship to ignore or belittle this area of Chinese literary history. In consequence, a major portion of this study is devoted to an overall consideration of the *shih* poetry of the Yüan and to the criticism of Kuan's own classical verse. Those who are not familiar with post-Sung *shih* poetry may be pleasantly surprised by some of the things which are presented in these parts of the book.

Kuan is an interesting and remarkable figure. The original plan of this work was merely to provide brief sketches of his biography and the times in which he lived and to concentrate on a strictly literary study of his *shih* and *san-ch'ü*, but, impressed by the contributions a full biographical treatment might have for general historical perspectives on the Yüan, I decided to try to unearth every fact and hint of fact concerning Kuan's life that the sources might contain. Although Kuan was not a figure of major political or intellectual consequence, he was still close enough to the center of trends and events in both these areas to be representative, in several important ways, of the values and the sensibilities of his age. Therefore, the chapter concerned with Kuan's biography should prove of some interest to students of Yüan society, government, and intellectual history, as well as serving as the background for the verse and the lyrics presented in the later chapters.

Kuan's lyrics, like those of all Yüan authors of the genre, exist now in a critical edition in the *Ch'üan Yüan san-ch'ü* (Complete Lyrics of the Yüan). This meticulous collection lists all extant sources of, and all known textual variants for, the lyrics recorded. In addition, problems of authorial attribution are thoroughly treated, and so the section devoted to Kuan's *san-ch'ü* is the source for my translations. The order of the translations follows that of the originals in the *Ch'üan Yüan san-ch'ü*, and, except in a very few instances, follows Sui's critical version of the texts; when variant readings are preferred, this will be indicated in my notes to the lyrics involved.

No such critical edition of Kuan's *shih* exists. His collected *shih-wen*, the *Suan-chai shih-wen* or *Suan-chai wen-chi*, was never printed and is now apparently lost. The largest selection ever made of Kuan's classical verse is that done by Ku Ssu-li and published in Ku's *Yüan-shih hsüan* (An Anthology of Yüan Verse) in 1702. Ku's selection, however, fails to list many variants and in at least two instances has wrongly attributed *shih* to Kuan. Examples of Kuan's *shih* have been discovered in fourteen other anthologies (eleven of which predate the *Yüan-shih hsüan*) and in several other kinds of sources, such as *pi-chi* ("notebooks" or "jottings") and inscriptions on stone. My original intent in trying to track down Kuan's verse in these other sources was to determine all known textual variants and to find more examples. Although only two additional *shih* have turned up, other things emerged which shed light on the nature of Kuan's lost works. These finds and the speculations which they seem to allow us to make are presented at the end of Chapter Three—after the translations of Kuan's *shih* as they appear in the *Yüan-shih hsüan*—as well as a Finding List of all known occurrences of the *shih* in the anthologies. Integral translations of the five principal documents that were used in the preparation of Kuan's biography are appended to the end of Chapter One. Presenting them in this way is convenient for the citation of sources.

In this study, "poem," "poetry," and "verse" refer to *shih* poetry, and "lyric" and "song" refer to *san-ch'ü*. For the lyrics, except for occasionally isolating *ch'en-tzu* (extrametrical syllables) which occur at the head of a line as a separate line in the translations, the punctuation of the texts in the *Ch'üan Yüan san-ch'ü* has been followed throughout. Translations of the lyrics follow the order as they appear in the *Ch'üan Yüan san-ch'ü*. The *hsiao-ling* (single songs) are numbered in Arabic numerals, and the *t'ao-shu* (song-sets) are numbered in Roman numerals with the individual songs numbered in Arabic numerals; VI.3, for example, is the third lyric in the sixth song-set. After the number of each lyric, I indicate to which musical mode the tune belongs. For single songs, this is followed by the name of the tune, the title of the lyric (if any), and the source by page number in the *Ch'üan Yüan san-ch'ü*. For song-sets, the name of the musical mode is followed by the title of the song-set (if any) and the source by page number. The names of the tunes to which the song-sets were written are given after the number of each individual lyric in the sets.

Except for the passages of vernacular exegesis in Kuan's *Hsiao-ching chih-chieh* (Classic of Filial Piety with a Vernacular Exegesis), I have translated every piece of writing that can be attributed to Kuan in the sources; I am reasonably confident that I have overlooked nothing in this respect. As for his *shih* and *san-ch'ü*, this study then presents his complete works as they exist today. Inevitably, some poems and lyrics have not easily lent themselves to translation, and some others are of lesser quality. Nevertheless, I feel that the benefits derived from translating all pieces far outweigh the disadvantages. Kuan's work is not so extensive that it cannot be accommodated easily in the space of a single monograph, and rather than attempt to present his work in terms of a selection which risks distorting some of his qualities and neglecting others, I have preferred to let the poems and lyrics speak for themselves.

RICHARD JOHN LYNN

Macquarie University, Sydney

Acknowledgments

This study began as a master's thesis at the University of Washington, Seattle, under the direction of Hellmut Wilhelm (1966). Vincent Y. C. Shih also provided criticism of the project at this stage. However, little progress was made after the completion of the thesis until 1971, when additional materials concerning Kuan were assembled and work, though still intermittent, began anew. The following friends and colleagues have criticized, corrected, and in countless other ways contributed to, the realization of the final version of this study; their kindly assistance is here acknowledged with gratitude: James J. Y. Liu, Herbert Franke, Frederick W. Mote, Donald Holzman, Hiraoka Takeo, Paul Y. M. Jiang, Liu Ts'un-yan, Cheng Ch'ing-mao, Alvin Cohen, K. T. Wu, Matsuda Shizue, Liu Wu-chi, William Schultz, Ch'iu K'ai-ming, George Potter, Yang Lien-sheng, and Patrick Hanan.

Several research grants which provided for the purchase of books and materials on microfilm essential for this study were made by the University of Auckland (New Zealand) during 1971–72, and the interlibrary loan service of this university and that of the Australian National University, Canberra, did much to further the progress of research at that time, as did the interlibrary loan service of the University of Massachusetts, Amherst, during 1972–75.

Yang Tsung-han, "Hsiao-Yün-Shih Khaya (1286–1324)," *MS* 9 (1944), pp. 92–100, has been a useful source of bibliography. Ch'en Yüan, *Yüan hsi-yü-jen hua-hua k'ao*, translated by Ch'ien Hsing-hai and L. C. Goodrich as *Western and Central Asians in China under the Mongols; Their Transformation into Chinese* (Los Angeles: University of California Press, 1966), contains many references to Kuan. As a compilation of materials and as a source of bibliography, this work has been very helpful. However, many passages of primary source material included in it have been abridged by Ch'en from the originals, and since the translations are based on these abridged versions, the work's usefulness is considerably diminished. I have therefore preferred to provide new translations, based on the original sources, for all the passages concerned. The massive index to names and terms in the *Yüan-shih* (History

KUAN YÜN-SHIN

of the Yüan Dynasty) prepared at Kyōto University, the *Genshi goi shūsei*, has proven to be an indispensable reference tool. Translating colloquial expressions which appear in the lyrics has been particularly troublesome, and while I have consulted all the available studies which attempt to gloss such expressions, I have found Chang Hsiang's *Shih tz'u ch'ü yü hui-shih* (A Glossary of Terms Found in *Shih, Tz'u,* and *Ch'ü,* Taipei, 1960) to be especially helpful.

Some of the material which appears in this study has appeared in the following publications: *Literature East and West* XVI, No. 3 (1974); *Sunflower Splendor: Three Thousand Years of Chinese Poetry,* Liu Wu-chi and Irving Lo, eds. (New York, 1975); Ronald C. Miao, ed., *Studies in Chinese Poetry and Poetics I* (Taipei, 1978); and *Papers on Far Eastern History* 18 (September, 1978). Permission from the editors concerned to reprint these materials in revised form is greatly appreciated.

Although this study owes much to those mentioned above, it goes without saying that only the author is responsible for the opinions expressed and for any errors of fact, translation, or judgment that may have been committed.

Chronology

Yellow Sea to the mouth of the Yangtze, then journeys up river to the Tung-t'ing Lake region, visiting scenic places and writing poetry. Apparently spends the rest of the year and the early part of the next in this area.

1318   Arrives in Hangchow, probably in late spring. After spending the summer in a retreat on Phoenix Mountain, decides to make his home there and purchases two residences—the main one at the foot of the mountain and a summer place, "Retreat Perched in the Clouds," at the summit. For the next six years devotes himself to a life of seclusion and self-cultivation punctuated by outings to the West Lake, Hangchow, and the surrounding area. Most extant lyrics date from this period.

1324   Dies at his residence outside Hangchow on May 30.

CHAPTER 1

Life

I *Family Background*

K UAN YÜN-SHIH was born in the twenty-third year of the Chih-yüan era (1286) of the Yüan dynasty, since it is recorded that he died at the age of thirty-nine *sui* (i.e., at the age of thirty-eight years) during the first year of the T'ai-ting era (1324).[1] His original Uighur name is rendered in the Chinese sources as Hsiao-yün shih hai-ya, which is the Turkish Sewinch Qaya (Joy/Thankfulness Cliff).[2] We know a great deal about his ancestry, which was most likely completely Uighur, and can trace his lineage back to his paternal great-grandparents and to his great-grandfather's grandfather on his mother's side. Kuan's paternal great-grandfather's name is rendered variously as Yeh-hsien-huo-che,[3] O-sen-ho-cho,[4] and A-san-ho-ch'e.[5] He was a native of Pei-t'ing,[6] which is identified with the city of Pieh-shih-pa (Beshbaliq). Beshbaliq (Five Towns) was situated to the northeast of present-day Urumchi, the capital of the Sinkiang Uighur Autonomous Region.[7] His paternal great-grandmother's name is rendered T'u-ch'in hu-tu-lu,[8] or Tu-chien hu-t'u-lu.[9] Nothing is known about her except that she had to give birth to Kuan's grandfather by Caesarian section and that she persuaded her husband to spare the child's life when he wanted to have it put to death, believing that such an unnatural delivery was a portent of misfortune.[10] This was in 1227. The child's name was A-li hai-ya, which is the Turkish Arigh Qaya (Pure Cliff), and he lived to his fifty-eighth year to die by his own hand in 1286, the very year in which Kuan himself was born.

Arigh Qaya was one of the most important historical figures of thirteenth-century China.[11] As a military leader and as a civil administrator, his contributions to the Mongol cause were enormous,

17

almost rivaling those of Po-yen (Bayan) (1227–1295), the great Mongol general who was in charge of the assault on the Southern Sung and who presided over its capitulation in 1276.[12] He is supposed to have tilled the fields as a young man, but, soon realizing the lack of opportunity in this, he turned to the study of Uighur writings and became a tutor to the son of a Uighur general, who then recommended him to Qubilai before Qubilai became Qaghan (Supreme Overlord) and emperor. Qubilai placed him in his personal guard, and his star began to rise, for he soon impressed his master with his skill with weapons and his bravery. His first major appointment came early after Qubilai's ascendency when he was made a *chung-shu-sheng lang-chung* (Bureau Director in the Central Chancellery), which meant that he was already in the upper ranks of the political and military leadership of the empire. His promotions came quickly, and we soon find him in the provinces of North China supervising the governments of the *lu* (circuits). Between 1268 and 1273, Arigh Qaya was one of the leaders of the siege of Hsiang-yang in Hupeh and was personally responsible for its surrender; he went to the foot of the city wall and persuaded the commander of the Sung defenders to accept terms.[13]

In 1274 he was appointed *yu ch'eng-hsiang* (Chief Administrator of the Right) of Ching-hu (later to be called Hu-kuang) Province and assisted the *ch'eng-hsiang* (Viceroy) of the province, Bayan. The "province" (which was to comprise Hupeh, Hunan, Kwangsi, and Kwangtung) did not yet exist since it still had to be wrested from Sung control. In October 1274 the armies assembled at Hsiang-yang, and the advance against the South began.[14] After the Mongol forces crossed the Yangtze, Bayan proceeded east toward Hangchow and the Southern Sung court, and Arigh Qaya secured the rear by subjugating the middle Yangtze region from his base at O-chou (Wu-ch'ang). He forbade all looting and maintained strict standards of law and order, and it was this policy which quickly won the sympathies of the people of the O-chou region, as well as influencing the surrender of many cities in the months to come. A short time later he took Chiang-ling, the core of Sung resistance in the Yangtze region above Tung-t'ing Lake, and with it collapsed all Sung hopes of turning back the invasion and cutting off the forces of Bayan as they advanced east.

Arigh Qaya then requested that Qubilai dispatch a high official to establish a civil government on the provincial scale for this region with its capital at Chiang-ling. Qubilai agreed and selected Lien Hsi-hsien (1231–1280), a Uighur who had already established himself in the upper hierarchy of the central government. He also happened to be related to Arigh Qaya by marriage; Arigh Qaya's son, Kuan-chih-ko, had married the daughter of Lien Hsi-min, Hsi-hsien's elder brother.[15] Since Kuan-chih-ko was Kuan Yün-shih's own father, this made Lien Hsi-hsien Kuan's maternal great-uncle. Lien arrived at Chiang-ling in June 1275, at which time Qubilai had Arigh Qaya return to O-chou. However, at the beginning of 1276 we find him laying siege to T'an-chou (Ch'ang-sha in Hunan). After considerable resistance on the part of the defenders, he took the city. Although some of his officers wanted to slaughter the population because the city had refused to surrender, Arigh Qaya forbade it, opened up the granaries, and fed the starving survivors. He apparently did this as much out of enlightened self-interest as out of compassion, since he believed that to put the city to the sword would be counterproductive in stiffening resistance in other cities. His policy proved correct, and city after city down the Hsiang River surrendered, with the result that his control soon extended into eastern Kiangsi and northern Kwangtung. When Hangchow fell to Bayan's forces and the Sung capitulated, Arigh Qaya was summoned to Qubilai's presence and, along with Bayan and the other leaders of the successful campaign in the South, was lavishly rewarded with riches and honors. He himself was promoted to Chief Administrator in August 1276 [16] and returned to Hu-kuang to finish the task of conquest, for there remained many areas in southern China which still held out. This task was finished in 1279.

Arigh Qaya's conquests were enormous; in extent of area they were many times larger than the territories Bayan had taken in the course of his march on Hangchow. However, sources outside his spirit-way stele inscription (which by its very nature had to be an uncompromising eulogy) are mixed in their evaluation of his conduct during the later stages of his campaign in the South. While all mention the many temples erected in his honor throughout the South by a population grateful for his preference for persuasion over bloodshed, his prohibitions against looting and slaughter of defeated soldiers and civilians, and his policy of light taxation,[17] some state that he made thousands of captives his serfs and that he refused to free them even when a censor from the central government demanded their release. He had been made Viceroy of Hu-kuang

Province in 1280, but whether he actually ever involved himself greatly in the civil affairs of the province is open to question, since we know that in 1281 he was engaged in further military operations in Kwangsi, where he subjugated the various aboriginal tribes, and in 1284 it is recorded that he was put in charge of an army to initiate a campaign against Annam.

In any event, the end came for him in 1286. A charge of embezzlement of state funds and property was brought against him, and he was summoned to Qubilai's summer palace in Shang-tu, the "Upper Capital" in Chahar. The case went against him, and he fell ill. Qubilai detained him at Shang-tu and had his own physicians tend to him, but whether out of despair brought about by his illness or out of chagrin at his reversals, he suddenly committed suicide on June 18, 1286.[18] His property was subsequently confiscated,[19] though later on posthumous ranks, titles, and offices were conferred on him,[20] and his descendents, Kuan Yün-shih among them, were appointed to high office through the *yin* (inheritance) privilege.

Arigh Qaya is known to have had six sons and five daughters, born variously of three wives and two concubines. His first wife's name was T'e-li. She appears to have had only one son, Hu-shih hai-ya,[21] also rendered Ho-ssu ha-ya[22] (Qus Qaya, "Bird Cliff"). Arigh Qaya probably married her while still fairly young, since this son was already old enough to hold the rank of *wan-hu* (Myriarch) and was right in the thick of the fighting during Bayan's campaign against Hangchow in 1274–1276,[23] when he himself was in his late forties. However, sometime after 1260, Qubilai decreed that the eldest daughter of Hao Ch'ien, then the *yüan-shuai* (Marshal) of a district comprising Po-chou and Ying-chou in Ch'en (i.e., western Anhwei), be given to him in marriage as reward for his achievements. Madame Hao does not seem to have lived longer than to give birth to one son, Kuan-chih-ko,[24] also rendered Ko-ch'i-ko,[25] Kuan Yün-shih's father. Upon her death, Qubilai decreed that her younger sister be married to Arigh Qaya in her place. The younger Madame Hao had one son, Ho-shang,[26] also rendered Hua-shan,[27] who later became *hsüan-wei-shih* (Pacification Commissioner) for Hunan Circuit.[28] Arigh Qaya also had three other sons by concubines. His five daughters all married prominent members of the Yüan administrative establishment.

Kuan's father must have been born during the 1260s, so that he was in his twenties when Kuan himself was born in 1286. For some reason, probably his early death, Arigh Qaya's first son, Qus Qaya, is not mentioned again in the sources,[29] and Kuan-chih-ko became his chief son and principal heir. After he reached his maturity in the 1280s, he was appointed a *ta-lu-hua-ch'ih* (Garrison Commander)[30] and general in charge of the Liang-huai Division with headquarters at Yung-chou (present-day Ling-ling on the Hsiang River in Hunan).[31] At this time Arigh Qaya himself was Viceroy of Hukuang, and it was surely because of this that his son was given this appointment. It is likely that Kuan-chih-ko's family resided with him at Yung-chou and that it was here that Kuan Yün-shih was born.

As was mentioned above, Kuan-chih-ko married a daughter of Lien Hsi-min. Lien was the eldest son of the prominent Uighur official Pu-lu hai-ya (1197–1265). On the same day Pu-lu hai-ya was appointed *lien-fang-shih* (Censor), his second son, Lien Hsi-hsien, was born (1231), and out of deference to these twin blessings he took the first character in the title of his office, *lien*, as a Chinese surname, as did his descendants after him. Lien Hsi-min held the posts of Pacification Commissioner for Ch'i-chou and Huang-kang Circuits in Hupeh.[32]

Kuan's great-uncle Hsi-hsien, of course, was far more prominent; indeed, his place in Yüan history rivals even that of Arigh Qaya.[33] In 1249 at the age of eighteen he became a personal attendant (*shih*) to Qubilai. His association with Arigh Qaya must date from that time, but whereas Arigh Qaya was the bodyguard-warrior who accompanied Qubilai in the field, Hsi-hsien was his tutor in the Confucian Classics. This came about apparently by accident, for one day Hsi-hsien was reading the *Mencius* and, summoned unexpectedly by Qubilai, absentmindedly took the volume along with him. Qubilai noticed it and asked him to explain Mencius's teaching, and Hsi-hsien was able to expound with such perception and zeal that Qubilai gave him the nickname Lien Meng-tzu (Mencius Lien). From that time on Qubilai became his patron, and he began to rise rapidly in official service. In 1254 he was made Commissioner in Charge of Maintaining Good Order for Ching-chao, the Metropolitan District; that is, he was made de facto governor of Yen-ching, the capital of North China which had been placed under Qubilai's control by his elder brother, the Qaghan Mönke. Although the Mongols had captured Yen-ching, from the Jürched Chin dynasty in 1215, it had not been brought under proper civil control and remained under the fragmented jurisdiction of the feudatory estates of various princes, the people a confused mass of mixed nationalities difficult to govern. Lien Hsi-hsien succeeded in curbing the exploitation and injustice which had plagued the area for so long and is credited with bringing it peace and stability.

His program for rehabilitation was assisted by the counsel of two prominent Chinese scholars, Hsü Heng (1209–1281) and Yao Shu (1203–1280), who had been advisors to Qubilai for some time.[34] Hsü and Yao did much to influence and encourage the readoption of Chinese-style government, first as advisors to Qubilai before his ascendancy and later as officials in his Central Chancellery.[35] They were thoroughgoing Neo-Confucians,[36] forerunners of that generation of scholar-bureaucrats which oversaw the reimplementation of the civil service examination system in 1314–1315 and which dominated the selection of its subject matter, primarily the *Four Books* with Chu Hsi's commentary.[37] Hsü was also the teacher of Yao Shu's nephew, Yao Sui (1238–1313), the most prominent Confucian scholar of the late thirteenth and early fourteenth centuries and the man who was the leader and teacher of those who actually drafted the regulations of the new examination system: Ch'eng Chü-fu (1249–1318), Yüan Ming-shan (1269–1322), and Kuan Yün-shih, who had become Yao's pupil in 1308/9 and who was appointed to the Imperial Academy (*Han-lin hsüeh-yüan*) in 1313.[38] As we shall see later in this chapter, Kuan's Confucianism had clear connections with Hsü Heng. The fact that his maternal great-uncle had studied with Hsü and had employed his counsel two generations earlier is surely more than mere coincidence.

Lien Hsi-hsien's next important task was set during Qubilai's abortive campaign against O-chou in 1259 when he was placed in charge of keeping accounts of goods and property taken in the course of the occupation (Qubilai's army surrounded but did not take the city itself). In this capacity, Hsi-hsien had more than 500 captured literati released and returned to their homes, an act which was to enhance Qubilai's image as an enlightened ruler and Hsi-hsien's reputation as a minister sympathetic to Chinese culture and to the plight of the literati during those later years of the campaign against the South (1274–1279). Between 1260 and 1270, Hsi-hsien served both as governor of provinces in North China and as an Assistant Chief Administrator in the Central Chancellery; he was one of the most powerful ministers during this early period of Qubilai's rule. In 1264 his mother died (Kuan Yün-shih's maternal great-grandmother), and he caused something of a sensation by going into strict mourning and following the traditional Chinese rites. For three days he took no food or drink, slept on straw in a hut next to his mother's grave, and declared that he intended to retire from office. Qubilai issued an edict that he return to his duties, which he dared not refuse though he appeared in plain attire and changed immediately into mourning clothes when he went home at the end of the day. Later, at the time of his father's death, he did the same thing.[39]

In 1270, Hsi-hsien was dismissed from office because he had mistakenly released from prison during a general amnesty a criminal whom Qubilai had not meant to release. He was out of office until 1274, when he was appointed Chief Administrator of Pei-ching (i.e., Liao-yang) Province. The next year he was transferred to Chiang-ling and became Chief Administrator of Hu-kuang Province. This position he filled until the spring of 1277, when he fell seriously ill. Since it was then very hot in Chiang-ling, Qubilai summoned him to Shang-tu. His administration was so well thought of by the people of Chiang-ling that they are said to have filled the streets, moaning and weeping, at the news of his recall, and when they discovered that there was no hope of retaining him, they had portraits painted of him and sacrificial temples erected in his honor. When Qubilai learned that Lien Hsi-hsien was almost penniless, having only his zither and a few books in his baggage, he conferred 5,000 taels of silver and 10,000 strings of paper cash on him and, upon his arrival in Shang-tu, had a famous physician summoned to look after him. The medicines had their effect, and Hsi-hsien was soon able to get around with a staff. However, he never held formal office again, but he seems to have been kept on at the Central Chancellery and near Qubilai's side as an informal advisor. He finally passed away on December 12, 1280, at the age of forty-nine, six years before his great-nephew Kuan Yün-shih was born. Nevertheless, his life seems to have been as much a model for Kuan's as that of Arigh Qaya, especially when Kuan was serving in civil office. More will be said below about the influences Kuan's paternal grandfather and maternal great-uncle had on him.

Little is known about Kuan's father. Kuan-chih-ko's position in life and the offices he held were probably entirely due to the fact that he was Arigh Qaya's son. He does not seem to have inherited either his father's energy or his talents, merely his office. He assumed the post of Chief Administrator of Hu-kuang Province in

1306.[40] Prior to this it is likely that he continued to hold the office of Garrison Commander at Yung-chou, to which he had been originally appointed in the early 1280s. All we know of his life as a garrison commander is contained in a statement in Kuan Yün-shih's spirit-way stele inscription: "Previously his father had been so lenient and kindhearted that his troops were undisciplined. . . ."[41] He retained this post until 1308, and we do not find him again in the official lists until 1321, thirteen years later, when he appears as Chief Administrator of Kiangsi, a position he filled until 1325.[42] His last post seems to have been that of Chief Administrator of Chiang-che Province, this in 1326.[43] There is no record of him after that.[44]

II Kuan Yün-Shih

If Kuan was born in Yung-chou at the garrison command headquarters, it is likely that he grew up there as well. The spirit-way stele inscription informs us that at the age of eleven or twelve years (1296 or 1297) he was already physically stronger than most grown men, suggesting that he had led a vigorous outdoor existence as a child.[45] As the garrison commandant's eldest son, he would have had the run of the camp, every officer and trooper his willing teacher and companion. He was far from being a pampered brat, however, since it appears that he excelled at riding, archery, and the use of various weapons.[46] His life so far seems to have been modeled upon that of his paternal grandfather, Arigh Qaya, a man he had never known but about whom he is sure to have heard every exploit. Kuan might have led a life of idle luxury, but he did not. While it may have been a discipline others forced on him, it is more likely that it was the image of his grandfather that inspired his early prowess in the martial arts. Kuan must also have been well aware of his illustrious ancestry on his mother's side. His great-grandfather Pu-lu hai-ya, his great uncles, such as Lien Hsi-hsien, as well as his maternal grandfather, had served the state with distinction.[47] Kuan's mother had every right to be proud of her uncles, especially Lien Hsi-hsien, who was to her side of the family what Arigh Qaya was to her husband's. If Arigh Qaya was Kuan's warrior ideal, Lien Hsi-hsien must have been his ideal statesman.

Considering the enormous accomplishments Kuan achieved in Chinese scholarship and letters while still quite young, he must have begun his studies while a small boy. Perhaps his mother was his earliest tutor; at least as a Lien she must have encouraged him to learn and arranged to have him tutored so that he could continue the scholarly traditions of her family.[48]

Such a dual role as a scholar-warrior, though perhaps unusual, would have seemed reasonable to Kuan because his grandfather Arigh Qaya, after all, had made his start by becoming expert at Uighur letters and making his way first as a tutor, and this certainly did not detract from his success as a military man. As a young man, Kuan's great-uncle Lien Hsi-hsien also was expert in the martial arts. He is said to have once impressed the whole court when he ran off three consecutive bull's eyes with an exceptionally stiff bow during an archery contest in Qubilai's presence.[49] It is likely, therefore, that Kuan had considerable scholarly attainments as a youth in addition to his skills in the martial arts. There is no proof that his mother had any hand in this, however, though one poem he wrote later in life, "Longing for My Mother" (Poem 13), suggests that he had a close relationship with her.

Poems 12 and 13 suggest that Kuan left home for government service about the year 1303, when he was seventeen, though if it were not for a document preserved in the *Yüan tien-chang* (Casebook of Yüan Administrative Law; see Appendix V)[50] we would know nothing of his life between the hunting and martial exploits of 1296–1297 and the time he assumed his father's post of garrison commander in 1306. It appears from this document that for a time (from about 1303 to 1306) Kuan served as a *lu-shih-ssu ta-lu-hua-ch'ih* (Police Commissioner) in a commandery in Kiangsi, this probably a kind of apprenticeship for the more important provincial offices he was expected to occupy later. However, no mention of this appears in the biographical sources, though this should not be surprising since all of them are based on his stele inscription. Considering the poor light this experience throws on Kuan's early career, it is unlikely that Ou-yang would have mentioned it even if he knew about it, which he probably did not. Kuan's family would have had to supply Ou-yang with the facts of his early years, and mention of this unfortunate episode would have detracted from the desired characterization of Kuan. The fact is that Kuan was found guilty of misconduct in office and dismissed from his post. He and other ranking members of the commandery had mismanaged a murder case so that an accessory whose degree of culpability in the affair

was very minor—in comparison to that of the actual murderer—had
been improperly kept in prison so long that he grew despondent
and committed suicide. Kuan's later disenchantment with official
life and his ultimate resignation from office may have stemmed in
part from this sordid experience.

Kuan probably assumed his father's office of Garrison Commander
at Yung-chou when Kuan-chih-ko became the Chief Administrator
of Hu-kuang Province in 1306, and he appears to have held this
office at least until February 1308, for his preface to his *Classic of
Filial Piety with a Vernacular Exegesis* closes with the statement:

Dated the sixteenth day of the first month of spring of the new Chih-ta era
[February 8, 1308]. This is the author's own preface, the Commander of
the Liang-huai Division, Hsüan-wu [Promoter of Martial Prowess] General
Sewinch Qaya, whose sobriquet is Ch'eng-chai [Owner of the Studio of
Accomplishment].[51]

From the stele inscription, we know that Kuan was a strict dis-
ciplinarian who was able to bring his troops up to a fine degree of
efficiency, this in great contrast to the lax command of his father.
Ou-yang states, however, that Kuan did not live for military effi-
cency alone and that when he had time off from duties he would
"sing in an elegant fashion and play the game of pitching arrows
into the pot." In other words, he enjoyed music, feasting, and
elegant drinking games. The game mentioned here involves one
player's, the host or one of the guests, holding a pot into which the
others take turns tossing an arrow; a miss forces the loser to drink.
Ou-yang suggests that this reveals the streak of eccentricity and
individuality that was later to lead to his withdrawal from worldly
affairs, as well as to his earlier resignation from the military. Ou-
yang gives him "several years" in this post;[52] this fits with the period
1306–1308 which I have suggested above.

The stele inscription tells us that after his resignation Kuan wandered about for a while, visiting scenic places and writing poetry,
but that before long he was in the North studying with Yao Sui.[53]
During 1308 Yao was appointed *t'ai-tzu pin-k'o* (Chief Counselor
to the Heir-Apparent), that is, to Ayurbarwada, the future Jen-
tsung, but was transferred before the end of the year to the office
of *ch'eng-chih* (Transmitter of Directives) in the Imperial Academy.[54] The inscription goes on to tell us that when Yao became an

attendant of Ayurbarwada, he recommended Kuan to him several times, and this was *after* Ayurbarwada had heard that Kuan had resigned his military post.[55] This seems to indicate that Kuan must have resigned early in 1308, taken a few months to wander about the South, and then arrived in Peking sometime before Yao had been transferred out of the Heir-Apparent's residence, since it is unlikely that Yao would have recommended him to Ayurbarwada before he had actually become his pupil. In any event, when he decided to resign, Kuan handed over his office to his younger brother Hu-tu hai-ya (Quduq Qaya) and informed his father of his action by letter. He then left the military life behind, never to return to it.

It was probably Kuan's vernacular exegesis of the *Classic of Filial Piety* that both secured him a place as Yao's student and a position in Ayurbarwada's household. Thanks to Yao's recommendation, Kuan was able to submit his work to Ayurbarwada, and when it met with his approval he appointed Kuan tutor to his son and heir, Shidebala, the future Ying-tsung.[56] Since Shidebala was born in early 1303,[57] he would have been five or six when Kuan became his tutor in late 1308 or early 1309. Kuan was to hold this post until February 1313, at which time he was appointed to much higher office.

Besides its intrinsic interest as an example of Yüan dynasty vernacular language, Kuan's edition of the *Classic of Filial Piety*, especially his preface to it, contains some important biographical information.[58] In particular, it can help us assess Kuan's role in the Neo-Confucian movement which had been rekindled by Hsü Heng and Yao Shu some sixty years earlier and which in his own day was receiving added impetus from Ayurbarwada's patronage of it, this both before and after he became emperor.[59] Unfortunately the text of the preface is damaged in a number of places, and some of the characters are missing. However, except for a section of four characters in the second column of the first page, it has been possible to reconstruct the missing characters from the context; these are indicated in the translation by putting those portions of the English into italics. The text is as follows:

Master Confucius said, "Of all man's actions, none is greater than filiality."[60] *He also said, "For transforming manner and influencing customs,* nothing is better than music. For making rulers secure and keeping the people well governed, nothing is better than ritual.[61] One————[62] there is no greater crime among those governed by the five punishments. For these reasons, this particular work, the *Classic of Filial Piety*, truly incorporates the great moral principles which make up the gateway to sagehood. The student can usually learn to recite it word for word, but often fails to grasp its meaning in his heart and mind, so how much the worse off are the mass of common people who suffer from unenlightened ignorance! How can we endeavor to enlighten them by means of the written word? As for the filial son in antiquity, when his parents loved him, he rejoiced and forgot them not, and when they tormented him, he was patient and bore no resentment.[63] This is the filiality which derived from [what was then simply] customary proprietry, and those who thus established themselves, practiced the Way and perpetuated their names throughout future generations are, oh, how remote from us now! I once observed how Mr. Lu-chai [Hsü Heng] adapted the language of common *speech* to explain the *Ta-hsüeh* [*The Great Learning*] in the vernacular,[64] so that even simple farmers and woodgathers could all understand it. People nowadays *regard* it as a treasure, and among the literati none find fault with it, either in the way they perceive Lu-chai's intention of transforming *the people* and developing good morals or in respect to its actual moral influence. How indeed could it be called a mere minor remedy! Although I am unlearned, I always lack *a sense of modesty* and so now make bold to imitate him and do a vernacular exegesis of the *Classic of Filial Piety* in order that all ordinary men and women can achieve enlightenment, come to understand the Way of Filiality and Fraternal Love, and that, to some extent at least, those who do not understand *li* [principle] and *i* [righteousness] might not fall into *the way* of unfiliality. Never once did I think to set it down for proper students of Confucianism! However, if some might say, 'Is it not true that you want to outdo Mr. Lu-chai?' I would say, 'How could I dare?' and if others say, 'Are you not insulting the words of the Sage?' I would again reply, '*How could* I dare!' " [Signed and dated as given above.][65]

We noted earlier that Kuan's Confucianism had clear links to his maternal great-uncle's teacher and counselor Hsü Heng.[66] Evidence for this assertion should be now apparent: Kuan's annotated edition of the *Classic of Filial Piety* is an avowed and explicit imitation of Hsü's popular edition of *The Great Learning*. Other vernacular editions of the *Classic of Filial Piety* may have preceded Kuan's during the thirteenth century,[67] for translations into Mongolian of this work and the *Lieh-nü chuan* (Lives of Noted Women) were published in illustrated editions under imperial auspices in July 1307 and distributed at the court of Ayurbarwada's elder brother Qaishan (Wu-tsung).[68] This was perhaps a year or so before Kuan submitted his own annotated version in Chinese to Ayurbarwada. The printed edition of Kuan's version that has survived is, in fact, completely illustrated (*ch'üan-hsiang*), the upper third of each page being given over to a scene intended to enhance the meaning of the text below.[69]

Yoshikawa Kōjirō has proposed the theory that Kuan's vernacular exegesis, because of certain grammatical features, was primarily intended as as crib to assist the direct translation of the text proper into Mongolian during oral tutoring, citing evidence that the combination of *chih-chieh* or *chih-shu* (vernacular exegesis) in Chinese and translation of the Confucian Classics into Mongolian was a common practice at the Mongol court as early as the time when Yeh-lü Ch'u-ts'ai (1189–1243) was an advisor to Ögödei.[70] Kuan's idea of doing a vernacular exegesis of the *Classic of Filial Piety* may have derived as much from this apparently common practice as from his specific familiarity with Hsü Heng's work, a familiarity which probably began in his youth when he was very likely taught the *Ta-hsüeh* and the *Chung-yung* (Doctrine of the Mean) with Hsü's annotated editions in the vernacular. Kuan's interest in Hsü's works surely enhanced his relationship with Yao Sui—Hsü's own pupil a generation before. Yao may have come to look upon Kuan as his successor, just as he himself was Hsü's, but since neither man refers to the other in the writings which have survived, we can only speculate on the real extent and depth of their relationship.

However, Kuan's acknowledged debt to Hsü Heng, his effort at producing a popular version of the *Classic of Filial Piety*—which could help spread Confucian principles among both the non-Chinese ruling elite and the masses—his association with Yao Sui, and his patronage by Ayurbarwada all seem to place Kuan in the so-called "Neo-Confucian Faction" of mid-Yüan times.[71] His association later with Ch'eng Chü-fu and Yüan Ming-shan in 1313–1314 in their joint drafting of the regulations for the reinstitution of the examination system, which was throughly oriented to Chu Hsi's commentaries on the classics and to Neo-Confucianism in general, also identifies him with this faction at a time when it was enjoying one of its high points of influence at court. Kuan became a leader of this group when Ayurbarwada, who had become emperor in 1311, appointed him *Han-lin shih-tu hsüeh-shih* (Reader-in-Waiting in the Imperial Academy), with the rank of *Chung-feng* Grandee (*tai-fu*), Drafter of Imperial Edicts and Proclamations (*chih-chih kao*),

and Drafter of the History of the State (*hsiu kuo-shih*) in the second
month of the second year of the Huang-ch'ing era (February 26 –
March 27, 1313).[72]

Lyrics 56–59, especially 58, express a strong Confucian ethic and
may well date from these years in Peking before Kuan received his
appointment to the Imperial Academy. They affirm a strong commitment to duty and a confidence in the future satisfactions he
expects from the career of a Confucian stateman. Poem 4, "Song
on Painting a Dragon," is in essence a patriotic celebration of the
Yüan state whose rule Kuan compares favorably with that of the
ancient sage-kings Yao and Shun, and it too dates from about this
time, as does the patriotic panegyric of Song-Set VII. Poem 12,
"At the Capital, Sent to a Friend," on the other hand, reveals Kuan's
satisfaction, indeed triumph, at being appointed to the Imperial
Academy: "Recently, I've become embarrassed/That while hair still
black/I've managed to have people call me/'Young Member of the
Academy!' "

After his appointment to the Imperial Academy, Kuan's circle of
friends and colleagues surely expanded. We know that in addition
to Yao Sui, Kuan was then acquainted with the above mentioned
Ch'eng Chü-fu (his senior by thirty-seven years)[73] and Yüan Ming-
shan (seventeen years his senior),[74] as well as Ou-yang Hsüan (three
years older)[75] and Teng Wen-yüan (1239–1328), who was twenty-
seven years older.[76] He seems also to have known Li Meng (1255–
1321), Chao Meng-fu (1254–1322)—probably the most prominent
official-literatus of the day—and Yü Chi (1272–1348).[77] All these
men were members of the Imperial Academy while Kuan held his
appointment there.

Outside the academy, Kuan had among his acquaintances Ch'a-
han (Chahan), a native of Balkh in Afghanistan who had had a long
and distinguished military career and who, when Kuan knew him,
was serving as a Chief Administrator in the Central Chancellery
(1312). Chahan was a noted translator of Chinese texts into Mongolian and also enjoyed a high reputation as a writer of classical
poetry and prose in Chinese.[78] Kuan also seems to have been on
close terms with Ch'en Hao (1261–1324) at this time. Ch'en was the
son of the noted Southern Sung Confucian Ch'en Yu (*chin-shih* of
1259) who had brought fame to his family by his study of the *Li-chi*
(*Record of Rites*). Ch'en Hao continued his father's work after the
fall of the Sung and eventually brought out a *Li-chi chi-shuo* (Col-

lected Explanations of the *Record of Rites*) in thirty *chüan*. He was also a noted painter.[79]

What all these men and Kuan seem to have had in common was their love of writing, especially poetry, and their scholarship. They were among the most famous men of letters of their day, and Kuan was the youngest member of their circle. From the remarks of those who knew him at the time, Kuan appears to have been a highly respected scholar and writer, a man whom his older friends thought would go far.[80] Kuan should have had a long and distinguished official career, but something went wrong, and we find him just a few years later resigning his posts and titles once again, this time never to return to government service for the rest of his life.

Kuan's posts—Reader-in-Waiting in the Imperial Academy, Drafter of Imperial Edicts and Proclamations, and Drafter of the History of the State—were taken over from him and filled by a Mongol, O-le-che pu-ha, also rendered Wan-che pu-hua (Öljä-buqa), on March 24, 1317. Öljä-buqa had been a personal attendant of Ayurbarwada and now was appointed to these posts by special decree (*t'e-shou*), just as Ayurbarwada had appointed Kuan to them four years previously.[81] It is probable that Kuan resigned shortly before this, because it is unlikely that these important posts would have been allowed to remain vacant for long.[82]

Although we know almost the exact dates of Kuan's tenure of office in the Imperial Academy, we know little about his activities there. The stele inscription indicates that he was involved in drawing up the regulations for the reimplementation of the civil service examination system.[83] Ayurbarwada probably began to consider this in 1313 when he ordered the members of the Central Chancellery to begin debate on the matter at the end of October. By early December, the essentials of the content had been determined and the times of the first examinations had been fixed. The *hsien* (county) and *chün* (commandery or prefecture) examinations were scheduled for the eighth month (September-October) of 1314, and the metropolitan examination was to be held in March 1315. After that, examinations were to be convened every three years. The commentaries of Ch'eng I and Ch'eng Hao and those of Chu Hsi were to provide the basis for questions concerning the Confucian Classics, and literary style was to be judged by the standards of T'ang and Sung prose. Mongols and other non-Chinese who wanted to take the examinations set for Northern Chinese (*Han-jen*) and Southern

Chinese (*Nan-jen*) were to be given the advantage of being graded one level higher than the one actually achieved.[84] Once these general guidelines were set by the Central Chancellery, it must have turned the actual drafting of the regulations and examination questions over to members of the Imperial Academy, and this task seems to have fallen principally on three men, as we noted above: Ch'eng Chü-fu, Yüan Ming-shan, and Kuan Yün-shih. It is likely that their work was completed by the end of the summer of 1314, in time for the September examinations.

There is no way to determine the actual projects on which Kuan worked at the *Kuo-shih yüan* (Bureau of State Historiography), but after his retirement he claimed that he had been so busy there that he was gradually losing vigor and growing old.[85] However, sometime after his work on the examination system was completed, he found time to compose a memorial to Ayurbarwada which ran to over 10,000 characters. The memorial itself is now lost, but the stele inscription does list the six matters with which it was concerned:

The first was "Disband the Frontier Guards so that they may Cultivate Civil Virtues." The second one was "Educate the Heir-Apparent in Order that the Foundations of the State be Rectified." The third was "Appoint Remonstrators to Assist His Majesty." The fourth was "Publicly Honor People by Proper Surname so as to Distinguish the Descendants of Meritorious Officials." The fifth was "Standardize Dress so as to Transform Public Morality." The sixth was "Promote the Worthy and the Talented so as to Enlarge the Most Excellent Way."[86]

Each of these topics is concerned with the reestablishment of orthodox Confucian government in China. The first suggests that much of the military be disbanded and that emphasis be placed on civil rather than military activities. In the second, probably in keeping with his own experiences as a tutor to the heir-apparent, Kuan emphasizes the importance of imbuing future emperors with the proper ideological stance, a stance firmly fixed in Neo-Confucianism. The third attempts to limit the absolutism of the emperor and to increase the power of the bureaucracy. If the emperor were to allow remonstrators and censors to direct, limit, and even overturn his own decisions, the bureaucracy, through its highest ranking members at least, would gain effective control over the state—an age-old dream of the Confucian literati. The fourth item, while obviously directed at the sinicization of Mongol rule in China, may have had some specific personal significance for Kuan himself. Either at this time or earlier he adopted the first character of his father's name, *kuan*, as his own Chinese surname followed by the second and third characters in the transliteration of his own Uighur name, *Yün-shih*, as his *ming* (given name). What he had done as an individual he now advocated as a general policy for non-Chinese of distinction in the Yüan state. The fifth item, like the fourth, is an attempt to further the process of sinicization of non-Chinese elements in Yüan society, as well as to reestablish a standard of social behavior which had apparently been allowed to fall into disuse under Mongol rule. The standardization of dress, reflecting the hierarchy of status in the Chinese state, is an old Confucian idea. To have all people governed by such rules would help break down distinctions between non-Chinese and Chinese, with Chinese culture as the standard for all. The sixth suggestion, if adopted, would have transformed Mongol rule in China. It is an appeal to return to one of the most cherished precepts of Confucianism: only the most talented and worthy should staff the bureaucracy. Such standards of talent and worth would be drawn from the Chinese tradition, especially the Neo-Confucian view of it. Although the civil service examination system had been restored, still only a relatively small number of people gained office through that route and fewer still were appointed to high office. The Mongol systems of *ch'ieh-hsieh* (a kind of spoils system) and *yin* (the inheritance privilege) were still—and continued to be for the rest of the dynasty—much more widely employed.

The sum of these six suggestions would have been substantially to transform Mongol rule in China, and to make the dynasty conform to the sociopolitical pattern laid down by earlier Chinese dynasties. It is doubtful if any ranking Chinese official would have dared make such suggestions in the form of a memorial to the emperor. Kuan, as a Uighur and the scion of some of Qubilai's most prominent and trusted ministers, may have been the spokesman for a radical group of Chinese statesmen within the Neo-Confucian faction at Ayurbarwada's court. By virtue of his birth and background, he could advocate what they could not. In any event, the memorial failed. Ayurbarwada is supposed to have "scrutinized it, sighed in admiration, but taken no action on it."[87] The implication here is that the emperor wanted to put Kuan's ideas into effect but that he could not, perhaps out of concern for the dangerous counteraction that would be sure to come from strong anti-Confucian elements at court.

It may well be that he realized that his dream of a Confucianized Yüan state, governed by a coalition of worthy Chinese and sinicized non-Chinese ministers, was a hopeless cause, at least in his own time, and that this prompted him to leave office. He may also have realized that the policies he advocated could place him in considerable danger, not merely the danger of losing office but actual physical danger. Considering what happened six or seven years later under the reign of Shidebala, such fears would have been justified.[88] There is more than a hint of distaste for the dangers of high office in some of the lyrics Kuan wrote after his resignation. Lyrics 41, 48, and 50 are particularly noteworthy examples of this.

Kuan's desire to leave office was apparently heightened by a need to spend more time and effort at the writing of lyrics. He makes the claim in his preface to the anthology *Yang-ch'un pai-hsüeh*, written after his retirement, that he was ashamed not to have been able to keep up with other lyricists of the day because of his official duties. For whatever reasons, Kuan seems to have been a dissatisfied and frustrated man *even before* he became a member of the Imperial Academy, for we know that he had changed his sobriquet from Ch'eng-chai (Owner of the Studio of Accomplishment) to Suan-chai (Owner of the Sour Studio) by the time he took up his appointment there. Thanks to the preface to Kuan's *Classic of Filial Piety*, we know that he called himself Ch'eng-chai when he arrived in Peking. However, by the time Ch'eng Chü-fu wrote his *pa* (colophon) to Kuan's collected poetry and prose he had begun to call himself Suan-chai. It is clear from this colophon (Appendix IV) that Ch'eng wrote it soon after Kuan had become his colleague in the Imperial Academy early in 1313. *Suan*, which basically means "sour," can also mean "caustic," "acrimonious," or "cynical," ideas diametrically opposed to the feelings associated with *ch'eng*: "success," "accomplishment," "confidence," "optimism," and "trust." Kuan probably intended this new sobriquet to represent a new outlook on life: dissatisfaction with the realities of political life rather than the idealistic expectations he had had as a young man arriving in Peking. In fact, we have it in Kuan's own words that he meant the *suan* in Suan-chai to characterize his personality, character, and attitude toward life:

Once in the past, Suan-chai, Mr. Kuan, was passing the time with Tan-chai [Owner of the Placid Studio—Yang Chao-ying (fl. 1300–1325)], and he said, "If I am *suan*, then you ought to be *tan*." And so he gave it to him as a sobriquet.[89]

Kuan referred to himself by two other cognomens when he wrote the preface to his *Classic of Filial Piety*: Ssu-yu t'ang (Owner of the Hall of the Four Friends) and Shu-lan yeh-jen (The Wayward and Lazy Rustic).[90] The term "Four Friends" can refer to the four things associated with and essential to a studio: *pi* (brush), *mo* (ink), *chih* (paper), and *yen* (inkstone). It may also refer to the four friends of King Wen of the Chou (end of the second millennium B.C.): Hung Yao, T'ai-kung Wang, Nan-kung Kua, and San-i Sheng, if he had loyalty to sovereign and cultivation of civil virtues in mind, or to the favorite disciples of Confucius: Yen Hui, Tzu Kung, Tzu Chang, and Tzu Lu, if love of the Confucian Classics and devotion to Confucius were the intended implications. Of course, this studio name might have been intended to connote all of these, suggesting that the man who dwelt therein was utterly devoted to scholarship and writing in the service of the state.

Shu-lan yeh-jen is very different. *Shu-lan* is an allusion to Hsi K'ang's (223–262) famous letter to Shan T'ao, *Yü Shan Chü-yüan chüeh chiao shu* (Letter to Shan Chü-yüan Breaking Off My Friendship with Him), in which Hsi enumerates the reasons why he is ill-suited to an official career and declares he cannot put up with the hypocrisy and vulgarity, the sycophancy and the empty decorum necessary for official "success." He goes on to state that the basis of his unsuitability was already fixed in his youth when, as he put it, he was "already wayward [*shu*] and lazy [*lan*] by nature."[91] Since this phrase was used in one of Kuan's sobriquets while he was still a garrison commander, we have to assume that he was already rather cynical toward officialdom, though that cynicism was directed specifically at the military life. It is an attitude that he seems to have carried to Peking in 1308 and which appears to have taken over completely when his career there turned "sour." His preface to *Yang-ch'un pai-hsüeh*, as we shall see, also shows a marked lack of respect for official duties and an admiration for those who manage to escape to a life of freedom in the country. Though it was written after his retirement, it surely expresses sentiments that had been with him for some time.

When he was writing the preface, someone noticed that he had
written critiques of only a few of the many lyricists represented in
the anthology and asked him why he did not deal with the rest.
Kuan's reply was: "In the western mountains when morning comes,
there is such invigorating air."[92] This quotes a statement attributed
to the eccentric Wang Hui-chih (died A.D. 388):

Wang Tzu-yu [Hui-chih] was Administrator of Cavalry for the General of
Transportation and Cavalry Huan [Ch'ung (died 385)]. Huan once said to
Wang: "You have been at your office for a long time, so now you ought to
be really efficient in dealing with your duties." For some time Wang did
not reply, but then looking high in the air and resting his chin on his tablet
of office, he said: "In the western mountains when morning comes,there
is such invigorating air."[93]

Specifically, Kuan's reply meant that a morning walk in the mountains would be a better way to spend one's time than sitting in a
studio doing critiques of the work of others, but it is also likely that
it refers in general to the dissatisfaction he felt at being compelled
to tend to endless and tedious official paper work. Poem 21, "Inscribed in Lien-ch'uan's Calligraphy on His Screen Wall," may have
been written while Kuan was at the Imperial Academy; it seems to
be a high official's poem which both celebrates and envies the life
of a mountain recluse, sentiments appropriate to this stage of Kuan's
life.

Thus Kuan used four different cognomens between the time he
reached his maturity (about 1303) and the time he entered the
Imperial Academy (1313), and this suggests that he may have been
suffering from some kind of identity crisis, since the names involved
connote such different attitudes and ideals. Ch'eng-chai and Ssu-yu
t'ang belong together; they involve a combination of expectation of
success, idealism and devotion to serious scholarship and writing
in the service of society and the state. Shu-lan yeh-jen and Suan-
chai also belong together but imply just the opposite: irresponsi-
bility, cynicism, eccentricity, and self-centered individualism, as
well as contempt for official duties and the official establishment.
If these pairs of cognomens represent opposite sides of the same
personality, it is not surprising that it took until 1317 for Kuan to
decide, once and for all, what he really wanted out of life. The
actual frustrations and disappointments he seems to have encountered in 1313–1317 apparently pushed him to what the second pair

represented and forced him to the conclusion that since official life held neither present satisfaction nor hope, it would be well to be out of it.

Hard facts about Kuan's life after his retirement are few. There is the broad outline provided by the stele inscription, which constitutes the framework into which various pieces of biographical information from other sources can be fitted. To begin with, we know from Poem 5 that Kuan visited Pao-t'o Mountain, a precipitous islet east of Ning-po just off the coast of Chekiang, between April 12 and May 11, 1317. This was probably soon after he left Peking. The poem not only describes the sunrise he came to see but also appears to allude to his voyage from the North by ship. It is likely that he started out from the southern coast of Shantung and arrived at some nearby port at the mouth of the Yangtze.[94] It is significant that in the preface to this poem he mentions a Buddhist monk, a certain Lu-shan, who is unknown as far as the sources are concerned. His associates are no longer the rich and the powerful, but people of the lower classes, such as this unknown monk. Except in a very few instances, his new acquaintances are far removed from the non-Chinese ruling elite and the prestigious Chinese literati with whom he previously associated.

From the mouth of the Yangtze, Kuan would have traveled up river toward the Nanking area. If so, Poem 6 may have been written during the summer of 1317, since its setting along the Yangtze from Ts'ai-shih shan (Pick Rocks Mountain)—slightly below what was then Chin-ling (Nanking)—to Hsin-t'ing (New Pavilion), slightly above it, would fit well with such an itinerary. There are certain lines of the poem that suggest sentiments appropriate for his initial period of retirement: "I too do not stay in White Jade Hall,/Since the capital's wine is weak and Hsiang clouds linger long."

Poem 9, an autumn poem, is still set on the river and expresses sentiments of both relief and regret, and, as such, probably dates from Kuan's early months of retirement—a time when he appears to have been unable to resolve the various conflicting emotions which stemmed from his resignation.

Teng Wen-yüan's preface to Kuan's collected poetry and prose (Appendix III) states that it was at least a full year after Kuan left Peking before he came to live in retirement at Hangchow. The stele inscription is very laconic at this point and merely tells us that Kuan was attracting so much attention between the time he resigned and the time he came to Hangchow that he feared that he would get into trouble. (He had resigned his office on the pretext of illness.) One item of information that Ou-yang does give us here is significant: after wandering about for a time, Kuan decided *to travel east* to Ch'ien-t'ang (Hangchow). West of Hangchow lies the middle Yangtze and Tung-t'ing Lake region. It is likely, therefore, that Kuan spent most of his time after coming south from Peking in this region, traveling from place to place by boat. The time would have been the summer, autumn, and winter of 1317. Poems 3, 7, 19, 20, 22, and 23 seem to date from this time, as well as Poems 5, 6, and 9. These are all "travel" poems, poems written at various sites from the mouth of the Yangtze to the middle Yangtze and Tung-t'ing Lake areas.[95]

Although where he actually was during most of 1317 must be conjectured, we do know that he arrived at Hangchow in 1318 and that he probably remained in or near this scenic city for the rest of his life. It is not certain exactly when he arrived, though the statement in Teng's preface to his collected works that "after we had been parted for a year, he came to visit Ch'ien-t'ang and came by to see me" suggests that Kuan was there by early spring, if we count a year from the time he must have left office (February 1317). On the other hand, Poem 26, "On First Arriving in the South, I Pass the Summer Resting on Phoenix Mountain," implies that he did not arrive until either late spring or early summer. In either case, Kuan would have gone to visit Teng, his former colleague in the Imperial Academy, soon after his arrival, and he may have stayed with him for a time. The heat of the summer would have begun by May, and then Kuan would have moved to Phoenix Mountain. Poem 26 suggests that at this time he was not yet free from the dual fetters of duty and ambition, even though it was over a year since his resignation. He was now thirty-two and had six more years to live, years he was to spend in the writing of lyrics and music, with women and wine, in the pursuit of the meaning of Ch'an (Zen) Buddhism, and in the quest for Taoist immortality. The events of his life during these six years defy any attempt at dating. Therefore, this last period of his life will be presented as an undifferentiated whole.

Before we begin to explore the years 1318–1324, however, a few words should be said about Kuan's family life, if indeed he now had one. We know he married a daughter of Shih T'ien-lin (1219–1310),[96] but we do not know when. Kuan's elder son, A-ssu-lan hai-ya (Arslan Qaya; "Tiger Cliff"), was still alive in 1368, when, in his capacity of Chief Administrator of Hu-kuang Province, he surrendered the remnants of the provincial forces to the Ming.[97] By the time Ou-yang Hsüan wrote the stele inscription in 1349, this son had already had an extensive official and military career.[98] It seems likely, then, that Arslan Qaya was born about the year 1310, so that he was in his late thirties in 1349 and in his late fifties in 1368. Kuan's wife is supposed to have come from a "famous Peking family," and if he married shortly after his arrival in Peking (1308/9), the birth of his first son might have occurred in 1310. Kuan also had a second son, Pa-ssu hai-ya (Bars Qaya; "Leopard Cliff"), about whom nothing is known, and a daughter who married Tuan Ch'ien, the Garrison Commander of Huai-ch'ing Military Prefecture (in Honan) at the time Ou-yang's inscription was written.[99] The fact that neither of Kuan's sons assumed the character *kuan* as a Chinese surname and that the elder son apparently spent all his life in provincial military and quasi-military posts suggests that Kuan's family may have been entrusted to the care of his younger brother Quduq Qaya, who had taken over Kuan's post of Garrison Commander of Liang-huai in 1308. Otherwise, if Kuan himself had had a hand in their upbring-ing, one would expect the sons of such a scholarly and sinicized father to have turned out quite differently. When Kuan resigned his office, he may have left his wife and children behind in Peking for a time, perhaps with his wife's relations, then later had them join his younger brother in Yung-chou. In any event, there is no-thing in the sources that suggests that he had his family with him in Hangchow during his years of retirement, but there is evidence that suggests just the opposite.

The image we gain from reading those lyrics which seem to date from this period is overwhelmingly either that of an eccentric bon vivant who carried on a seemingly uninterrupted round of feasting, music-making, and excursions to the pleasure quarters or outings to the West Lake (complete with singing girls and fellow lyricists), or that of an equally eccentric lay Buddhist or amateur Taoist wan-dering the hills and streams in search of self-transcendence or im-mortality. He is said to have slept into the late afternoon, and his residence remained closed to visitors until evening—his servants picked up his habits and "changed day into night."[100] This implies, of course, that they changed night into day as well. It could hardly have been the place to maintain a proper domestic existence and rear children. While Kuan's lyrics sometimes mention singing girls and fellow lyricists, they never so much as allude to his wife or children. However, he did not live alone with just servants for company. It appears that he had two concubines, one named Tung-hua (Cave Blossom) and the other Yu-ts'ao (Secluded Shrub). They were with him when he died. This, at least, is the interpretation T'ao Tsung-i (c. 1320 – c. 1410) places upon the appearance of these two names in Poem 29, a *tz'u shih shih* (A Valedictory Poem to the World) which he attributes to Kuan.[101]

Kuan kept two residences at Hangchow. His summer home was called Ch'i-yün an (Retreat Perched in the Clouds) and was located on Phoenix Mountain to the southwest of the city and about halfway between West Lake and the Ch'ien-t'ang River.[102] His main residence was a villa at the foot of Phoenix Mountain, a place which in later times became the Hai-hsien (Freshness-of-the-Sea) Temple.[103] As the name implies, the site faced Ch'ien-t'ang River and the sea, with the mountain at its back and behind that West Lake. Although situated in the rugged hill country to the southwest, Kuan's residences were not far from the city and the lake, and he had easy access to both. It was to Phoenix Mountain that he first came in 1318; he must have formed a lasting affection for the place at first sight. Lyrics 66–69 seem to be idealized depictions of his life there, and various others may have been set there as well: Lyrics 40–42, 48–51, 63–64, and perhaps 70.

If we take the stele inscription literally, Kuan often left home and wandered about the Hangchow region employing disguises and aliases and mixing with the ordinary folk.[104] He did this, presumably, to protect himself against the charge that he had resigned from office under false pretenses (i.e., that he had become ill and needed to live a life of seclusion and rest). We do not know how elaborate this subterfuge was or whether he actually kept it up for all the years he was at Hangchow. In any case, his attempts to remain unknown seem to have failed, since his place later became so prominent in the lore of West Lake.[105] He must have become a well-known local figure during his lifetime, and the high regard in which he was held by other well-known lyricists of the day indicates that his fame as a literary figure continued to grow after his retirement from office. There are indications, in fact, that he was a genuine local celebrity.[106] The only way to reconcile this fact with the statement in the stele inscription is to assume that he went out in disguise only during the early period of his residence at Hangchow, and then, after enough time had passed and his resignation was no longer a fresh concern of the authorities, he ceased to do so. It is also possible that he may have continued to do so on occasion, disguised for example as a medicine peddler or as an old man dragging a staff, two instances which are actually recorded in the sources.[107]

The famous Yüan lyricist Chang K'o-chiu (c. 1270 – after 1348) was a man who held several minor posts in various local governments earlier in his life and who seems to have come to Hangchow to live while Kuan was there.[108] He may have been Kuan's closest friend at this time. After Kuan's death, Chang wrote a lyric entitled "An Apologia for Suan-chai," which seems to be both a eulogy and an attempt to refute those critics who apparently thought that Kuan had wasted his later years:

> Our Sovereign once gave him a banquet in Jade Grove Park,
> But he had three gallons before he had his first audience at court.
> Very lazy about documents for the Bureau of Editing,
> His personal letters were written on decorated red paper,
> His lyrics on white taro paper,
> And essays on paper as orange as tangerines.
> He learned the Way of Immortality
> And was thoroughly versed in poetry and in Ch'an.
> Hating the din of the vulgar world,
> He freed himself from fame and self-advantage.
> At the mouth of a cave on T'ien-t'ai Mountain
> And at the foot of Mount Ti-fei
> He learned to refine Pills of Immortality.
> Together we sold ink,
> Talked about the abstruse mysteries of the Way,
> Our high spirits effervescent—
> And we'd take naps in winehouses!
> "Cave Blossom and Secluded Shrub,
> Make good marriages for yourselves!"
> I myself deceived others for forty years—
> Over the sea the moon in the sky will remain just as round.[109]

The second line follows closely a line in Tu Fu's (712–770) *Yin-chung pa-hsien ko* (Song on the Eight Immortals of Drinking): "Ju-yang had three gallons before he had his first audience at court."[110]

Lines 3–6 allude to the time when Kuan was at the Bureau of State Historiography and imply that while he was slapdash about his work in the bureau, he took great and elaborate pains with personal correspondence and belletristic compositions. The rest of the lyric, except for the last three lines, which were taken from Kuan's "Valedictory Poem to the World," deal with his eccentric life as a student of Ch'an and Taoism and his habitual patronage of wineshops. T'ient'ai Mountain is in Chekiang to the southeast, and Ti-fei Mountain is in Kiangsu to the north, both a fair distance from Hangchow. If we take Chang's reference to them seriously—they may be merely conventional allusions to Taoism—it suggests that Kuan was an ardent student of the Taoist quest for immortality, ardent enough to make pilgrimages to these shrines of Taoist lore. If so, then it may have been on such an excursion that Kuan encountered the old fisherman of Poem 8 and his reed-floss quilt (*lu-hua pei*)— for which Kuan traded this poem and so acquired the sobriquet Lu-hua taojen (Reed-Floss Taoist).[111] The mention of selling ink in line 14 is probably an allusion to the story of Lü Tung-pin, one of the Eight Immortals of Taoist lore, who is supposed to have disguised himself as an ink peddler. He is so represented in the popular Yüan drama *Yüeh-yang lou* (The Yüeh-yang Tower) by Ma Chih-yüan (c. 1260 – c. 1324).

The wandering Taoist eccentric seems to have been a favorite pose of Kuan's; he even went so far as to set up shop in the marketplace of Ch'ien-t'ang as a peddler of medicines, though once when he did this he seems to have intended merely to play a harmless though pointed joke on his "customers."[112] Taoism is often mentioned in Kuan's *shih* poetry, both philosophical Taoism and the "popular" magical-alchemical variety.[113] On one occasion Kuan appears to have been present at a send-off party for the Taoist Master of the T'ung-yüan kuan (Temple where the Ultimate Mystery is Revealed), Yü Hsing-chien. Yü's temple was on nearby Mount Wu, and the party seems to have taken place at a pavilion along the Ch'ien-t'ang River. Present on this occasion were Yü Chi, with whom Kuan was probably acquainted during his Peking days, and Chang Chu (1287–1367). Chang was a famous Confucianist who was teaching privately at Hangchow at this time; later he was appointed to the Imperial Academy (see Poem 30 and its commentary in Chapter Three).

Philosophical Taoism, of course, has close affinities with Ch'an

Buddhism, and Kuan seems to have divided his time equally between the search for physical immortality in the techniques of popular Taoism and in an attempt to achieve psychological or spiritual
self-transcendence in philosophical Taoism and in Ch'an. In effect,
he was trying to come to grips with the problem of life and death
in two different and, one might imagine, mutually exclusive ways.
Popular Taoist techniques are concerned with *preserving* the self
(albeit a "refined" version of it), and Taoist philosophy and Ch'an
are concerned with *extinguishing* it, with bringing about an enlightened state in which one discards the self and its fear of death. Kuan,
in practicing both, seems to have wanted it both ways: if popular
Taoist techniques failed to save him from death, perhaps philosophical Taoism/Ch'an could teach him to transcend the fear of it.
Poem 18 (probably written during Kuan's association with Ch'en
Hao in Peking before 1317) seems to suggest that at that time Kuan
had more faith in the latter method, but after his retirement the
attractions of popular Taoism seem to have compromised this faith.

While Kuan's deathbed poem, Poem 29, does suggest that he
finally managed to transcend the self, as late as the preceding autumn he was still apparently struggling to free himself from the
fetters of emotion and attachments to mortal existence.[114] He seems
to have been a passionate and human individual who had chosen
a hard road to travel. He was greatly attracted to sensual and aes-
thetic experiences, wine, women, music, poetry, the beauty of scenery, and the companionship of bosom friends with whom he could
share these delights. The conflicts that might have arisen between
these attachments and the need for self-transcendence must have
been intense. However, we are assured by the stele inscription and
by the values and sentiments expressed in some of his lyrics—Lyrics
20, 40, 41, 48, and 49—that he did manage to transcend the desire
to serve in office, and this, at least, must have given him some
measure of peace and freedom, regardless of what other frustrations
he might have had.[115]

Kuan's study and practice of Ch'an consisted of private meditation
in his retreat on Phoenix Mountain,[116] reading the scriptures,[117] and
at least one visit and debate with the most famous Ch'an master of
the day, Ming-pen (1263–1323), whose sobriquet was Chung-feng
and who was a native of Ch'ien-t'ang.[118] In addition to their discussions of Ch'an, Kuan and Ming-pen may also have talked about
poetry and exchanged poems, for the Buddhist was a famous poet.[119]

He also counted among his friends the foremost literatus of the age, Chao Meng-fu.[120] Kuan does not seem to have written any explicitly Ch'an poems or lyrics, though certainly some of the lyrics which might be regarded as "transcendent" in the Taoist sense could equally be interpreted in Ch'anist terms.

We have little means of measuring the extent and depth of Kuan's relationship with such fellow lyricists as Chang K'o-chiu. Ou-yang's inscription does not deal with this aspect of Kuan's life, and none of Kuan's prose writings of this period, apart from the preface to *Yang-ch'un pai-hsüeh* seems to have survived. Chang K'o-chiu refers to Kuan in no less than nine lyrics, at least four of which seem to have been actually composed in his company.[121] Since some of these illuminate the nature of their relationship, they are translated here. One was written at a party to see off the Lord of the East (Tung-chün, the God of Spring). The location was a tavern on the shore of the Ch'ien-t'ang River, or possibly on a floating restaurant and is entitled "At a Banquet Provided by Scholar Suan-chai":

> A breeze from the shore splits open river clouds and
> Allows a slanting ray of sunshine to burst through,
> Shine on our farewell cups,
> Hesitate on the pavilion to the west,
> Linger over the sea to the north
> And send off for good the Lord of the East.
> Jade-fair, slender fingers pass 'round gold cups for drinking games,
> As the others, in silk headresses and with feather fans, scorn our
>   poetry circle.
> Waking the God of the Waves
> And rousing Plum Spirits from slumber—
> Our beauty in kingfisher-green sleeves
> And our "White Snow of Sunny Spring" songs![122]

They are obviously at an establishment which catered to the wealthy. Kuan, Chang, and perhaps others composed lyrics for the occasion, which a beautiful singer attired in green sang for them. The other customers ostentatiously defiled this poignant moment for the aspiring poets by playing drinking games.

Another lyric, entitled "Out on the Lake—Composed at Suan-chai's Request," gives an account of an incident during a day's boating on West Lake:

Busy looking for love affairs,
Golden whips cast reflections in the water,
And kingfisher-green sleeves emanate perfume.
Out on the lake, filling decorated note paper with poetry,
We floated by mistake to a house of pleasure
And became surrounded by a drunken land filled with spring delights.
What romantic allure this place has!
There—someone hungry for pleasure,
His horse left neighing among green willows,
Monopolizes the charms of a "Purple Cloud" maid![123]

"Purple Cloud" (Tzu-yün) is the name of a famous courtesan of late T'ang times. West Lake was lined with such places as the one described in this lyric. Two lyrics entitled "Following the Rhymes of Suan-chai" are translated in the commentary to Lyric 70 in Chapter Five. The first alludes to their long friendship and sympathy for each other and praises Kuan's capacity for wine and his talent for poetry. The second pokes fun at Kuan and lightheartedly accuses him of still secretly wishing to become a great general or statesman, thus implying that Kuan still talked about affairs of state during his retirement. [124]

A lyric composed at another party and entitled "Listening to the *Hu-ch'in* at a Banquet Provided by Suan-chai" reads:

Jade whip and
Kingfisher hair ornaments
Remind me of the face of Chao-chün on horseback.
One stroke across silver strings breaks up ice in silver
    springs,
Shatters strings of black dragon pearls,
Makes wild geese dance in autumn mists,
Orioles sing in spring gardens and
Wounds the hearts of those in frontier grasslands.
It's our drunken immortal,
On decorated note paper,
Capturing the chagrin of passes and mountains thousands of
    miles away![125]

"Our drunken immortal" is, of course, Kuan himself, the host of this gathering who has composed the music for the *hu-ch'in* (a two-stringed violinlike instrument played upright) and the lyrics to go with it. Perhaps Kuan even played the instrument himself. More will be said below about Kuan's interest in music. For Chao-chün (Bright Consort), see the commentary to Poem 22 in Chapter Three; for "black dragon pearls," see Poem 4.

One lyric which mentions Kuan is actually concerned with someone else—Yang Chü-erh (Yang the Colt), a musician and possibly a playwright, who seems to have been a close friend of both Chang and Kuan.[126] The lyric is a lament for Yang's passing and is entitled "At Yang Chü-erh's Graveyard":

> Moss covers the grey, mist-shrouded path.
> I leave the little red pavilion—
> The lyric inscribed there still the one Suan-chai wrote,
> And now I too have written one to the same rhyme:
> He used to criticize calligraphy and painting
> While leaning on the railing,
> But here's his tea stove blocked up with dust
> And his ink turned to ice.
> As I shut the secluded gate
> My thin shadow hangs suspended—
> A companion to the lonely lamp.
> I'm a Po Ya who has already destroyed his zither,
> And my wine will never reach this Liu Ling.
> With a short piece of vine for a cane
> I'll take advantage of this evening scene,
> Express my feelings in song,
> Write a new lyric and
> Have a spring oriole take it to him.
> Next year when I come to celebrate the Clear and Bright Festival,
> Windows shut, it'll be quiet here in the pear blossom garden,
> But who will share the sound of wind and rain in this little house![127]

"The lyric inscribed there" translates t'i-ch'ing, which literally means "on the subject of my feelings." Here it should be understood in the sense of t'i-mu, a poem inscribed at the grave of a loved one which expresses one's feelings about the departed. Po Ya lived during the Spring and Autumn era (722–481 B.C.) and excelled at the zither. He had a good friend, Chung Tzu-ch'i, who could interpret his music. When Chung died, Po never played the zither again, since there was no one in the world who could appreciate what he played. For Liu Ling, see the commentary to Lyric 49. There is a curious passage in the Ch'ing-lou chi (Collection of Anec-

dotes about People of the Pleasure Quarters) which also links Kuan
to Yang Chü-erh. However, since Kuan seems to have been a friend
of Yang's, it may be spurious:

Yang Mai-nu [Bought-Slave Yang] was a daughter of Yang Chü-erh. She
had a beautiful face and figure and sang well. Officials and scholars in great
numbers doted on her. By nature she was fond of wine. Later on she
married the musician Ch'a-ch'a kuei [Chattering Devil] Chang Ssu [Chang
the Fourth] as his proper wife [ch'i], but, worn out with illness, she died.
Kuan Suan-chai once mocked her with the lines: "Hair coiled up in conch-
shell shape, her skirt trails a white sash [pai-tai]"—probably because she
suffered from pai-tai disease [leucorrhea].[128]

There is a certain meanness in this passage and in another one from
the *Ch'ing-lou chi* which seems uncharacteristic of Kuan.[129] It seems
unlikely that he could have stooped so low as to lampoon old and
sick singing girls, one of them his father's concubine and the other
the daughter of a dear friend.

These lyrics cast some light on Chang's relation to Kuan: Chang
was often present at parties given by Kuan and often accompanied
him on boating excursions on West Lake. On these occasions, they
wrote lyrics to each other's rhymes. Chang seems to have been both
an especially close friend and an ardent admirer, and it is likely that
their acquaintance lasted over the entire period of Kuan's retirement
at Hangchow, for, as Chang writes: "At the fishing pier/We haven't
roused the doubts of gulls for ten years" (from the first of two lyrics
translated in the commentary to Kuan's Lyric 70). The mention of
ten years is an exaggeration, since Kuan did not live that long after
his retirement, but it does indicate that the two were close friends
for as long as they knew each other—some six years. Chang's lyrics
also reveal that Kuan took his music and lyric writing very seriously
and was no mere hedonist who wasted his time and money in the
pleasure quarters. The sensual delights available there seem to have
been the inspiration for the lyrics rather than an end in themselves—
at least this is what Chang would have us believe. Also, Chang
indicates that Kuan knew Yang Chü-erh well, and perhaps he was
acquainted with other musicians, actors, actresses, and playwrights,
not just as a customer but as a friend, patron, and even collaborator
in their theatrical and musical endeavors. It is true that Kuan is not
known to have written a play himself, but many of his lyrics, short
songs as well as song-sets, have a distinctly dramatic orientation.

If he had lived longer, it is not unlikely that he would have produced his own dramas.

A-li hsi-ying is another lyricist with whom Kuan was acquainted (see Poem 22 in Chapter Three and Lyric 79 in Chapter Five). He seems to have come from a background not unlike Kuan's, though certainly more modest. His name indicates that his family originated in the Western Regions, and his father, A-li yao-ch'ing, was also a writer of lyrics.[130] A-li hsi-ying seems never to have served in office and probably used an inheritance (perhaps the spoils of conquest of his forebears) to set himself up in what appears to have been an elegant and luxurious retreat which he called the Lan-yün wo (Lazy Cloud Refuge). This was situated in the northeast corner of the city of Wu-ch'eng overlooking the Yangtze. That A-li hsi-ying was acquainted with several of the more prominent lyricists of the day is indicated by the numerous lyrics which echo his famous composition entitled "Lazy Cloud Refuge." Kuan wrote one (Lyric 79), Ch'iao Chi wrote six,[131] Wu Hsi-i wrote six,[132] Wei Li–chung wrote one,[133] and Yang Chao-ying, the compiler and editor of Yang-ch'un pai-hsüeh and Ch'ao-yeh hsin-sheng t'ai-p'ing yüeh-fu (New Sounds from Court and Country: Yüeh-fu [Ballads] of the Age of Great Peace), wrote six, changing the title to Pai-yün wo (White Cloud Refuge).[134]

Kuan may have been A-li hsi-ying's guest at Lazy Cloud Refuge during his trip south from Peking in 1317, since his route up the Yangtze would have taken him there, and it is there that Poem 22 and Lyric 79 seem to have been written. Kuan and A-li hsi-ying appear to have shared a love of music as well as the same kind of life-style. Lyric 79 may signal a critical point in Kuan's attitude toward his abandoned career; the last three lines give an account of Kuan's despair and A-li hsi-ying's advice:

[Kuan says,]
"I've finished my ten thousand mile roc's journey and I'm broken,"
But he faces the misty rose-tinged clouds and laughs his scorn—
"Let the affairs of the world go to hell!"

From what we know of the rest of Kuan's life, it appears that he took A-li hsi-ying's advice.

Yang Chao-ying and Kuan were close friends. This is attested by Teng Tzu-chin in his preface to T'ai-ping yüeh-fu.[135] Teng was a native of Pa-hsi (Mien-chou in Szechwan) whose family had moved to Ch'ien-t'ang a generation or two before him. He was, in fact, a relative of Teng Wen-yüan, Kuan's old colleague from the Imperial Academy, who in 1317 had become Supervisor of Branch Censorates in the Circuits of Che-hsi and had come to reside in Hangchow, where the Teng clan had settled. Teng Wen-yüan remained there for the next two years. Teng Tzu-chin's preface is dated 1351, and Teng Wen-yüan died in 1328. Depending on whether Tzu-chin was an old or a young man when he wrote the preface, he would appear to have been either a son or grandson, or nephew or grand-nephew, of Wen-yüan.[136] We can date Kuan's association with Yang Chao-ying to his period of retirement at Hangchow because the *Yang-ch'un pai-hsüeh*, Yang's first anthology of lyrics, contains many of Kuan's lyrics set at West Lake or nearby. Kuan's own preface to it must therefore date from this period of 1318/19–1324.

It was fortunate that Kuan was acquainted with this first anthologist of Yüan lyrics. Through Yang, it is likely that Kuan became familiar with the work of lyricists he did not know personally and could keep up with the latest developments in the genre. At the same time, his own lyrics were included in the anthology; if they had not been, much of Kuan's work might have been lost. The same holds true for the *T'ai-p'ing yüeh-fu*, in which Yang included many of Kuan's lyrics as well.

I have been unable to find any links Kuan might have had with other Yüan lyricists. His name is often linked with that of Hsü Tsai-ssu, whose sobriquet of T'ien-chai (Owner of the Sweet Studio) stands in amusing contrast to Kuan's Suan-chai. It seems that Kuan's and Hsü's lyrics were often spoken of together and perhaps even published together as the *Suan-t'ien yüeh-fu* (Sweet and Sour Lyrics), but there is no evidence that they ever knew each other. (Jen Na brought the two men's lyrics together under this title in the twentieth century.)[137]

An interesting passage appears in the *Lo-chiao ssu-yü* (Private Chats from the Happy Land) by Yao T'ung-shou (late Yüan):

Many of the young men of our *chou* [subprefecture/department] are good at singing lyrics [*yüeh-fu*]. This tradition stems completely from Mr. Yang from Kan-ch'uan [i.e., Kan-p'u in Hai-yen District, Chekiang]. During Mr. K'ang-hui's [Yang's] lifetime he was honorable and courageous and had a romantic personality [*chieh-hsia feng-liu*]. He was good at music and formed a close friendship with Yün-shih from Wu-lin [Hangchow], the son [*sic*] of Arigh Qaya. Yün-shih was an elegant and dashing young man, and, no matter what he wrote, either *yüeh-fu* [single lyrics] or *t'ao-shu* [song-sets], they were *chün-i* [spirited and free] and were the very best of the age. His voice was high pitched [*kao-yin*] and could reach even the Milky Way. It was K'ang-hui alone who carried on his tradition. [138]

Yang K'ang-hui was Yang Tzu; K'ang-hui is a posthumous title. Yang served in various administrative positions during the first part of the fourteenth century, first in Fukien and then later in Chekiang. As a young man he had even taken part in the Mongol expedition against Java in the 1290s. [139] He is also the author of three extant Yüan dramas: *Huo Kuang kuei chieh* (The Ghost of Huo Kuang Remonstrates, *YCHWP*, No. 136), *Yü Jang t'un t'an* (Yü Jang Swallows Charcoal, *YCHWP*; No. 137) and *Ching-te pu-fu lao* (Ching-te Does Not Give in to Old Age, *YCHWP*, No. 138). The passage then goes on to describe Yang's contributions to the development of the Hai-yen *ch'iang*, the Hai-yen style of staging and singing *tsa-chü* (dramas), which included the incorporation of *nan-pei ho-tiao* (medleys of northern and southern tunes). [140] If this account of Kuan's influence on Yang Tzu is accurate, then Kuan seems to have made a major contribution to the development of *nan-hsi*, Southern Drama, which began to flourish in places such as Hai-yen during the fourteenth century.

Kuan was a man of many talents. In addition to his accomplishments in classical verse and prose, in lyrics and singing, in composing music and perhaps playing various instruments, he claims to have played the *ch'in* (zither) (Poem 12). He also was a calligrapher of considerable repute and may even have been a painter as well. Ch'en Chi (1314–1370) wrote a colophon to a piece of calligraphy by Kuan, "Colophon to a Copy of [T'ao Ch'ien's] *Kuei-ch'ü-lai tz'u* (Returning to Live in the Country) in the Calligraphy of Kuan Suan-chai":

Mr. Suan-chai was like a wild goose in splendid isolation or a magnificent steed running free beyond the reach of harpoon-arrow or of bridle, and he emancipated himself from the vile state of common humanity as a cicada sheds its skin. Utterly free and unrestrained, he kept company with the very processes of Nature itself [*tsao wu-che*]. In recent times there has been no one to equal him. He himself once said that it was his lifelong policy not to copy out ancient- and modern-style verse written by others, but he so admired the character of T'ao Ching-chieh that he copied out his "Returning to Live in the Country." Those who examine it will never be able to find anything like it along the paths trodden by run-of-the-mill calligraphers. This critique was written on the second day of the fifth month of the tenth year of the Chih-cheng era [June 6, 1350] by Ch'en Chi of Lin-hai [Chekiang].[141]

T'ao Tsung-i, who identified the names of Kuan's concubines in his *Cho-keng lu*, also admired Kuan's calligraphy. He includes a critique of it in his *Shu-shih hui-yao* (Compendium of Essential Materials Concerned with the History of Calligraphy):

Kuan Yün-shih hai-ya: His sobriquet was Suan-chai, and he was a native of Pei-t'ing. In office he attained the post of Reader-in-Waiting in the Imperial Academy. Magnanimous by nature, he had an inspiring personality [*hao-shuang yu feng-kai*] and had rich talents as an author, as well as being a superb calligrapher. Famous compositions and beautiful phrases that have flowed out of the tip of his brush are so utterly marvelous [*kuai-kuai ch'i-ch'i*] that they appear to have transcended the very brush and ink which made them. As soon as you see his calligraphy, you can realize what he nourished in his breast.[142]

According to the *Mo-yüan hui-kuan lu* (Record of Collected Views of Notable Contributions to Painting and Calligraphy) by the wealthy art connoisseur, the Korean bannerman An Ch'i (born c. 1683), Kuan's calligraphy emulated that of the distinguished monk of the T'ang Dynasty, Kao-hsien, but since nothing of Kao-hsien's work has survived, there is no way of telling what this means.[143] In fact, only one piece of Kuan's own calligraphy is known to have survived into modern times. This consists of the two characters which have been published in Yang Tsung-han's article "Hsiao-Yün-Shih Khaya (1286–1324)," *MS* 9 (1944), plate XVIII, and which appear as the frontpiece of this book. One piece of calligraphy bears the seal of the Prince of Ch'ien-ning, which means that it was once owned by Mu Ying (1345–1392), the adopted son of the founder of the Ming, Chu Yüan-chang. Mu served with such distinction in the overthrow of the Yüan and in the early years of the consolidation of Ming rule that he was rewarded with a princely fief.[144] The piece of calligraphy may, of course, have come into the family during the tenure of a later descendant. The other piece bears the signature, Suan-chai. Yang Tsung-han informs us that at the time of publication these pieces of calligraphy were in the possession of a Mr. Yüan Li-chun of Peking.[145] Their present whereabouts are unknown.

In Hsü Tsung-yen's biography of Liang T'ung-shu (1723–1815), a native of Ch'ien-t'ang and one of the most famous calligraphers of the Ch'ing dynasty, it is recorded that Liang once managed to obtain possession of two characters in Kuan's calligraphy, *shan* (mountain) and *chou* (boat), and in consequence adopted the two of them as his sobriquet.[146] These too are now lost. However, Kuan's reputation as a great calligrapher seems beyond question; it is a pity that we now have only the photographic reproduction of these characters as the sole examples of his work.

It is possible that Kuan was a painter as well, though evidence for this is very slight. A *Kuan Suan-chai sung-t'u* (Painting of Pines by Kuan Suan-chai) is recorded in Wang K'o-yü's (born 1587) *Shan-hu-wang hua-lu* (A Painting Catalogue as Intricate and Sturdy as a Coral Network), but Wang adds the note: *wei-ch'üeh* (authenticity uncertain).[147] Although the titles of Poems 25 and 26 state that the author is a painter, these poems are actually not by Kuan (see the commentary which accompanies these poems in Chapter Three). Kuan might conceivably have painted the picture of the dragon which is the subject of Poem 4; in view of his great calligraphic skill, it is not unlikely that he was also a painter.

After Kuan's death the following ranks, titles, and offices were conferred posthumously: *Chi-hsien hsüeh-shih* (Scholar in the College of Assembled Worthies), *Chung-feng tai-fu* (Chung-feng Grandee), *Hu-chün* (General in the Imperial Guard), *Ching-chao kung* (Duke of the Metropolitan Commandery), and *Wen-ching* (Promoter of Peace through the Civil Arts).[148]

Before closing this chapter on Kuan's life, something should be said about Kuan's family and descendants. His younger brother Quduq Qaya seems to have served with distinction in the post of Garrison Commander of Liang-huai, for in 1333 we find him called to the capital to be promoted to *ts'an-chih cheng-shih* (Assistant Administrator in the Central Chancellery), a post he is listed as holding until the next year.[149] His name does not appear again in the sources until 1352 and 1353, when he is listed as a Chief Administrator in the Central Chancellery.[150] He is mentioned as well in the *Basic Annals* of Hsün-ti (Toqon Temür) for the fourth month of the twelfth year of the Chih-cheng era (May 14 – June 13, 1352), where it is recorded that "the Chief Administrator Quduq Qaya, because of his age and poor health, is ordered by the Emperor to be excused from morning audiences."[151] Quduq Qaya must have been in his sixties at that time. If he had been born a year or two after Kuan, he would have been sixty-three or sixty-four. After this, nothing more is heard of him. Nevertheless, his official career was unquestionably a great success, since the rank of Chief Administrator in the Central Chancellery was at the very top of the central bureaucracy.

This was a post which his elder brother Kuan Yün-shih surely aspired to before his disillusionment with an official career. Quduq Qaya's own career seems to have begun with his assumption of Kuan's office of Garrison Commander in 1308. When Kuan turned it over to him, he appears to have sincerely encouraged his younger brother to be a diligent and honest official of the state—so Ch'eng Chü-fu tells us in his *Colophon to the Poetry and Prose of Suan-chai* (Appendix IV): "When I read his 'Preface to [the poem] Seeing Younger Brother off to Yung-chou,' I thought it was such a sincere piece of moral advice." It is impossible to tell what the effects of this advice were over the rest of Quduq Qaya's life, but it is likely that he became what the family hoped Kuan himself would become, and managed to achieve for himself, in the process, at least a part of what Kuan's early career promised.

While nothing is known about the second of Kuan's two sons, Bars Qaya, the eldest, Arslan Qaya, had a long and distinguished career in both the military and civil administrations of various provinces.[152] He eventually became Chief Administrator of Hu-kuang Province during the last few years of Yüan rule in China. We know that he held this post during 1367 and 1368, right up to the very collapse of Yüan rule.[153] An entry in the *Ming shih-lu* (Veritable Records of the Ming Dynasty) for August 3, 1368, reads:

Chief Administrator Arslan surrendered Hsiang-chou. At first, after his defeat at Ch'üan-chou, he led what remained of his troops back to protect Hsiang-chou. When Generalissimo of our Southern Campaign [*cheng-nan chiang-chün*] Liao Yung-chung's [1323–1375] forces arrived at Wu-chou, he dispatched Commander Keng T'ien-pi [died 1374] and others to attack him. When Keng's forces reached the border of Pin-chou, Arslan sent his Company Commander Li, Assistant Chief Administrator of the Left, to meet them and block their advance, but T'ien-pi attacked and defeated him. His situation then untenable, Arslan sent his son Seng-pao to offer surrender, and then, leading all his subordinates, he came personally to

Yung-chung to surrender. He handed over his silver seal of office, three bronze seals and thirty-seven golden tallies, and with that the five districts of Kwangsi were pacified.[154]

It is ironic that Arslan Qaya, the great-grandson of Arigh Qaya who had conquered this region for the Yüan during the 1270s, was now the one to surrender it to the Ming. Perhaps the seals of office which he presented to General Liao were the very ones which Arigh Qaya himself had used during the days of Yüan glory. Arslan Qaya's son, Seng-pao (Guardian of Monks), is not included in the list of Kuan's grandsons which appears in the stele inscription of 1349; those given there are Nan-shan, Ning-shan, and Pao-shan (a fourth is unnamed).[155] We do not know which of these grandsons was born of which son. Seng-pao could have been the unnamed grandson, or he could have been born after the inscription was written, or he could be the same person as Pao-shan. Pao-shan sounds like a Chinese-style given name, and Seng-pao, the second syllable of which is homophonous with the first syllable of Pao-shan, may have been the Uighur name of the same individual. In any event, nothing more is known of Seng-pao, of his father, Arslan Qaya, or of any other of Kuan's descendants. If any of them survived in China into the Ming, it is likely that they were eventually completely assimilated into Chinese society and in time lost all recollection of their origins.

Kuan's own fame, however, did last. His name continued to appear in discussions of the *ch'ü* up to the end of the traditional era, and now, during the modern upsurge of interest in the Yüan lyric, much life is being breathed back into his reputation. It might be fitting to close this account of Kuan's life with a poetic eulogy by the famous Mongol poet and lyricist Sa-tu-la (born 1308) entitled "A Poem Written on the Wall of the Posthouse at Lu-kang, Following the Rhyme of One by Kuan Suan-chai Written There":

His new song turns "Maid of Wu" and "Water Song" into
    something fresh.[156]
What a fine figure on horseback this gentleman must have been!
Since the noble fellow's gone, spring grasses have grown deep,
Though the wild reputation he built by chance still fills the
    world.
Chanting his poem, I shout for wine at the riverside pavilion,

Then, spray from my brush a flying rain, the river's no longer
clean!
Overhead, the river wind tears apart a crescent-eyebrow
moon—
Like him, I too am a wanderer to the four corners of the
earth![157]

Appendix I *The Spirit-Way Stele Inscription of Mr. Kuan of the
Yüan Dynasty, Former Member of the Imperial Academy, Chung
Feng Grandee, Drafter of Imperial Edicts and Proclamations, and
Drafter of the History of the State*[158]

1. In the autumn of the third year of the Chih-chih era, the year
kuei-hai [1323], I served as an examiner in Chekiang, and when my
duties were finished, I went out and roamed about amidst the
mountains and the lakes. My old friend from the Imperial Academy,
Mr. Kuan, wandered with me for more than half a month. When
I was about to leave Hangchow, it being toward evening, he brought
along wine to see me off and said to me: "When I was young,
whenever I took leave of dear friends, I always felt the lingering
pain of separation for several days afterwards, but these last few
years I have been reading Buddhist writings and so have learned
that the Buddhists forbid this kind of sentiment, saying that 'memory
becomes rooted in it.' Consequently, I have come to regard it as
an abstention, but, here parting from you, I really cannot help it!"
Then we sadly parted.
2. In the summer of the next, the *chia-tzu* year [1324], Mr. Kuan
passed away at his residence at Hangchow. When the news of his
death reached me several months later, overcome with grief I wept.
Since then, whenever I go to Hangchow and meet with old friends
of his, I remember the time when we were about to part and, never
failing to be moved to tears, I call for a libation of wine to offer up
to him.
3. Twenty-five years after Mr. Kuan's death [1349], his son Arslan
Qaya, upon visiting his grave in Yen [Hopeh, i.e., Peking] and
observing that his father's spirit-way stele still lacked a memorial
inscription, came to see me and entrusted its composition to me.
How can I bear to write it!
4. Mr. Kuan's family originally came from Pei-t'ing. His given name
is Yün-shih, and he gave himself the sobriquet Suan-chai. He is the

grandson of Arigh Qaya, the former Viceroy of Hu-kuang Province
and upon whom were posthumously conferred the ranks: Meritorious Minister who Extended Imperial Majesty, Subdued Distant
Regions, Supported Virtue and Assisted Fate, Great Teacher, Grand
Commander Equal in Dignity to the Three Great Officers of State,
and Exalted Pillar of the State, and who was posthumously enfeoffed
as Prince of Chiang-ling and given the posthumous title of Pacifier
By Means of Military Arts. He is the son of Kuan-chih-ko, the
former Chief Administrator of Chiang-che Province and upon whom
were posthumously conferred the ranks of Great Officer in the Court
of Imperial Entertainment, Chief Administrator of Honan Province
and Pillar of the State, and who was posthumously enfeoffed as the
Duke of Ch'u and given the posthumous title of One Who is Loyal
and Kind. His mother was posthumously enfeoffed as Lady of the
State of Chao. She was the daughter of the former Chief Administrator Lien Hsi-min.
5. Before Mr. Kuan was born, his mother had a dream in which a
divine being took a star from the sky, turned it into a bright pearl
and gave it to her. After toying with it in her hand, she swallowed
it. Then she became pregnant. When he was born, he had an extraordinarily striking appearance, and when he was eleven or twelve
years of age, his physical strength already surpassed that of ordinary
men. He excelled at riding, archery and used the cavalry lance with
great skill. Once he had some young braves spur on three fierce
horses to a fast gallop while he held his lance at the ready and
waited for them. When they reached him, he jumped up at them,
and, leaping over two, he straddled the third—twirling his lance
he fanned up a breeze and scattered the onlookers in all directions.
Using a stiff bow, he would pursue wild animals up hill and down.
6. At first he inherited his father's office and became Garrison Commander and General of the Liang-huai Division with headquarters
at Yung-chou. When in camp, he clearly defined right and wrong
and meted out punishments without fail. Previously his father had
been so lenient and kindhearted that his troops were undisciplined,
but when Mr. Kuan arrived, his orders were strict, the soldiers
were respectful, and military affairs were well ordered. In his leisure
time, he would sing in an elegant fashion and play the game of
pitching arrows into the pot. He was inclined to do whatever pleased
him, as if he would not allow himself to be inhibited by circumstances. Thus his ambition to transcend the impure world was al-

ready established at this time. One day he summoned his younger brother Quduq Qaya and said to him: "I have been born with a weak desire for an official career, but I did not dare refuse to accept our grandfather's office. Now I have been at it for several years, and according to regulations it now ought to be handed over to you." On the selfsame day he informed his father by letter and submitted official papers to inform those in charge. He untied the golden tiger tally which had been bound on him and gladly gave it over to his brother.

7. He then retired to where he could wander about amidst beautiful mountains and waters with literary men and exchanged poems with them all day long. He was so free and happy that he forgot all about ever returning. Later he went to the North and pursued studies under Yao Wen-kung [Yao Sui] who then came to the opinion that his prose in the ancient style was austere but full of strong feeling and according to form, and that his songs and poetry in the ancient ballad form were rich in profound feeling and poignantly moving. He greatly marvelled at his talent.

8. When Emperor Jen-tsung [Ayurbarwada] was still Heir-Apparent, he had heard about Mr. Kuan's yielding his rank and office to his brother and said to the officers in attendance: "It is indeed difficult to find a person of such virtue as this who comes from a family of ministers and generals!" When Mr. Yao became his attendant, he also recommended him several times. Not long after this, Mr. Kuan presented his *Classic of Filial Piety with a Commentary in the Vernacular*, and it met with Imperial approval. He was then appointed Licentiate Lecturer of the Confucian Classics in the residence of the future Emperor Ying-tsung [Shidebala] and served night guard duty in His Presence. When Jen-tsung ascended the Throne, Mr. Kuan, by special Imperial order, was appointed Member of the Imperial Academy, *Chung-feng* Grandee, Drafter of Imperial Edicts and Proclamations and Drafter of the History of the State. Immediately, the other members of the Imperial Academy, who had already heard of him, were so anxious to meet him that each competed with the other to be the first to do so.

9. When the Court held meetings to deliberate the re-implementation of the civil service examination system, Mr. Yao had then already retired from Court, but Mr. Kuan together with the Transmitter of Directives, Mr. Ch'eng Wen-hsien [Ch'eng Chu-fü], and the Expositor-in-Waiting, Mr. Yüan Wen-min [Yüan Ming-shan],

determined what the regulations should be. Mr. Kuan provided the most assistance. Now they are written into law.

10. Soon after this, Mr. Kuan submitted a memorial which enumerated six matters. The first was "Disband the Frontier Guards so that They May Cultivate Civil Virtues." The second one was "Educate the Heir-Apparent in Order that the Foundations of the State be Rectified." The third was "Appoint Remonstrators to Assist His Majesty." The fourth was "Publicly Honor People by Proper Surname so as to Distinguish the Descendants of Meritorious Officials." The fifth was "Standardize Dress so as to Transform Public Morality." The sixth was "Promote the Worthy and the Talented so as to Enlarge the Most Excellent Way." Altogether it consisted of more than ten thousand characters and often hit exactly upon what was wrong with the times, the Emperor scrutinized it, sighed in admiration but took no action on it.

11. Mr. Kuan then thought to himself: "Worthy men of the past declined high positions and occupied low ones. The position I now hold in the Imperial Academy is higher than the military post I gave up. People will therefore say that I lived for a fine reputation and coveted high office, and so I should resign." After he resigned on the pretext of illness, he returned to the South and for more than ten years toured famous scenic places one after the other. His writings also filled his house. Wherever he went, retired officials in their red sashes, young aspirants to officialdom in their billowing sleeves, and gentlemen of leisure who lived outside the bounds of propriety [lay Taoists] followed him about in clouds. Anyone who obtained a composition of his, even if it were only a letter a few words long, would treasure it as if it were a large jade circular plaque. In the light of this, Mr. Kuan said: "My aim was to escape from fame, but fame has followed me here. I will certainly come to harm because of this. The Chiang-Che region is prosperous and large, so I can hide my tracks there." Consequently he travelled east to Ch'ien-t'ang [Hangchow] and sold medicine in the marketplace, assumed aliases, altered his manner of dress and mixed in with the local inhabitants. Once he was passing through Liang-shan Marsh and saw an old fisherman weaving a quilt out of reed-floss. He took a fancy to it and offered to trade a piece of silk for it. The old fisherman, seeing that he would exchange something expensive for something cheap, regarded him as an unusual person, and, as if in jest, said: "If you, sir, want my quilt, you shall have to compose

a poem for it too."Mr. Kuan took up writing brush and finished one on the spot, got the quilt after all, and took it away with him. The poem then circulated among the people, and they came to call him the "Reed-Floss Taoist." When Mr. Kuan reached Ch'ien-t'ang, he therefore took it as his own sobriquet.

12. He once went up to the T'ien-mu Mountains and visited the Ch'an Master [Ming-] pen, Chung-feng. They took delight in discussing the Great Way, matching wits which were as sharp as arrows or lances with each other. Every summer he sat in Ch'an meditation on Pao Mountain; only when summer was over would he start back to town. Thereafter, day by day, he became broader in learning and more accomplished in the writing of prose, and his classical verse also became self-transcendent and dispassionate, modest and remote. In calligraphy he derived his style somewhat from the ancients but transformed it and became a master in his own right. When he discussed affairs of state, he got at the real essentials and was unpretentious. Those with discerning judgment were delighted with him and said that he was going to be of service to the world once again, but Mr. Kuan's footsteps gradually withdrew more and more from the world's entanglements. When the afternoon arrived, he would still be wrapped up in his bedclothes and remain fast asleep, and so there were many visitors who did not get to see him. His servants picked up his habits and they changed day into night. His taste for the Way increased day by day, and his taste for the world daily waned. Not only did he untie his official's sash, he put it aside and turned his back on it.

13. On the eighth day of the fifth month of the first year of the T'ai-ting era [May 30, 1324] he passed away at his residence at Ch'ien-t'ang at the age of thirty-eight years. From members of the scholar-official class to children and people of the lower classes, there was none who did not mourn his passing. A certain time afterwards all his bereaved children accompanied his coffin for internment in the family burial ground at Hsi-chin [southwest of Peking].

14. He married a woman from the famous Shih family of Peking. Her father, Shih T'ien-lin, was once the Commandant of Chiang-ling Circuit [Hupeh]. She possessed wifely virtues and was posthumously enfeoffed as Lady of the Metropolitan Commandery. He has two sons. The elder, Arslan Qaya, has served successively as Garrison Commander of Lan-hsi Military Prefecture [Hupeh], a Tea-tax Inspector and as Garrison Commander of Tz'u-li Military

Prefecture [Hunan]. In all the offices in which he served he became famous for his incorruptability. The younger son is Bars Qaya. He has four grandsons. The eldest is Nan-shan, the second is Ning-shan, and the third is Pao-shan. All of them are preparing for the *chin-shih* examination. He has one daughter. She married Tuan Ch'ien, the Garrison Commander of Huai-ch'ing Military Prefecture [Honan]. She is learned and knowledgeable and can write in an accomplished style.

15. I once gave an evaluation of Mr. Kuan as someone who employed the strategy of attack and subdue in military affairs and who had the talent to excel at administration in civil affairs. From the military he proceeded to the civil and helped manage the affairs of the Empire. He certainly was the kind of person it is difficult to find in a world such as this, though it might not be uncommon for someone who had been born into an age which has enjoyed peace and into a family which has enjoyed official salaries for generations. The fact that he lightly regarded high position, lived in seclusion beyond the confines of the impure world, made his way through life without hesitation and acted as if he were poor—thus living out his life in tranquillity—is something which is even difficult for gentlemen recluses who dwell in the wilderness to do. This indicates the high quality of his character. How can we ever manage to measure him by our insignificant standards!

16. There are still in circulation in the world today several *chüan* of his writings; namely, *pei* [funerary inscriptions], *ming* [memorial inscriptions], *chi* [records], *hsü* [narratives], *tsa-chu* [miscellaneous writings], *shih* [classical verse], *tz'u* [lyrics], and his *Classic of Filial Piety with Commentary in the Vernacular*, which he once presented to the Court.

17. His Memorial Inscription reads:

Alas! Mr. Kuan is a unicorn, a phoenix—
Since his departure lies beyond inquiry, was not his appearance
    unpredictable!
Alas! Mr. Kuan is a divine dragon, a Pegasus—
Since his transformation is unfathomable, does not his constancy lie
    beyond investigation!
The Noble Spirit of the Universe condenses and disperses as do clouds,
    diffuses as does thunder.
It moves things and the gods, influences both military and civil affairs.

In both action and in repose, is it not always perfectly fitting without the
  least effort!
He came and went with the marvelous powers of a flying genie or an
  arhat and passed through the world as if it were sport.
All of a sudden he had enlightenment—
Do we not meet and part as if in an instant, assemble and disperse in a
  flash!
Since between life and death lies the boundary of darkness and light,
How can we know that what most delights Mr. Kuan is what the world
  finds most sad.
Alas and alack! There are things we can know and things we cannot.
What we can know is that the graveyard in Yen conceals his body here.

Although I have composed this memorial verse, how can I possibly
give an adequate account of Mr. Kuan's greatness? I can only, for
a time at least, hope to bring comfort to the thoughts of those he
left behind.

Appendix II *Biography of Hsiao-Yün-Shih Hai-Ya (Sewinch Qaya),
  Reader-in-Waiting in the Imperial Academy*[159]

[The first half of this biographical notice fails to provide any information not found in the spirit-way stele of Ou-yang Hsüan—Appendix I.]

After Suan-chai surrendered his office and gave up his salary, he
sometimes concealed himself among butchers and wine-sellers and
sometimes befriended woodgathers and shepherds. Often in the
marketplace of Lin-an [Hangchow] he would set up an advertising
signboard which said: "The World's Very Best Pills to Make You
Happy." When a customer would come, he would stretch out his
two hands and give a great big laugh—by way of demonstration.
Those who understood what he meant would also begin to laugh
before they went away. One day, several of the local gentry from
Ch'ien-t'ang came for an outing to Tiger Run Spring. While they
were drinking they tried to compose poems which employed the
character *ch'üan* [spring] as the rhyme. One of them could only
mumble, "*Ch'üan, ch'üan, ch'üan,*" and for a long time could not
bring it off, when suddenly there appeared an old fellow dragging
a staff who said by way of response:

The spring, the spring, the spring
Randomly spews precious pearls—each one of them
    round.
It's jade axes chipping out the essence from witless stones,
Golden hooks snatching up saliva from an ancient dragon!

They were all startled and asked, "Sir, are you not Kuan Suan-chai?" He replied, "Yes, yes, yes [jan-jan-jan]." They then invited him to drink with them, and when he had become thoroughly drunk, he left. The way he used disguises and sported with the world was often like this.

Appendix III *Preface to the Collected Writings of Mr. Kuan, Reader-in-Waiting in the Imperial Academy*[160]

1. Formerly when I worked at correcting errors in documents at the Imperial Academy, Mr. Yao [Sui], Imperial Academician for the Transmission of Directives, had little approval for the writers of the day, but he always praised Mr. Kuan as a young man of tremendous ability who deserved to be singled out as a spokesman for our current age. I took secret delight in the hope that I might have the good fortune to associate with Mr. Kuan so that from what he said and from what he wrote I might be able to verify whether Mr. Yao's judgment was to be trusted. Not long afterwards, Mr. Kuan joined the Imperial Academy as Reader-in-Waiting, but by then I had been transferred to a post outside the court and thus did not have the opportunity to fulfill that hope. Two years later, as Vice-Director of Education, I was assembling students day after day and had to listen to their empty recitations by rote—something which was always disturbingly noisy! I was otherwise busy with different matters, and so again we did not have an opportunity to meet.
2. When we finally met, it was as if we "lowered our carriage covers," as people of old used to say [i.e., a close and immediate friendship was formed]. As far as friendship is concerned, even if run-of-the-mill scholars knock on my door every day in countless numbers, I would never exchange this for the pleasure of knowing that. Shortly afterwards, Mr. Kuan and I returned to the South in close succession, and after we had been parted for a year he came to spend some time in Ch'ien-t'ang and paid me a visit. Our reunion

was as happy as if we had been lifelong friends. When he showed me the poetry and prose he had written, I read every piece and realized that Mr. Kuan's ability was indeed tremendous—exactly as Mr. Yao had said. His writing even gallops up and down like a Pegasus which has thrown off its bridle and can cross a thousand *li* in one bound. Wang-liang and Tsao-fu [two famous horsemen of antiquity] would have stared at him in amazement and turned their heads for a better look! Oh, he is indeed marvelous! Confucians used to have the saying that famous generals of antiquity only came from among those who had marvelous ability, for only then were they able to be victorious. However, if one were not well versed in tactics as well, he could not do it. Perfection lies in quick action, and quick action lies in daring. This is the way that men of the world ought to behave—something which people constrained by ordinary limits cannot understand.

3. Mr. Kuan's grandfather was the Prince of Ch'ang-sha, a Viceroy of a province and our Commander-in-Chief of the Expedition against the South. His merit was in military affairs, and Mr. Kuan inherited from him these same blessings. He once served as a Myriarch and in military tactics was very skillful. Could it be that the versatility of his literary art benefited from his experiences there? Li Kuang and Ch'eng Pu-shih of the Han Dynasty both had reputations as great generals. On the march, Kuang did not have his troops arranged in any proper order, and, in camp, he did not have cooking pots struck for the sake of alarm—as he examined dispatches in his tent headquarters. The way he managed things was very casual and careless, yet his reputation has always been higher than that of Pu-shih. People like me, who have been fond of composing literature since we were very young, are barely able to keep to the rules, and with this limitation, we cannot accomplish anything comparable to Mr. Kuan's work. How can I help but feel ashamed of myself! I have observed that throughout ancient and modern times gifted writers for the most part have come either from among those who were in distressed circumstances due to forced travel or from among those who lived in humble circumstances in the country. Now, Mr. Kuan has been born into and has been raised in great wealth and high status, but he does not put any value on getting drunk at banquets or living a life of carefree frivolity. He only takes delight in matching skills with common folk and laborers. This is truly something which ordinary men are unable to do. Fame is a public

commodity for anyone in the world—Mr. Kuan should be careful not to take too much of it!

Appendix IV *Colophon to the Poetry and Prose of Suan-Chai*[161]

The above *chüan* [sections] of poetry and prose are by Suan-chai, the grandson of the later meritorious official, [posthumously enfeoffed as] the Duke of Ch'u who holds the [posthumously conferred] title of Pacifier by Means of Military Arts. In the second month of the second year of the Huang-ch'ing Era [February 26 – March 27, 1313] he was appointed Reader-in-Waiting in the Imperial Academy, and we became colleagues. It was then that he brought out the manuscript of this to show me. When I read his "Preface to [the poem] Seeing Younger Brother off to Yung-chou," I thought it was such a sincere piece of moral advice! His five- and seven-syllable ancient-style verse and his *ch'ang-tuan chü* [lyrics] effect a profound attainment in the fusion of emotion and scene. I have to sigh and declare: Since what he has already achieved in his youth is as good as this, how much more can we expect from him in the future!

At first, Mr. Kuan inherited the office of Myriarch, and law and moral suasion formed equal parts of his administration. However, after a short time he yielded his office to his younger brother. Through his learning and his personal conduct he then came to the attention of the Emperor, thus he came to hold this appointment. I have listened to his words and so know that fame and wealth lack sufficient means to make him easily happy. How indeed can we ever fix limits for the way virtue is passed down in a family from one generation to the next!

Appendix V *Entry in Yüan Tien-Chang (Casebook of Yüan Administrative Law): "Unjustly Imprisoned, Someone Despairs of Life and Commits Suicide"*[162]

1. In the sixth month of the eleventh year of the Ta-te era [June 30—July 29, 1307] the Provincial Governor of Kiangsi received a communication from the Central Chancellery: "The delegated official, Li Chü-chin, the former Secretary in the Ministry of Justice, has reported: 'In accordance with the order given by the Central Chancellery, I went to the offices of the Provincial Government of

Kiang-si, where—together with the Vice-Commissioner of Jui-chou Commandery, Cheng Chao-lien, who had been so delegated by the Provincial Government—I inspected the dossiers of convicts incarcerated in prisons.' "

2. Among such criminal cases there was one which involved a man detained by the Department of Police of Chi-chou Commandery: "The jailers Hsiao Te and Ch'en Wan put Chung the Third in prison where he killed himself by hanging." We went through the various files and came across a deposition made by the Commissioner of Police Sewinch Qaya [Kuan Yün-shih]: "On the fourteenth day of the eleventh month of the ninth year of the Ta-te era [November 30, 1305], in response to a plaint made by Li A-liu that a certain Liu Chi-san, in the company of a salt merchant of unknown name and surname, had come looking for her husband, and, when they had called him outside, they kicked him to death, I, with the assistance of the Police Magistrate and the Assistant Magistrate of the said commandery, carried out an investigation. We determined that the principal malefactor, Liu Chi-san, as already accused, had indeed kicked Li Chung-erh to death. The accessory, Chung the Third, gave the following evidence in a deposition: '[Liu Chi-san] had cursed Li Chung-erh with the words, "You lying beggar's bastard! You owe me money and won't pay it back!" When I tried to save [Li] by dissuading [Liu from killing him], he wouldn't listen. It was Liu Chi-san who kicked Li Chung-erh to death.' A report was then sent up to the Garrison Commander of Chi-chou Commandery for the purpose of cross-examination. Since Chung the Third was the key to the case, it was necessary to interrogate a number of people, and now all of them had to undergo interrogation for a second time. However, their depositions contained no discrepancies. Since it was also necessary to determine the lesser and the greater degrees of guilt [i.e., between Liu Chi-san and Chung the Third], a decision was reached according to law. Unfortunately it was repeatedly charged by the principal plaintiff, Li A-liu, that her husband had been kicked to death by Chung the Third, and she would not sign the proceedings. Therefore, we locked up Chung the Third in prison for more than sixty days, which resulted in his despairing of life and killing himself by hanging. This deposition conforms to the facts."

3. The depositions made by Police Magistrate Chi Lu, by the Assistant Magistrate Chiang Hsiang, by the Office Errand-Runner Liu

Hsien, by the clerk of Chi-chou Commandery Teng Wen-hsin, and by others contain no discrepancies. Since the decision [to incarcerate Chung the Third] had been arbitrary, this case should be declared to be "Death of a Person Caused by Strangulation during Incarceration."

4. The matter was brought before the Ministry of Justice, whose deliberations concluded: "According to the depositions made by the Commissioner of Police Sewinch Qaya, by the Police Magistrate Chi Lu, by the Assistant Magistrate Chiang Hsiang, by the Office Errand-Runner Liu Hsien and by others, they all knew that Chung the Third had given the evidence: 'The reason why Liu Chi-san kicked Li Chung-erh to death was because I did not do my best to save the one and dissuade the other.' However, they did not properly distinguish between the lesser and the greater degrees of guilt in deciding the case and so unjustly incarcerated Chung the Third for more than eighty days [sic], with the result that while in prison he despaired of life and hung himself. Each official involved, as punishment, is to be dismissed. All are to be released from the offices to which they have been appointed and should apply for office elsewhere. As for the clerk Liu Hsien and the others, each is to be dismissed from his post, and the employment lists in general circulation are to contain an account of their demerits."

5. "As should be done, the Central Chancellery decrees in this communication that the matter be dealt with in accordance with the above."

CHAPTER 2

The Classical Verse of a Yüan Poet

I The Verse of the Yüan Era

K UAN YÜN-SHIH is not well known as a writer of classical verse (*shih*); indeed, the *shih* poetry of the Yüan era has been little studied, either in the West or in China and Japan.[1] Therefore, in this respect Kuan is an obscure figure in an almost equally obscure field of study. Before we can begin to make a meaningful analysis of him as an individual *shih* poet, we must first try to sketch out the general features of Yüan *shih* and attempt to determine both its links with earlier stages of the genre, especially with the T'ang and the Sung, and its standing in the eyes of critics of the Ming and Ch'ing eras. It is during the Ming and the Ch'ing, in fact, that we find the reasons why Yüan *shih* is almost totally unknown today. Before providing a general view of what Yüan verse was like, it is appropriate that we first look into these reasons.

During the 600 years since the fall of the Yüan dynasty, Yüan *shih* seems to have enjoyed a period of high esteem only during the later Ch'ing dynasty, from about 1690 to the end of the nineteenth century. It was in the 1690s that Ku Ssu-li's *Yüan-shih hsüan* (An Anthology of Yüan Verse) appeared. The first *chi* (collection or series) was published in 1694, the second in 1702, and the third in 1720. Kuan's own *shih* is included in the second *chi*. Each *chi* contains the poetry of 100 authors. A supplementary (*kuei*) collection was published after Ku's death during the Chia-ch'ing era (1796–1820). These four collections constitute the single most important source for the study of Yüan *shih*; without them the works of many a Yüan poet would certainly have been lost, and the convenience they offer the researcher is immeasurable. Moreover, the *Yüan-shih hsüan* is not an accident of literary history but something which seems to have been an inevitable product of both the general trends

of *shih* development in the Ming and the early Ch'ing and the
general historical and political views of Ku's own age. It was, in
fact, a product of literary and political culture. The age which produced it, the mid-Ch'ing, was intensely concerned with legitimacy
and orthodoxy, both in the literary and the political realms, and
Yüan *shih* poetry, as curious as this might sound, was an important
ingredient in the constitution of both.

The Manchus, in inaugurating another era of non-Chinese rule
of the empire, naturally looked to the Mongols for precedents that
might enhance the legitimacy of their own rule, and the Chinese
themselves looked to the Yüan period for precedents that might
help justify, or at least rationalize, life under the Manchus. In light
of this, Ku's *Yüan-shih hsüan* can be explained in part as a monumental attempt to prove that Chinese culture flourished during the
Yüan,[2] and, by analogy, to convince his contemporaries that it could
flourish again under the Manchus. As such, the *Yüan-shih hsüan*
could attract the sympathetic attention of ruler and ruled alike: the
Manchus, and the Chinese who identified with their rule, could
regard it as a monument to the excellence of literary culture during
an era analogous to their own. Disaffected Chinese, whose attitudes
to Manchu rule ranged from outright resentment and frustration to
resigned acceptance, could see it as monumental proof that traditional Chinese culture could survive in spite of non-Chinese rule.

After it appeared in print, the *Yüan-shih hsüan* was widely read,
and it remained a popular work throughout the rest of the eighteenth
century. It was the stimulus for a number of smaller, more compact
anthologies of Yüan verse,[3] and Yüan *shih*, for a time at least, enjoyed a popularity which it had never known since Yüan times.
When anti-Manchu sentiment began to manifest itself during the
period of dynastic decline and foreign imperialism during the nineteenth and early twentieth centuries, the whole process of legiti-
mizing or rationalizing Manchu rule in terms of the precedents of
the Yüan became unpleasant for the Manchus and superfluous for
the Chinese: the Manchus now found any analogy between their
rule and the shortlived rule of the Mongols odious, and the Chinese,
reformers and revolutionaries alike, looked not to the Yüan for
inspiration, but instead, if they looked to the past at all, to earlier
periods of legitimate Chinese rule, especially to the Ming, the dynasty which had crushed the Mongols and had driven them out of
China. In the context of political attitudes such as these, Yüan *shih*

poetry had little or no role to play and the eclipse of interest in it as a period genre by the early years of the Republic seems to have been inevitable.

However, the entire phenomenon of the growth, apogee, continuance, and final disintegration of interest in Yüan *shih* during the Ch'ing and the early Republic can also be explained in different, though complementary, terms. It was also the result of intrinsic forces within the tradition of *shih* poetry itself and within the various attitudes toward literature in general which developed during this time. We must go back to the Ming (1368–1643) to appreciate how these forces emerged.[4] During most of the Ming, *shih* written after the T'ang (618–906), both that of the Sung (960–1279) and the Yüan, was almost completely ignored. The so-called "archaist" or "neoclassical" *(fu-ku)* movement which centered around the *ch'ien-hou ch'i-tzu* ("The Former and Latter Seven Masters") dominated the world of poetry until the end of the sixteenth century, and this movement decreed, following the dictum attributed to Li Mengyang (1472–1529): "Prose must be in the style of the Ch'in and the Han, and poetry [*shih*] must be in that of the High T'ang."[5] It insisted that after the T'ang there was no *shih* worth reading, and the *shih* of the Sung and the Yüan (if attended to at all) was judged solely in terms of how well or ill it followed in the paths laid down by the T'ang masters. This movement was challenged finally by the Kung-an school led by Yüan Hung-tao (1568–1610) and his brothers (natives of Kung-an in Hupeh). They attacked the archaists on a number of grounds, including: a condemnation of their imitation of T'ang masters, something which too often had degenerated into plagiarism (an unfortunate and seemingly inevitable result of some of the key theoretical tenets of the movement); a complaint that the archaists lacked real and individual expressiveness in their poetry; and a rejection of the claim that no poetry worthy of emulation was written after the T'ang. Yüan Tsung-tao, the eldest of the Yüan brothers, emulated in particular two poets from whom the archaists largely withheld approval: the Middle T'ang writer Po Chü-i (772–846), who anticipated much of the Sung "style" of poetry—its casual, offhand atmosphere, its loose narrative qualities and its prosy descriptions of everyday life—and the Sung master Su Shih (1037–1101). The Kung-an school was very partial to the poetry of the Sung dynasty, and it is likely that the late Ming interest in Sung and Yüan poetry, which occasioned the appearance of several anthologies, can be traced to the literary circle centered in the Yüan brothers.[6] The Kung-an school did not seem to regard Sung and Yüan poetry as separate entities and considered the one to be largely a continuation of the other. It was interested in both as part of its reaction against the dictates and poetic practice of the archaists who, in general, insisted upon exclusive loyalty to models taken from the High T'ang period. Although its view of Yüan poetry was largely erroneous (as we shall see), the Kung-an school did help to emancipate it from almost total obscurity and, as such, did much to stimulate the more accurate and sophisticated critical attention which was addressed to Yüan verse during the late Ming period and later during the Ch'ing era.

The fall of the Ming in 1643 did not end the influence of the Kung-an school, but it considerably diminished it. It was not until the appearance of Wu Chih-chen's (1640–1717) anthology of Sung verse, the Sung-shih ch'ao, in 1671 that Sung poetry began to recover the popularity it had enjoyed during the days of the Yüan brothers. In fact, it became so popular that many poets, for a time, exclusively imitated Sung rather than T'ang models. In the meantime, however, an interest in Yüan poetry was also building—now not in terms of the erroneous view that it was simply an extension of that of the Sung. By the second half of the seventeenth century people were beginning to realize that Yüan verse, in both technique and spirit, was very close to the shih of the T'ang masters. This was something which the Ming archaists seem to have realized as well, but, totally committed to the T'ang as they were, they had very little to say about it. For the most part, they were willing to admit that Yüan poetry was better (i.e., more cheng: "correct" or "orthodox") than that of the Sung, but that marked the limits of their interest in it. Of all the Ming archaists, only Hu Ying-lin (1551–1602) devoted a major portion of his critical writings on poetry to Yüan verse.[7] Hu went to great lengths to demonstrate how Yüan shih reversed the "pernicious" tendency of Sung poets to depart from the correct standards set down by the T'ang masters. Since he was active during the heyday of the Kung-an school, it is likely that Hu, unlike his archaist predecessors whose views went largely unchallenged in their own times, was prodded to defend the "orthodox" tradition of poetry by enlisting Yüan verse as an ally. To do so, of course, he first had to establish its "orthodox" credentials. Even so, Hu can hardly be called a champion of Yüan verse, since he regarded it, orthodox as it may be, as decidedly inferior to that of the T'ang itself. He thought it was too "imitative" (*lin-mo*), too "shallow" (*ch'ien*), lacking in "seasoned maturity" (*lao-ts'ang*), and deficient in "surprising variations" (*pien-huan*),[8] but, whatever these failings, it was still his view that Yüan *shih* was very much superior to that of the Sung—something which he dismissed as mere "rhymed prose." The popularity of the pro-Sung views of the Kung-an school seem to have struck him as a genuine danger, and, needing all the help he could get, he willingly accepted the poetry of the Yüan as an ally in the fight against the Sung and for the T'ang. Although Hu's interest in the poetry of the Yüan was largely opportunistic and peripheral, many of his observations about it make sense, and his general assertion that it should be regarded as a renaissance of the T'ang "style" seems beyond question.[9]

Critics of the second half of the seventeenth century took a much closer and fairer view of Yüan *shih* than did the Ming archaists, Hu Ying-lin included, and what they saw convinced some of them that a revival of the poetry of the Yüan was appropriate and necessary, not only to combat the excessive interest in Sung verse which the *Sung-shih ch'ao* was generating, but to bring about as well a salutary effect on current poetic practice. Some critics of the time thought that the study of Yüan poetry could retrieve the best features of T'ang verse—something which they felt the Ming archaists, as much as they may have championed T'ang poetry, had failed to do. Influential critics such as Wang Shih-chen (1634–1711) and Sung Lo (1634–1713) seem to have begun at this time to advocate a kind of "progressive classicism," a view that saw the tradition of *shih* poetry as a living, ever-growing stream to which all periods had contributed. They were much more open-minded and catholic in their literary tastes and standards than the Ming archaists had been before them. Although, like the Ming archaists, they regarded T'ang *shih* as the apogee of poetic excellence, they also readily admitted what they considered to have been the "best" of successive ages (from the Sung, the Yüan, and the Ming, as well as their own age) into the "orthodox tradition." They seem to have been more interested in discovering proofs that "true" poetry continued to be written after the T'ang than in regarding the T'ang as possessing a unique monopoly over "true" poetry as such, as had the Ming archaists. For them, "true" or "correct" poetry may have first achieved real and universal status under the T'ang, but they also regarded this "true" poetry as a mode of expression which potentially could be recovered in every age. They deplored both the neglect of later *shih* poetry in the training of contemporary poets as well as the blind imitation of earlier individual poets and period styles, whether it be of the T'ang or the Sung.[10]

Sung Lo in his later years seems to have turned away from this progressive attitude and to have adopted a critical stance much more in line with the Ming archaists. For example, he insisted in his preface to Ku Ssu-li's *Yüan-shih hsüan* (1694) that the principal value of Yüan *shih* poetry was as an antidote to that of the Sung, since it could lead the student of poetry back to the "truth" of the T'ang:

In my opinion, poetry in this present day and age has reached a juncture where it must undergo a change. It must change by going back to the T'ang. It must also change by keeping up with the flow, that is, by going back to the Yüan.[11]

Ku himself was even more adamant in his insistence that the tradition of *shih* poetry was a closed circle (always returning to the T'ang) rather than an open-ended process accessible to each and every age:

The great flowing current of the tradition of poetry has its source in two ancestors: the *Feng* [i.e., the *Classic of Poetry* (*Shih-ching*)] and the *Sao* [i.e., the *Elegies of Ch'u* (*Ch'u-tz'u*)]. Poets who came after those who wrote the *Sao* went through successive transformations. Five-syllable verse reached its apogee with the T'ang, and its transformations came to an end with the Sung. Since, by the time it came down to the Yüan, poetry had exhausted all the possibilities open to it, it turned from what the Sung had done back to the T'ang, and, at this, all possible variations were complete with it.[12]

We might label these statements by Sung Lo and Ku Ssu-li "neo-archaist," since they are so similar to what the Ming archaists themselves advocated. Whatever sympathy such neo-archaist critics had for Sung verse seems to have evaporated by the early years of the eighteenth century. By this time the world of *shih* poetry was clearly divided between the pro-T'ang neo-archaists and the pro-Sung expressionist-individualists, and Yüan poetry in the views of both obviously belonged to the pro-T'ang camp.[13] Then, the Yüan *shih* came to be regarded as simply a latter-day version of T'ang *shih* and was either admired or condemned as such. Prefaces to eighteenth-century anthologies of Yüan verse all praise and recommend it as something which recovers the excellence of T'ang verse. For example, Shen Chün-te's preface to his own anthology, the *Yüan-shih pai-i ch'ao* (A Concise [i.e., "one out of a hundred"] Anthology of Yüan Verse), has this to say:

If one follows the brilliant example of Yüan poetry, he will not lose contact with the sounds of the T'ang and will furthermore be able to trace the source of poetry upstream to the *Feng*, the *Sao*, and to the verse of the Han and the Wei, thus obtaining something upon which to depend . . . . The pernicious qualities of poetry at the end of the Sung era consist of its *ts'u-shuai* [careless impulsiveness] and *sheng-ying* [crude rigidity]. The poetry of the Yüan reversed this trend completely. If one wishes to save himself from the pernicious influence of Sung verse and immerse himself in the Yüan, how can he do it? He should learn from the *Yüan-shih pai-i ch'ao.*[14]

It was this identification of Yüan *shih* with the most conservative views of the pro-T'ang neo-archaists that in part contributed most to its loss of reputation among advocates of literary reform and the vernacular language movement during the early years of the Republic. Even before this, the early nineteenth-century poet Kung Tzu-chen (1792–1841), progressive poets from the second half of the century such as Huang Tsun-hsien (1848–1905), and the poets of the Nan-she (Southern Society) all made a conscious effort to break with conservative tradition, and they deplored the "antiquarian" fetters of those of their contemporaries who persisted in identifying with the views of the Ming archaists and the later Ch'ing neo-archaists. As a result, Yüan *shih* poetry fell into neglect just at a time when native scholars were beginning the modern study of their own literary tradition.

In addition to his editor's preface and the *fan-li* (principles of compilation) section to the *Yüan-shih hsüan*, Ku Ssu-li has much to say about Yüan poetry in his collected remarks on poetry, the *Han-t'ing shih-hua.* One passage is of particular importance since in it Ku provides a catalogue of the major poets and attempts to establish critical guidelines for distinguishing overall trends:

Yüan poetry is a continuation of trends in existence at the end of the Sung. In the northeast, it began with Yüan Hao-wen, [*hao*] I-shan [1190–1257].

His followers Hao Ching, [hao] Ling-ch'uan [1223–1275], and Liu Yin, [hao] Ching-hsiu [1247–1293], continued a tradition which came to great fruition during the time between the Chung-t'ung [1260–1264] and the Chih-yüan [1280–1294] eras. However, they still failed to refrain from ts'u-hao [excessive straightforwardness]. In the southeast, it began with Chao Meng-fu, [hao] Sung-hsüeh. Poets such as Yüan Chüeh, [hao] Ch'ing-k'o [1267–1327], Teng Wen-yüan, [tzu] Shan-chih, and Kung K'uei, [hao] Yün-lin [1268–1329], followed his example and carried on what he had begun. Since they lived during an age of successive peaceful reigns, they purged poetry completely of the unfortunate habits left over from the Sung and the Chin dynasties and effected a major transformation of it. Between the Yen-yu [1314–1320] and the Ta-li [1328–1329] eras, the style of poetry [feng-ch'i] continually improved. Those who gloriously sang of the peace and prosperity of this age included Yü [Chi], Yang [Tsai (1271–1323)], Fan [P'eng (1272–1330)] and Chieh [Hsi-ssu (1274–1344)], all of whom equally regarded the poetry of the T'ang dynasty as their patriarch as they pursued literary elegance, and they should be regarded as representing the golden age of Yüan poetry, though sometimes people so designate Yü, Chieh, Ma [Tsu-ch'ang (1279–1338)], and [the two brothers] Sung Pen [1281–1334] and Sung Chiung [1294–1346]. Furthermore, opinion has it that only Ch'en [Lü (1288–1343)], Li [Hsiao-kuang (1297–1348)] and the two Chang's— Chang Chu [1287–1367] and Chang Hsien [fl. c. 1341]—were able to effect a renaissance of this tradition in the following period, and that Fu Jo-chin, [tzu] Ju-li [1304–1343] of Hsin-yü [Kiangsi], Kung Shih-t'ai, [tzu] T'ai-fu [1298–1362] of Wan-ling [Anhwei], and Chang Yü, [tzu] Kuang-pi [1289–1371] of Lu-ling [Kiangsi], all merely represent a branch development of their own. When we consider those who studied and assiduously emulated the poetry of the Six Dynasties era [third-sixth centuries A.D.] in order to arrive at a real grasp of the rules underlying T'ang verse and who worked as well at transforming common forms of language into startling and animated passages, we have to include Sung Wu, [tzu] Tzu-hsü [1260–1340] of Chin-ling [Kiangsu], Ch'eng T'ing-kuei, [tzu] Yüan-ch'ang [fl.c. 1338] of Kuang-ling [Kiangsu], and Ch'en Ch'iao, [tzu] Chü-ts'ai [1278–1365] of Tung-yang [Chekiang]. There were also those poets who independently became famous masters by aiming at unusual effects and trying to achieve the most graceful style [piao ch'i ching hsiu]. Among these there are some who had extraordinary ability and naturally endowed talent, but their recurrent demonic qualities [k'ai-ho pien-kuai] are so shocking that no one can get to the bottom of them. Here we have Kuan Suan-chai, Hsiao-yün-shih hai-ya, Feng Tzu-chen, [hao] Hai-su [1257–1327], Ch'en Fu, [tzu] Kang-chung [1240–1303], later on, Sa-tu-la, [tzu] T'ien-hsi [b. 1308], and finally, Yang Wei-chen, [tzu] Lien-fu [1296–1370]. During the military disturbances at the end of the Yüan, Lien-fu and my ancestor [Ku] Ying, Yü-shan chu-jen [Master of Jade Mountain, 1310–1369], as the foremost men of letters of their day, brought about a renaissance of literary excellence in the southeast, while in the region of the Sung and the Mao rivers [Kiangsu], poets such as K'o Chiu-ssu, [*tzu*] Ching-chung [1312–1365], Ni Tsan, [*tzu*] Yüan-chen [1301–1374], Kuo I, [*tzu*] Hsi-chung [1305–1364], and T'an Shao, [*tzu*] Chiu-ch'eng [fl. c. 1341], alternated the roles of leader and follower in another tradition, the lingering echoes of which have lasted down to the present day. In the ancient ballad form (*yüeh-fu*), Lien-fu went back to the Han and the Wei [second century B.C. – third century A.D.] for his models, and he was also thoroughly versed in the works of Shao-ling [Tu Fu (712–770)] and the two Li's [Li Po (701–762) and Li Ho (791–817)].[15] Although his followers numbered in the hundreds, only Chang Hsien, [*tzu*] Ssu-lien [dates unknown], really managed to learn his secrets. At the beginning of the Ming [1368], Yüan K'ai, [*hao*] Hai-sou [dates unknown], and Yang Chi [*hao*] Mei-an [c. 1334 – c. 1383], were the foremost literary courtiers of the day, and they too started out as followers of T'ieh-yai [Yang Wei-chen]. However, critics say that the T'ieh-*t'i* [the tradition of poetry associated with Yang and his followers] is so *mi-mi* [extravagant and decadent], reckless with the rules, and bitingly satirical that it should not be discussed as part of Yüan poetry.[16]

It would be illuminating, at this juncture, to provide a selection of poetry by the authors mentioned by Ku in his survey, but, unfortunately, limitations of space do not permit it. Instead, some comments on Ku's brief survey will suggest enough of the history of Yüan verse to make critical sense of Kuan's poetry.

To begin with, we have to note that Ku Ssu-li was essentially a pro-T'ang and anti-Sung critic of poetry, so when he talks about the style of poetry continually "improving" between the Yen-yu and the Ta-li eras, he means that it is becoming more and more like T'ang verse, and when he says that poetry was then "being purged of unfortunate habits," he means that it was becoming less like the poetry of the Sung dynasty. It is to be expected, therefore, that he equates the golden age of Yüan verse with the works of those poets— Yü Chi, Yang Tsai, Fan P'eng, and Chieh Hsi-ssu—whom he especially thought of as dedicated emulators of T'ang verse. It is also no accident that he mentions the "peace and prosperity" of the times in which they wrote; this, I believe, is an allusion to the poise and grandeur of style and the unselfishness and magnanimity of personal expression which characterize their poetry, qualities commonly attributed to poetry written during periods of social stability, economic prosperity and political strength by the Ming archaists and the Ch'ing neo-archaists, qualities they especially associated with the poetry of the High T'ang.[17] Much of Yüan poetry, however, is not characterized by a classical balance in emulation of the High T'ang style; for the rest of his survey Ku attempts to delineate various branch developments, regional schools, and independent masters.

Since this last category includes Kuan Yün-shih, it is of most interest to us. These independent masters—Kuan, Feng Tzu-chen, Ch'en Fu, Sa-tu-la, and Yang Wei-chen—have, according to Ku, several features in common: they aimed at unusual effects, had a graceful style (i.e., T'ang-like), had great talent and ability, and were demonic (pien-kuai). In another passage Ku discusses the non-Chinese poets of the Yüan period and says:

Kuan Suan-chai and Ma Shih-t'ien, [Ma] Tsu-ch'ang, began a school of poetry based on elegance and novelty [ch'i-li ch'ing-hsin chih p'ai], and Sa Ching-li, [Sa-] tu-la, brought this tradition to a real climax of excellence. It was refreshing but not impudent [ch'ing erh pu-t'iao] and gorgeous but not decadent [li erh pu-ju]—a development quite apart from the tradition of Yü, Yang, Fan, and Chieh.[18]

The mention of such things as unusual effects, novelty, elegance, and gorgeous (diction and imagery) and demonic qualities should make us suspect that this kind of poetry has something to do with the poetry of the Late T'ang period, especially with that of Li Ho and Li Shang-yin (813–858). Although Ku does not make this connection, there is a passage in the Yüan-shih tsung-lun (General Discussion of Yüan Verse) by the T'ao brothers (c. 1750) from Hsi-shan, Kiangsi, which does:

Many Yüan poets emulated the two Li's. T'ien-hsi [Sa-tu-la] was good at emulating I-shan [Li Shang-yin], Tsu-hsü [Sung Wu] was good at emulating Ch'ang-chi [Li Ho], and T'ieh-yai [Yang Wei-chen] was equally good at emulating both of them. As far as poets such as Feng Hai-su [Feng Tzu-chen], Kuan Suan-chai, and Wang Yüan-chang [the famous painter Wang Mien (1335–1407)] are concerned, although their diction certainly startles you,[19] it has not the least i-li [pattern to the thought], and one does not know whether it is an ox-demon or a snake-spirit [i.e., it is so bizarre that one does not know what to make of it]. It is just not fine work fit for the embroidered bag.[20]

Li Ho is said to have gone out riding every day on a donkey; composing lines of verse at random, he would write them down on slips of paper and stuff them into an old embroidered bag which he had strapped to the donkey's back. When he came home in the evening, he would have the bag emptied out and would put together as poems the lines which pleased him.[21] The implication is that the poetry of Feng, Kuan, and Wang, though attempting to emulate the eccentric and fantastic verse of Li Ho, is so random and disorganized in composition and so poor in intrinsic quality as far as individual lines are concerned that if it were Li Ho himself, he would not have saved them no matter how "startling" they were. It is true that the poetry of this "demonic tradition" of Yüan verse is, at times, terribly difficult to understand (some of Kuan's poems— 5 and 22 and certain lines in 2 and 4—are somewhat obscure and difficult to translate), but it seems unfair to say that it makes no sense at all. The T'ao brothers are very conservative critics who do not have much good to say about any poetry which is not cast in the High T'ang mold. They might allow the poetry of the Late T'ang into the realm of approved verse (but somewhere on the outer extremities of it), but later poets who try to take the innovations and peculiarities of the Late T'ang a step or two further receive only their condemnation. However, they are correct in identifying much of Yüan poetry with that of the Late T'ang and in singling out those poets who have especial affinities with Li Ho and Li Shang-yin.

Returning to Ku's own survey, we should note that the "demonic" tradition which began with such poets as Kuan and Feng Tzu-chen seems, in later years, to have become part of the mainstream of Yüan verse with the poetry of Yang Wei-chen, and that this reached an even more extreme stage of development at the end of the Yüan at the hands of some of Yang's followers. The golden age of Yü Chi and others—that brief period of classical balance—lacks basic elements of the characteristic Yüan style; it is, in fact, the poetry of such poets as Kuan Yün-shih which, through its close affiliation with the verse of the Late T'ang, most fully represents the age. Ku K'uei-kuang (1719–1764), a later kinsman of Ku Ssu-li, actually characterizes all of Yüan poetry as a latter-day version of Late T'ang verse:

Sung poetry is a transformation out of that of the T'ang–it changed and became Sung, while Yüan poetry is a transformation out of that of the Sung—it changed and became T'ang once again . . . . The poets of the Southern Sung called themselves "emulators of the T'ang," but in fact they merely ended up by turning T'ang poetry into an ancestral temple. Either they regarded *chüeh-ch'iang* [obstinate strength], *ao-che* [unnatural awk-wardness], *sheng-ying* [crude rigidity] as *lao* [mellow experience], or they took *ch'ien-chin* [shallow familiarity], *shuai-i* [impulsive facility], *lou-li* [low vulgarity] to be *chen* [sincerity]. They loved to be exhaustive in the form of expositions [*i-lun*] and were too unrestrained [*hao*] in the way they used their talents. Moreover, they paid little heed to tracing emotions with delicacy as fine as fine silk and to the restrained strength of expressive suggestion. They were really extinguishing the grand tradition of poetry! It is improper to emulate the ancient-style verse of the T'ang [i.e., it should be that of the Han and the Wei], but in regulated verse poets must regard the T'ang as their patriarch—and only the High and the Middle periods at that. The poetry of the Yüan corrected the pernicious tendencies of the Sung, but it failed in that it excessively imitated the faults of the Late T'ang: it is too detailed and intense [*hsien-nung*] and too complicated and involved (*fan-ju*). However, circumstances were such that it could not help but be this way [i.e., because it was a reaction against Sung poetry].[22]

We do not have to agree with this view of Sung poetry, but Ku seems to have hit upon something important regarding Yüan verse: it *is* often extremely detailed, intense, complicated, and involved, thus resembling much of Late T'ang poetry. But these qualities are not necessarily faults. It might be more meaningful to regard the verse of the Late T'ang and much of Yüan verse as attempts to explore complex states of mind and intricate sensibilities and to find the means, often in language rich in intellectual complexity and rife with symbolism, to articulate them. These qualities certainly exist in the poetry of Kuan Yün-shih, and, as the next section of this chapter will attempt to show, he was a typical Yüan poet in this respect.

II *Critical Introduction to Kuan's Verse*

A. ALLUSION

The first thing that will strike the reader is the extreme allusive-ness of much of Kuan's verse. Poem 22, for instance, would be almost incomprehensible without copious annotation. Allusion is a figure of speech, a rhetorical device that attempts to compress a complex of meaning, connotation, and association into a brief lin-guistic moment. When used honestly, it is a means by which the poet invites the reader to participate in a shared cultural motif, thus enriching the fabric of the poem and intensifying its meaning. As such, allusions should not be tampered with in translations but should be allowed to speak for themselves—with the aid of annotation when necessary—for to paraphrase them or gloss them over would be to dilute if not destroy their integrity.

Kuan rarely indulges in obscure, inappropriate, or misleading allusion. Although there is a great deal of it in some poems and some in almost all, his use of this device always seems to fit the progression of argument in the poem and to contribute to the integrity of the overall effect. Poem 1 is a case in point. An allusion that is not immediately apparent occurs in line 18: "And scorn the world for its lack of finery." The context, after consideration, should bring to mind a line from the "Summons of the Soul" in the *Ch'u-tz'u* (see the commentary to the poem), because this part of Kuan's poem involves an attempt to call the ghost of Li Po back to the land of the living. Some allusions, however, are not so easily grasped. In the eleventh line of Poem 2 there occurs an allusion which might have multiple associations. In cases such as this all possible tenors are given, since this multiplicity may have been exactly what the poet wanted to convey. This particular poem may also involve allegory, an aspect that will be discussed below.

Kuan's almost constant allusion to Li Po and his poetry seems to be more than a rhetorical device or stylistic feature of his poems. I think he was actually modeling his own personality on what he imagined Li Po to have been—the Li Po of Li Po's poetry. This leads us to the thorny problem of determining what the personality was that Kuan was trying to express in his poetry: was it his own, was it an assumed persona, or was it a combination of both? This will be discussed at length in Section E. Here I intend only to note Kuan's fondness for Li's poetry and to draw attention to how often he develops motifs that are designed to evoke immediate association with Li: for instance, "Unbuckling my sword, breaking into wild song beside a jug of wine" (Poem 1, line 15), "beauty from Wu" (Poem 2, line 2), riding the "back of the fish in the North Sea" (Poem 3, lines 1–2), and practically all of Poem 6 (an obvious eulogy to Li). Poem 20 seems to resemble Poem 6 in this regard as well. Poem 24 is not actually by Kuan, but Kuan seems to have appropriated it, and it is a veritable panegyric to Li, as, indeed, was the original author's intent (see the commentary).

No other poet figures so widely in Kuan's verse as does Li Po.

Allusions to Li Shang-yin's poetry occur in Poem 2, and allusions
to Li Ho's poetry occur in Poems 2, 3, and 5. Kuan also seems to
have been fond of the *Chuang-tzu*, since allusions to it appear in
Poems 3, 4, 11, and 19. Motifs associated with the general Taoist
tradition appear in Poems 2, 3, 11, 16, 17, 18, 19, and 30. Tu Fu
figures in Poem 3, line 1 (this line manages to create associations
with Li Po and the *Chuang-tzu* as well), in Poems 9, 22, and 23.
Allusions to the *Ch'u-tz'u* appear in Poem 1, lines 1 and 18–19, and
in the motif of the magical journey in Poem 3. The attempt to "call
up" Li Po's ghost in Poem 6 is reminiscent of Poem 1, lines 18–19.

Kuan draws as well upon conventional associations connected
with a particular site he happens to visit. These allusions draw upon
both history and myth, a practice of Chinese poets of all periods so
common that it needs no comment here. The reader is directed to
the commentaries to the poems involved: Poems 3, 5, 6, and 7.
Poems 24 and 25 can also be regarded in this light, since they are
concerned with sites important in the legends of the men to which
these eulogies are addressed. One allusion which probably was
immediately obvious to Kuan's contemporaries, but which is quite
obscure now, occurs in Poem 4, line 7. There Kuan alludes to a
couplet in a poem by the early Yüan statesman-poet Hao Ching.
Because of Hao's high reputation during the Yüan, it is likely that
this couplet would have been understandable at the time (see the
commentary).

B. IMAGERY

For an analysis of imagery in Kuan's *shih*, James J. Y. Liu's
distinction between "simple" and "compound" imagery will be used
as a basis for my discussion of the subject:

A simple image is a verbal expression that recalls a physical sensation or
evokes a mental picture without involving another object; a compound
image is one that involves a juxtaposition or a comparison of two objects,
or a substitution of one object for another, or a translation of one kind of
experience into another.[23]

In terms of this distinction, the imagery of Kuan's *shih* is overwhelmingly compound; he rarely depicts a sensation or an impression in simple and straightforward imagery. He prefers not to take

things as they are but *as he conceives them to be*, and for the most part he conceives them in such a way that our attention is arrested more by his conceits—often positively metaphysical in conception—than by the mental pictures and the sensations they invoke. Although he is certainly not the first to adopt this manner—this is a common feature of Late T'ang poets, such as Li Ho and Li Shang-yin—nevertheless, at times he brings off some remarkable examples that are worthy of the poets in whose mold he has largely cast himself. Consider for example Poem 2, lines 1–3, where a beautiful girl seems as if "carved from snow" or "trimmed from the moon," and whose coiffure in disarray, being "cloudlike," can be mended by "scudding clouds." Later we find (lines 5–6) that her eyebrows are painted to resemble "springtime mountains" (a cliché), but are so "weighed down" by chagrin that the "picture" (i.e., the spring-time mountains [landscape scroll] = her lovely eyebrows) cannot "unroll." Further on in this poem Kuan improvises on Li Ho's famous line "If Heaven had emotions, it would grow old too," and turns it into "She raises a hand to scratch Heaven, since Heaven also itches." That is, as stated in the commentary, if Heaven had her cares, it would suffer (itch) too, and, in a gesture of commis-eration, she scratches it!

In Poem 3, lines 9–10, Kuan employs a fantastic image of a sunset by playing on the Nü-kua myth, in which the goddess repairs a crack in Heaven's dome in the northwest quarter with multi-colored stones. Li Ho uses the same image to describe a sudden rainstorm: "Where Nü-kua fused stones and repaired Heaven/The stones break open, and Heaven, startled, pours down autumn rain." Kuan's ver-sion is even more "startling": "Nü-kua's hands were clumsy, the stones break open showing Heaven's ugly looks!" What is meant here is that dark rain clouds are gathering above the multi-colored sunset glow and the weather looks threatening in the west!

Simple imagery can also be occasionally found in Kuan's *shih*. A striking instance appears in Poem 2, line 7, where the beautiful girl is described: "On rich skin glossy with sweat rouge evenly lies." A rare example of simple landscape imagery occurs in Poem 11, line 1: "Wind soughing in the thatched roof there amidst water and rocks." "Soughing" translates *hsiao-hsiao*, which is onomatopoeia for the sound of the wind. By contrast, the "sadly moaning" trees of Poem 1, line 6, involve a compound image. In Poem 22, a poem saturated with allusion and compound imagery, lines 9–10 stand out in their stark simplicity: "With nightfall the god's wife passes around a cup made from a human head;/Taken off upside down, thus filthy with gore, they drink its fresh blood." The allusion tends to obscure the directness of the language, especially if the allusion is not immediately recognized (see the commentary). Poem 26 begins with a piece of simple imagery: "The path ends in verdant moss—that's as far as one can go." Then it quickly turns to compound imagery with: "Where spray from the spring, fine as hair, forms a jadelike mist."

The overall impression one gets of Kuan's use of imagery in his *shih* poems is that compound images outnumber simple ones by about ten to one. This fact alone clearly places him with practitioners of the Late T'ang style.

C. SYMBOLISM

Symbolism is distinguishable from imagery in the following ways:

. . . whereas a symbol represents the abstract and universal by the concrete and the particular, an image may involve only two physical and particular objects . . . . Therefore symbols have (or at least are meant to have) universal significance, but images have only local significance. Second, in symbolism, especially in private symbolism, the tenor (what is represented) cannot always be identified with ease, but the vehicle (that which represents) is always named . . . . With imagery, on the other hand, we can always identify the tenor, even if it is not mentioned (as in the case of substitution), but we may have difficulty in identifying the vehicle (as in the case of images of transference). Finally, imagery works on the sensual and emotional level, whereas symbolism functions mainly on the intellectual level.[24]

Many of Kuan's symbols are immediately accessible and their universal significance is readily apparent. The "west wind" in Poems 8, 9, and 23 symbolizes the advent of autumn and the passing of another year. The "white clouds" of Poem 3 and the "idle drift of clouds" of Poem 5 symbolize the freedom of travel, the random vagaries of journeys that bring one to this place or that. These are public associations, but these poems, written probably soon after Kuan's resignation from office, are intense expressions of personal feelings, and "clouds" may have had a private significance for him as well: his escape from a life he had come to dislike, the chance to indulge in unplanned and undisciplined activities that would have been impossible while he was an officeholder, etc.

The symbolic group of sword, wine, and song in Poem 1, line 15, besides the associations with Li Po that were mentioned above, represents the romantic swashbuckling hero, the unconventional individualist that Kuan seems to have fancied himself to be, even before his resignation from office. A postresignation poem, Poem 11, is constructed entirely around the "reed-floss quilt," which seems to be a symbol of rustic simplicity and innocence as well as emancipation from the entanglements of status, power, and luxury, things which, on the other hand, are symbolized by the silk quilt. Notice that the fisherman refuses the silk quilt—a "vile" object— and Kuan has to pay for the reed-floss quilt with a poem. His own poetry, then, becomes a symbol too: it becomes the means by which he can free himself from the "impure" world of rank and fame and thus realize a life of rustic simplicity. It is very likely that this poem is meant to be read primarily on this symbolic level, since, in sum, it appears to be an allegory of his metamorphosis from one state of being to another. It is the most thoroughgoing symbolic poem in Kuan's extant oeuvre, with the possible exception of Poem 2, which might also be read allegorically (see the commentary in the next chapter).

D. DICTION

Diction includes both word-choice and syntax. The syntax of Kuan's *shih* is almost entirely that of literary Chinese (*wen-yen*); in this respect, like most Yüan poets, he stays close to the T'ang poets he emulates and shuns those forays into vernacular syntax with which *shih* poets of the Sung era such as Yang Wan-li (1127–1206), sometimes indulged themselves. As later archaist and neo-archaist critics alike would say, he "kept close to the rules," rules applying as much to word-choice and syntax as to tonal prosody. The sole exceptions to this appear in Poems 29 and 31, two poems, by the way, which cannot be ascribed to Kuan with complete certainty.

Poem 29, Kuan's apocryphal death-bed poem, contains the line *pei-wo man t'a ssu-shih-nien*: "I myself deceived others for forty years." *Pei-wo* is a vernacular expression current during the Yüan which has the force of "I by myself" or "I, that's who."[25] The line cannot be construed as a violation of a grammatical rule, as a variant of *t'a pei wo man t'a ssu-shih-nien*: "Others have been deceived by me for forty years." *Pei-wo* is a binomial grammatical expression (function word), and its appearance here means that this is an example of vernacular syntax.

Poem 31 is really a humorous little ditty rather than a serious piece of poetry. It is a eulogistic inscription *(tsan)* said to have been inscribed on a portrait of Lung Kuang-han in celebration of his becoming a centenarian, and it contains the couplet *keng huo erh-pai nien/ch'ia-hao san-pai sui:* "If he lives another 200 years,/He'll be exactly 300 years old"! *Ch'ia-hao* is a vernacular expression still in use today which functions adverbially. Literary Chinese would express this with a single function word: *cheng* ("just so" or "exactly then"). Such usages are not to be found among the poems included in Ku Ssu-li's selection in the *Yüan-shih hsüan*, nor in Poem 30, a poem preserved in Juan Yüan's (1764–1849) *Liang-che chin-shih chih*, and which can, I believe, be safely attributed to Kuan.

In my translations of Kuan's *shih*, I have made a consistent effort to avoid paraphrasing the original Chinese and to preserve as much of the original syntax as possible. Much of the brilliance of *shih* poetry lies in its exploitation of the full range of syntactic possibilities of the literary language, and in surprising and unusual ways. One of Kuan's most successful ploys in this respect is his occasional use of the causative voice, as in Poem 14 in the couplet *ch'iu ming wu-shu Ch'in-o/ch'üeh pa ch'ing feng je shan-lo:* "Autumn sets singing an infinite number of Ch'in-o's [crickets]/And puts handle to a light breeze to tease the fan's gauze." *Ming* (cause to sing) and *pa* (get hold of, put the hand to) are both governed by the same subject— *ch'iu* (autumn). The result is startling, especially the second line. Since the poem is about a fan, one would expect the fan to "provoke" the breeze, not the other way around! (This line might also be rendered as "autumn used a light breeze to stir the fan's gauze," which, while still accurate, is not so graphic.)

As with syntax, Yüan poetry generally eschewed vernacular terms and expressions. The later pro-T'ang and anti-Sung critics were fond of distinguishing between T'ang word-choice: "elegant" (*ya* or *wen*), and Sung word-choice: "vulgar" (*su*), and they grouped Yüan verse with that of the T'ang. Elsewhere I have devised a scheme of analysis designed to fit the set of antithetical properties with which these critics associated the "success" of T'ang and Yüan verse and the "failure" of that of the Sung. "Success" and "failure," as such, were

taken to be products of the kinds of word-choices involved: connotation vs. denotation; concreteness vs. abstraction; the tendency
to use formal (*wen*) expressions as against the tendency to use colloquial expressions (*pai*); and the use of figurative, elaborate expressions—which often involve circumlocution or periphrasis—as against
the use of literal, simple, and straightforward expressions. T'ang
and Yüan poetry tends to utilize a poetic vocabulary of the former
kind, and Sung poetry the latter, though, to be sure, exceptions do
occur, as, for instance, in the poetry of the Middle T'ang poet Po
Chü-i, who "anticipated" the Sung style.[26] I do not suggest that
these lists of antithetical properties represent absolute rules about
the way Chinese poetry should be analyzed, but merely that period
"style" and individual "style," as far as word-choice is concerned,
can be understood in terms of whether they tend to one or the
other pole. This is a rule-of-thumb approach, in any case, and it is
not an attempt to establish an ontology of diction as such.

Kuan's verse, typical of Yüan verse in general, follows the T'ang,
especially the Late T'ang, and its vocabulary conforms to a large
extent to standards associated with the T'ang "style." Connotation
is preferred to denotation in all but a very few instances. Kuan
prefers to leave much unsaid which, however, can be understood
by a close reading of the implications and connotations involved.
Poem 5 contains an example of this: "Surprised to see, beneath the
moon, ink flowers fresh,/I want to write a new poem to give the
Dragon Maid." Besides being very allusive, these two lines contain
meanings that are not obvious even when one understands the
allusions. First, the fact that the moon is mentioned sets the time.
Since it is a poem on a sunrise (as indicated by the title), we know
it must be *before* dawn and *before* the moon has set. The "ink
flowers"—patterns of dried ink formed on the inkstone's surface
after the water has evaporated—are "fresh"; that is, the dried ink
on the inkstone from the day before has now "come to life" with
the moist sea air of the night. The "surprise" is that this would not
occur anywhere except at or near the sea. In consequence, the poet
writes a poem to the Dragon Maid—daughter to the Dragon King
who rules over and personifies the sea—since it is because of the
sea, her dwelling place, that the ink has "blossomed," thus providing
the stimulus for the poem. It is also significant that this is a *new*
poem; Kuan had apparently tried to write a poem at this site the
day or night before, but now, after seeing the glorious sunrise and

the fresh ink, which appears as if by magic, he is again inspired to write. Thus, the words "surprised," "moon," "fresh," and "new" all connote far more than they actually mean in "ordinary" discourse. The context has been structured in such a way as to allow the individual words to generate associations which reach well outside the poem in time and space. Much of Kuan's poetry works like this, but, rather than indulging in redundant analysis, it would be better to let the poems speak for themselves. When appropriate, the commentaries will draw the reader's attention to associations and connotations that might otherwise be overlooked.

In contrast to the high frequency of abstract ideas in Sung dynasty poetry, Yüan verse, like much of the T'ang verse it emulates, is more concrete. Sung poetry often engages in philosophical speculation or argument; mature Yüan verse (i.e., the poetry of roughly the third [Kuan's] generation of Yüan poets and later) seldom does.[27] To be sure, abstract ideas drawn from one or another tradition of thought do occasionally occur in verse such as Kuan's, but almost in passing, and then never in such a way as to become a characteristic feature. Examples of this appear in Poems 1, line 4; 2, line 21; 11, lines 2 and 7–8; 18, lines 1 and 4; 21, line 4; and 26, line 7.

Kuan does not employ colloquial expressions in his *shih* except as already noted, and thus nothing more needs to be said here about the distinction between formal and colloquial language. Of course, this is an important consideration in the analysis of Kuan's *san-ch'ü* (lyrics) where both kinds of expressions do occur, and that will be discussed at length in Chapter Four. However, before we turn to another final dimension of Kuan's poetry, the nature of his expression, we should note his frequent use of elaborate figures of speech. Circumlocution occurs throughout his verse. For example, to express the idea that a rooster has announced the dawn, Kuan has "a phoenix calls down the moon" (Poem 2, line 6); to say that a lady has sent a love letter to her man at the capital, he has "a bird flying, gripping chagrin in its beak, over Long Gate Palace" (Poem 2, line 13); to express the idea that he has just come down from the north by sea, he writes: "The back of the fish in the North Sea, thousands of miles long,/Carries me in a vast dream across Weak Water" (Poem 3, lines 1–2). The allusions here are dealt with in the commentary. Poem 5, lines 9–10, presents a tour de force in the use of elaborate figuration to describe the crash of waves against rocks: "Mighty *ao* turtles, nine feet broad, are melting frost-white drums,/As giant dogs, with slender stripes, leap up and dance." These are but several of many such examples of elaborate imagery in his *shih* verse.

E. EXPRESSION

A sensible approach to the problem of whether to interpret a poem as autobiographical revelation or dramatic situation appears in James J. Y. Liu, *The Poetry of Li Shang-yin*.[28] Faced with the ambiguity of many of Li's poems, Professor Liu concludes that in most cases a strictly autobiographical or allegorical approach may not only be misleading but also superfluous as far as understanding and evaluating the poem as poetry is concerned. As such, it would be better to try to reconstruct from hints within the poem itself the dramatic situation implicit in it. This can provide the critic with the means to make sense out of the poem and to evaluate it without having to resort to risky extrapolations from external biographical or historical materials. This means that the poem should be defined in terms of its objective status as a verbal object. However, when poems are not ambiguous, when they do contain explicit references to friends, relatives, or to biographical and historical data, they can and should be understood in the light of what we know of the poet's life and times. In these cases we cannot help but be concerned with the poet's *external* motive(s) or intention(s) in writing the poem, as opposed or in addition to his *artistic* intention, the guiding principle which has shaped the poem as such.

As expression rather than object, a poem is primarily concerned with defining and communicating values, ideas, and sensibilities, dimensions of the poet as person which come into existence from the poet's experiences in life. If we concentrate on the *general* attitudes expressed by the poems, it will be possible to assign all of Kuan's undated poems to various stages of his life, stages fixed by reference to his biography. In most cases the exact circumstances under which the poems were written are unknown, but it is still feasible to relate all of them to *general* circumstances and to discover in them his ways of thought and feeling. Although this will say nothing about him as an artist with words, which I have tried to treat in sections A through D above, it will help us to make sense of some of the poems, that is, to discern their *i-li* (pattern to the thought) that the T'ao brothers thought so lacking. In some cases it has not been possible to induce a coherent dramatic situation from the poem itself, and the only recourse in those instances has been to refer to the biography. Although there is certainly something of circular argumentation in the way such poems are analyzed, going around and around from poem to biography and back again, there simply seems to be no other way to do it. Since such analyses never try to do more than treat generalities, I think the benefits to interpretation should far outweigh any harm that might ensue.

We can propose the following outline of Kuan's life, divided into stages which seem appropriate settings for the *shih* poems which have survived. *Period One*: Youthful exuberance, confidence in himself and in the sociopolitical establishment as well as trust in the future. At this time Kuan seems to have had a strong faith in Confucianism and a firm commitment to duty, country, and emperor. Although hints of cynicism might occasionally appear, these are not sufficient to affect his basically positive attitudes. This period probably begins in youth and ends sometime during his stay in Peking—perhaps in 1314, a year or so after his appointment to the Imperial Academy. *Period Two*: Frustration and disappointment, expectations unfulfilled, attraction to the values of the recluse. This period dates from sometime during 1314, continues through the remaining years of his official appointment, and ends with his resignation in early 1317. *Period Three*: Although he has resigned from office, Kuan still remains tied to the values implicit in official service. He still has difficulty in reconciling himself to his retirement, even though he seems to have wanted it desperately. Certain of his poems which seem to belong here suggest that he may have had many regrets at having left office and that he may have been forced out against his will. This period begins with his resignation in early 1317 and lasts until at least the late summer of 1318 after he had settled in Hangchow. *Period Four*: Emancipation from the need for social status and from political ambition, growing serenity and freedom from the past. Little *shih* poetry survives from this period, and very little may have been written. However, a great many of his lyrics survive from this period of his life at Hangchow; these will be discussed below in Chapter Four. This period begins sometime after the summer of 1318 and lasts until his death in May, 1324.

The poems whose expression seems to fit *Period One* are Poems 1, 4, 12, 27, and possibly 14–18, though this last set might better be placed in *Period Two*. Poem 1 is datable to 1313 by reference to external sources (see the commentary in the next chapter). Since it is a eulogy of Li Po, Kuan's Li Po–like "voice" is here very intense, but there is a certain exuberance and confidence that seem lacking in the later poems inspired by Li. Poem 4 has such a proud and patriotic tone that it must reflect Kuan's early, predisillusionment state of mind. Poem 12 seems to have been written just after Kuan's appointment to the Imperial Academy in 1313; the ending contains more than a little tongue-in-cheek humility. The poet seems very pleased with himself and his new position. Poem 27 *may* be an allegory of Kuan's winning the emperor's favor and gaining an appointment to the Imperial Academy, though it may also be merely a literary exercise without any autobiographical value.

Those poems that seem to fit *Period Two* are Poems 2, 13, 14–18, and 21. It is possible that Poem 2 should be read as an allegory of Kuan's situation at the time: promised, or at least under the illusion that he had been promised, the trust and favor of the emperor, he has failed to obtain them in the measure he had expected. Perhaps this poem was written after the failure of his memorial. If so, in consequence of this disappointment, he now contemplates the life of Taoist seclusion, but not with happy anticipation. He views it with reluctance and even dread, for it will be a lonely existence fraught with the pain of disappointment and the frustration of ambitions unfulfilled. It seems to end with the idea that it might be better to bear the grief and to remain loyal to duty after all. Poem 13, "Longing for My Mother," is a problem. Was Kuan really this close to his mother, or is this simply a literary exercise, a simple imitation of Meng Chiao's poem on which part of it is so closely modeled? In either case, the poem was obviously written while Kuan was still serving in high office, but when he had begun to question the value of it all. Poems 14–18 have a thoroughly Taoist content. Since Kuan chose to write poems on the scenes depicted on fans, we can conclude that he must have identified to some extent with the scenes and the values they suggest, especially since after his own retirement he actually emulated the life-style they represent. Poem 21 both admires and envies the existence of the rustic hermit portrayed in it. It appears to be a high official's poem, an official who himself is contemplating retirement to a life of seclusion.

Those poems that seem to fit *Period Three* are Poems 3, 5, 6, 7, 9, 10, 19, 22, 23, and 26. Poems 24 and 25, though actually not from his hand, would have been appropriated by him now, for the

sentiments involved, those of identification with maligned and mis-
treated worthy men who were forced out of office by the machinations of petty evildoers, so closely fit what we should expect Kuan's
state of mind to have been at this time. Poems 5, 6, and 7 all express
a very strong "postretirement" sentiment, a sentiment which involves some ambivalence. There is some measure of relief at having
left office, but there is also some real regret. Poem 26 appears to
be the latest of this group, and was probably written at the end of
the summer of 1318, as much as a year and a half after his resignation, but it still contains a protestation of loyalty to the emperor.
Poem 23 is the only one of Kuan's poems which seems to have Tu
Fu strongly in mind, and here it seems to be Tu Fu the rootless
wanderer with whom he identifies. Poem 3, set at Tung-t'ing Lake,
suggests that Kuan is something other than the wretched and hapless
refugee from officialdom that some of the other poems make him
out to be. There is a genuine spark of exuberance here and a sense
of the pleasure he must have felt at having traveled so far to such
a lovely place. Poem 22 is of particular interest, since it may indicate
what Kuan thought about his non-Chinese origins. There is a certain
calculated barbarity here that seems meant to shock. It is significant
that this is the only *shih* in which Kuan refers to his Central Asian
background—in a poem written for another Central Asian, A-li hsi-
ying. The scene depicted is wild, savage, harsh, and cruel. It may
well be a denunciation of his own heritage, since the scene depicted
in it is cast in such uncomplimentary terms. The fact that it ends
with an allusion to Wang Chao-chün is particularly important. From
this I think we may conclude that Kuan identified with her fate,
that of being wrongly given over to the barbarians because of the
machinations of the emperor's unworthy advisors.

To *Period Four* belong Poems 8, 11, 28, 29, 30, and 31. Poems
8 and 11 seem to be serious attempts to express the author's interest
in Taoism; they even contain a distinctly didactic dimension in that
they both end with a formulation of basic Taoist principles. As such,
they seem to be manifestoes of his "other-worldly" life-style and his
commitment to it. Poems 28 and 30 appear to be examples of im-
promptu verse, more exercises in verbal ingenuity than statements
of self-expression. Poem 28 is Buddhist in orientation, whereas
Poem 30 is Taoist, and both are set at Ch'ien-t'ang (Hangchow),
where he had gone into retirement. Poem 31 is very much an
occasional piece of verse and rather devoid of any literary signifi-

cance. The centenarian Lung Kuang-han, to whom it is addressed, was a resident of Ch'ien-t'ang, so it must date from Kuan's period of retirement. Poem 29, Kuan's death-bed poem, is apocryphal, but we have no reason to doubt its authenticity. It reveals him to have been at peace with himself, with the world, and, most importantly, with the fact of his imminent death. There is, surprisingly, even humor here, something which is rather rare in Kuan's *shih* poetry.

CHAPTER 3

Translation of Kuan's Verse

Poem 1 Peach Blossom Cliff (*1313*)

O N Pai-chao Mountain is Peach Blossom Cliff, about which T'ai-pai once wrote a poem. Recently someone has established the Ch'ang-keng College there. When he came to the capital, Pai-yün, Chief Administrator in the Central Chancellery, was assisting in its completion and solicited dedicatory poems from us literary courtiers. Li Ch'iu-ku, Ch'eng Hsüeh-lou, Ch'en Pei-shan, Yüan Fu-ch'u, Chao Tzu-ang, Chang Hsi-meng, and I all contributed compositions.

The Fair One, once gone, should have stayed away three thousand
    years,
But thinking of the Fair One, oh, here he is before me!
Peach blossoms dye the rain as I start onto Pai-chao,
Surely believing he's escaped worldly dust in this realm of immortality.
This empty mountain, soaring above, is companion to rising and setting
    sun,
And its ancient trees, sadly moaning, beget foggy, crimson clouds.
On whose behalf has this been turned into an Immortal's realm?
For the river of windy mist, ten fathoms deep, it hangs banks fit for the
    Huai,
For whose warm greenery fragrance spreads and spring comes alive.
His hands fondle rosy sunset rays, all so delicate and fine, as there
From beyond the clouds, time and again, descends the sound of his
    clear whistling.
It is the Fair One in Heaven riding on a crimson crane.
His spirit may wander to the eight ends of the earth but it dwells on
    this mountain,
In flowing water, hidden from view, where his heart finds peace.
Unbuckling my sword, breaking into wild song beside a jug of wine,
92

I'm aware only of this Immortal's dwelling place and not the world of
   men.
Rapt with wine, I raise face to Heaven, shout "T'ai-pai"
And scorn the world for its lack of finery.
Bright moonlight fills the mountain, as I summon his departed soul,
But where in the spring breeze can I seek his face?

Commentary: Pai-chao Mountain, about ten miles west of Te-an
(present-day An-lu in Hupeh), is the traditional site of Li Po's *tu-
shu t'ang* (studio). Ch'ang-keng or T'ai-pai, the "star" Venus, is Li's
tzu (personal name), since his mother is supposed to have dreamt
of Venus just before giving birth. Ch'a-han, Pai-yün-shan jen (Man
of White Cloud Mountain) was appointed *p'ing-chang cheng-shih*
(Chief Administrator in the Central Chancellery) in 1312. In 1313,
he suggested to Li Feng-i, once assistant magistrate of Te-an and
then magistrate of Yao-chou (in Shansi), that he establish a college
on land Li had purchased on Pai-chao Mountain. Li agreed, and
construction seems to have begun soon afterwards.[1] The literary
courtiers are Li Meng, Ch'eng Chü-fu, Ch'en Hao, Yüan Ming-
shan, Chao Meng-fu, and Chang Yang-hao (1269-1329). The poem
by Li Po mentioned in the preface is "At Peach Blossom Cliff on
Pai-chao Mountain in An-lu, Sent to the Censor Liu Wan":

> I'll lie in clouds for thirty years,
> Loving leisure and the Way of Immortality.
> Although the Isles of the Blest are beyond all reach,
> The heart of this phoenix is at peace.
> Now returned to Peach Blossom Cliff,
> I can rest and sleep by my cloudy window—
> Here where people call from peak to peak,
> And ape after ape comes to drink in my mountain pool.
> Sometimes I climb to the verdant reaches of the summit
> Where the view is as Mount Lo-fo:
> Two ridges embrace a valley to the east,
> As one range stretches across the western sky.
> Trees so thick the sun's easily blocked out,
> Cliffs so steep the moon's hardly ever seen round.
> Fragrant shrubs take on a wild look,
> As trailing mosses set the spring mists quivering.
> Far out of the way, I've built a stone dwelling
> And picked a secluded spot to start a hill garden.
> I only want this forest here,

Sure I've no affinity for worldly existence.
I shall forever decline Your Honor's hospitality—
Only after a thousand years might we meet again![2]

Although Kuan's poem is obviously inspired by this one by Li Po, it is also heavily influenced by the *Ch'u-tz'u* (The Elegies of Ch'u). The "Fair One" (*mei-jen*) is employed throughout these "elegies" to signify the poet's prince, the ideal ruler for whom he is searching. In Kuan's poem, the *mei-jen* becomes the ideal poet, Li Po, or, more precisely, his deified spirit. The 3,000 years mentioned in line 1 seem to be an allusion to the magic peaches of the immortals whose tree bears fruit only once in every 3,000 years, appropriate since the setting is at Peach Blossom Cliff, and a poet like Li Po is as rare as the magic peaches. Line 8 describes how the green mountain, seen above and below a bank of mist, seems to provide "banks" for the river of "mist." The Huai River, far to the north, of course has nothing to do with the actual scene. Kuan surely has confused it for the Yüan River, which flows by the foot of Pai-chao Mountain, and this suggests in turn that he probably never visited there and that this poem is a studio piece rather than something derived from real experience. "Finery" in line 18 translates *hsien-wu*. This, I believe, is an allusion to a line in the *Chao-hun* (Summons of the Soul) in the *Ch'u-tz'u*: "Dressed in embroideries, clad in finest silks [*hsien*],"[3] where the poet tries to entice the soul of the departed to return by describing lovely girls who wear such finery. Here, Kuan scorns the world for lacking beauty enough to entice Li Po back to the realm of the living.

II *Poem 2* The Fair One *(1313–1317)*

Like a goddess carved from snow, so clear and warm,
She's a beauty from Wu trimmed from the moon, so slender and dusky.
Scudding clouds mend her coiffure, its verdant gleam shining,
As a phoenix calls down the moon from over lonely hills.
Fingers try to pull open the arched eyebrows knit by idle sadness,
But chagrin so weighs down the springtime mountains that the picture
    won't unroll!
On rich skin, glossy with sweat, rouge evenly lies,
Since, behind his back, she had wiped her tears to stop it from being
    ruined.
Fashioned by her own hand with a frost-white blade, the pomegranate
    skirt,

Behind these closed doors, will never know the sons of the mighty and
the rich,
Once drenched in the green-burning incense of Indigo Field Jade
And packed away with its fashionable silk sash, changed for something
else.
She sends birds flying, gripping her chagrin in their beaks, over Long
Gate Palace,
A fragrant blossom impatient with quarters where the best of its beauty
wastes away.
Interlocking rings swaying narrowly and jade pendants tinkling,
The sleeves of her rainbow dress broaden and stretch out in the spring
breeze.
With bracelets loose on her thin wrist from the heartbreak she suffers,
She raises a hand to scratch Heaven, since Heaven also itches!
Now the bedcurtains with their scented brocade are cold and the lamp is
dim,
But this fallen blossom still doesn't get under her hibiscus-spangled
quilt.
"The Road to the Three Mountains is dark, and the Milky Way is deep!
The high-pitched plaint of this colorful phoenix can break your heart.
Heaven gave this Fair One beauty enough to overturn a state,
But it would be better to give her a Fair One's fidelity as well,
So she can face the bright moon for the rest of eternity
With dreams filled with plum blossoms and a body which stays outside
of dreams!"

Commentary: Here "Fair One" indicates a beautiful woman, and
the poem as such should be read in part in the tradition of Li Po's
many poems on *mei-jen*.[4] However, I think it likely that it should
also be read as an allegory on Kuan's own status as a courtier estranged from his emperor. As an allegory, it can be divided into
three sections. Section one (lines 1–8) describes the beauty and
presents a brief vignette of her last meeting with her fickle lover.
Section two (lines 9–20) deals with the lonely lady as she suffers
grief and frustration alone in her boudoir, while in section three
(lines 21–26) we find the lady reluctantly toying with the idea of
renouncing the world and becoming a Taoist nun. The "Three
Mountains" (*san-shan*) refer to the three mythical mountainous
realms of the immortals: P'eng-lai, Fang-chang, and Ying-chou. The
"road" there is "dark" (i.e., arduous) for the student of immortality,
and the "deep" river of the Milky Way (*yin-ho*: "Silver River" in
Chinese) symbolizes the same thing. The poem seems to end with

a rejection of this way out of her dilemma—she will stay loyal to her man after all. For the lady read Kuan, the talented courtier of integrity, and for the lady's lover, read the emperor, mercurial player of favorites. As such, the poem must date from the period of Kuan's appointment to high office in the Imperial Academy. In line 2, "beauty from Wu" is a cliché for "beautiful woman," an expression which owes its popularity in poetry to its occurrence in the verse of Li Po, such as: "Wind blowing willow catkins fills the shop with fragrance;/A beauty from Wu pressing out new wine invites me to take a taste."[5] Line 11 seems to contain an allusion to Li Shang-yin's "The Ornamented Zither," in which there occurs the line "On Indigo Mountain, in the warm sun, jade engenders smoke."[6] In line 14, it is a cliché to say that love letters are carried to their destinations by a phoenix or a blue bird.[7] Long Gate Palace is an allusion to Ssu-ma Hsiang-ju's (179–117 B.C.) *Ch'ang-men fu*,[8] which he wrote on behalf of Empress Ch'en, the consort of Emperor Wu who had lost his favor and who was sequestered in the Long Gate Palace. The *fu* depicted the unhappy lady's grief in such poignant terms that when the emperor read it, he relented and took her back. Line 18 is modeled on Li Ho's famous line: "If Heaven had emotions, it would grow old too."[9]

III   *Poem 3* Song of Princess Mountain *(1317)*

The back of the fish in the North Sea, thousands of miles long,
Carries me in a vast dream voyaging across Weak Water.
P'eng-lai, in the blink of an eye, doesn't fill my hand,
As its fragrance fades from the azure sky beyond reach of the wind.
The scarlet skirted maid longs after this distant traveler
Who, going far never to return, has left the bright moon embarrassed!
Fastened with jeweled hairpin, the verdant locks about to flow,
Her phoenix ringlets, twelve in all, reflect late autumn's glow—
It's Nü-kua who's hands fused stones to repair Heaven,
But the hands were clumsy, the stones break open—showing Heaven's
    ugly looks!
Dramatine towers and jade mansions are here too in the world of men.
I'll point them out—don't you see them!
But in a flash the fish is gone, and I'm returned from the dream
To find myself amidst white clouds roaming on Princess Mountain!

Commentary: Princess Mountain (Chün-shan), also Hsiang-shan or Tung-t'ing shan (Grotto Court Mountain) is a mountainous island

in Tung-t'ing Lake in Hunan whose names derive from close association with the Goddess of the Hsiang River, one of two goddesses usually identified with the daughters of the sage-king Yao
who became the consorts of his successor Shun. Various names for
these goddesses include Hsiang-chün (Princess of the Hsiang),
Hsiang Fu-jen (Lady of the Hsiang), and Hsiang-fei (Consort of the
Hsiang). The Hsiang River was the center of a water complex presided over by the goddess, and Tung-t'ing Lake, the terminus of
the river, was the center of her cult, a cult which inspired a rich
representation in literature.[10] "The fish in the North Sea" is an
allusion to the giant K'un fish mentioned in the *Chuang-tzu*: "In
the North Sea there is a fish whose name is K'un; who knows how
many thousands of *li* its size is"![11] Kuan here imagines himself to
be a latter-day Li Po, one of whose epithets is *Ch'i ching-k'o* (The
Whale Rider), which derives from a poem by Tu Fu.[12] Kuan does
Li one better and rides a *k'un*, something which would dwarf any
whale! However, this *k'un* is elaborate periphrasis for the ships
which brought him south, then up the Yangtze to a point close to
Tung-t'ing Lake. I think that this poem was written during the late
summer of 1317, five months or so after his resignation from office,
when the wanderings of his first year of retirement brought him to
the central Yangtze River region. The "Weak Water" (Jo-shui) of
line 2 is a mythical river situated in the far west which flows around
the K'un-lun Mountains, the abode of the Queen Mother of the
West (Hsi Wang Mu). Its water is so "weak" that not even a goose
feather will float on it, so it cannot be crossed by mere mortals.[13]
By now, Kuan's *K'un* has changed into the giant P'eng (Roc),[14] so
he can simply fly across. P'eng-lai, the mythological mountains in
the eastern sea, is another place where immortals dwell. Its place
in the Chinese tradition is not too unlike the Isles of the Blest in
the Western tradition. Here Kuan is still flying on the back of his
P'eng, continuing on a magical circuit of the wondrous realms where
the immortals live. P'eng-lai does not "fill" his hand because he is
so high up in the air, up there (really atop the mountain) where the
fragrance of the countryside cannot reach him. In line 5, the red
skirt, the conventional trappings of a pretty girl, might be an allusion
to his own wife, if it is true that this poem was written after his
departure from Peking, where he would have left his family behind,
never to return. The moon would be embarrassed because it shines
on the lonely lady in vain; it is a light for lovers and married couples.

With line 7 there begins a description of Nü-kua in terms of the
attributes of the Goddess of the Hsiang as she manifests herself in
the misty vapors of the lake. Lines 13 and 14 are directly modeled
on a couplet in Huang T'ing-chien's (1045–1101) second of two
poems entitled "Climbing up Yüeh-yang Tower during Rain for the
View of Princess Mountain": "Wind-blown rain covers the flow as
I lean on the railing alone;/Binding up her hair the Hsiang Goddess
makes twelve ringlets."[15] The next couplet is modeled on one which
occurs in Li Ho's "Song of Li P'ing's Vertical Harp": "Where Nü-
kua fused stones and repaired Heaven/ [When the harp sounds] the
stones break open, and Heaven, startled, pours down autumn
rain."[16] Nü-kua is supposed to have patched the crack in Heaven
caused by the demon Kung Kung with multi-colored stones; it is
this variegated patch which causes the colorful sunsets. The "ugly
looks" of Heaven is an elaborate figure of speech for "storm clouds
in the West." The "dramatine towers and jade mansions" are cloud
formations. The entire poem should be read as an elaborate circumlocution for the trip Kuan has taken down from Peking and
which now finds him at Tung-t'ing Lake. The K'un/P'eng represents
the large (K'un-like) ships with sails (P'eng wings) that have brought
him here and which have now turned into Princess Mountain, as
big as a K'un swimming in the sea or a P'eng flying in the sky.

Poem 4 Song on Painting a Dragon (1309–1313)

Old ink makes a murky sky as sounds of thunder die, then,
His hand splits a bright pearl and turns it into the pupil of an eye.
Once submerged in the deep lake, it's been long since it's leapt up,
With mud-soiled windy whiskers tinged a deep purple hue.
The Curly Bearded Old Fellow, who lives in Yen City,
Angrily blows on the nine dragons till no lamps are left.
Raising icy water a hundred feet from out of the Dark Mountains,
He daubs in the body of a grey dragon which stretches right up to the
    clouds.
Forked teeth and claws and horns emerge with the speed of wind,
And its reverse scale shoots at the moon with the clatter of spears and
    shields.
While we on earth raise our faces and look, attentive with delight,
Orion and Lucifer shatter and fall, startling the immortals in Heaven.
Mount Omei floats lightly on the inky rivers Hsiao and Hsiang,
And T'ai-hang Mountain's just as green as P'eng-lai itself.

A fierce wind turns snow upside down and the Milky Way pours out,
But the coral cup's so broad it can't be quelled.
Drawing in and spurting out, the East Wind ushers in
Spring hues from the Dragon Court for the Ten Thousand States.
Only after seven years' drought was broken did Yao give his people life,
And for nine years of flood Shun could not plow.
Now all this has changed with the blessings of gentle rain—
Well enough for the mountains and rivers of Our Great Yüan Dynasty!

Commentary: The mention of Yen City, the palace setting, and the
extreme patriotism all indicate that this poem dates from Kuan's
early period in Peking before his disillusionment. Lines 1 and 2
seem to contain two allusions. There is a parable in the *Chuang-tzu*
which tells of the Black Dragon that lives in the deepest depths and
which has a priceless pearl beneath its throat. One can only hope
to take it, at life's peril, while the dragon sleeps.[17] Here the "bright
pearl" serves as a symbol for the painter's priceless skill. However,
something more is involved. The act of "splitting" the pearl and
turning it into the pupil of an eye refers to the placing of a stroke
or dot in the blank eye socket. This is an allusion to the story of the
four dragons painted in the An-le Temple in Chin-ling during the
Southern Ch'i dynasty (479–502). The dragons did not have pupils
dotted in because the temple authorities feared that if they were,
the dragons would come to life and fly away. When this was done
for two of them, in a flash of thunder and lightning, they flew up
into the sky, leaving the other two behind.[18] Here the painter's skill
is so great he can bring the dragons to life. The next line refers to
the idea that the dragon remains hidden deep in water during times
of bad government, but when good government returns, it leaps
out of the water and soars. "The Curly Bearded Old Fellow" translates *chiu-jan lao-tzu.* I have been unable to discover to whom this
refers. There is a possibility that Kuan is here referring to himself
and that he painted the picture. In line 6, I take it that the "dragons"
refer to *lung-teng* (dragon lamps); i.e., lamps upon which dragons
have been painted. The painter of this picture "angrily" blows them
out so that his own dragon, which does not have to rely on light
from within a lamp for its effect, could receive the undivided attention it deserves. The fact that nine dragons are involved suggests
that this dragon picture hangs in a palace, since groups of nine
dragons have been associated with palaces at least as early as A.D.
235 when a Nine Dragons Palace was built during the Wei Dynasty.

Groups of nine dragons were also decorative motifs within palaces.
For instance, female musical performers at court during the Yüan
sometimes wore a so-called Nine Dragon Cap (*chiu-lung kuan*).[19]
The Dark Mountains (Yin-shan) of line 7 stretch across Suiyuan,
Chahar, and northern Jehol (Inner Mongolia), and here Kuan seems
to have a couplet from Hao Ching's "Song of Chü-yung Pass" in
mind: "Fire rages on the Dark Mountains, putting the hibernating
dragon to flight;/Carrying the Pole Star on its back, it opens up the
vast primordial plain!"[20] In Hao's poem, as in Kuan's, the dragon's
flight signifies the advent of good government under the Mongols.
In Hao's, the fires of war (the battle for Chü-yung pass against the
Chin) startle the dragon to flight. It is an ingenious twist that Kuan
works into his poem when he has the painter draw up water from
the very bedrock of the Mongol people to mix the ink to paint the
dragon which symbolizes the realization of the Mongol cause. In
line 10 is an allusion to the parable in which the dragon is described
as having a reverse scale (*ni-lin*), one that thrusts forward instead
of lying back like the rest. One can ride the dragon, but if he should
happen to touch this, the dragon's most sensitive spot, the dragon
will kill; i.e., one should be careful not to "rub" the ruler the wrong
way.[21] Here the dragon (the Mongol Yüan Dynasty) has been irri-
tated by the injustices in the world, which it will now conquer
through force of arms and so bring justice to it. Lines 13–16 present
a magical microcosm where ink-forms create massive mountains
that float on great rivers of ink, and landscape representing real
topography is so beautiful that it rivals even P'eng-lai. The snow,
the Milky Way, and the coral cup (a vortex?) suggest the sweeps
and swirls of wind-driven clouds that usually provide the setting for
dragon pictures. The end of the poem declares that the accomplishments of the Yüan are comparable to those of the ancient sage-
kings, though, like theirs, success did not come easily but only after
long years of strife and hardship.

Poem 5 On Viewing the Sunrise *(1317)*

In the third month of the *ting-ssu* year [April 12 – May 11, 1317]
I visited what is called Pao-t'o Mountain. On top there is a rock
known as the "Rugged One" from which one can view the scene.
At first, one doubts this vastness could ever be fathomed. When
I arrived back at my lodgings, I had just completed the line begin-

ning with "as at midnight," and the poet-monk Lu-shan composed
the rest with me.

The six dragons are reined up, and the sea turns hot,
As at midnight the Golden Raven changes its color.
Lightning drenched in the Milky Way breaks the *ao*-turtle's leg in two,
Like a knife striking coral—the shattered pieces flowing snow.
This rustic traveler from the North, following the idle drift of clouds,
Rode the wind and traveled to this mountain in the sea.
Soaring up and pulled through space I crossed over fragrant waters
To a place apart from that Central Plain where sages have to mix with
the vulgar.
Mighty *ao*-turtles, nine feet broad, are melting frost-white drums,
As giant dogs, with slender stripes, leap up and dance.
Surprised to see, beneath the moon, ink-flowers fresh,
I want to write a new poem to give the Dragon Maid.
We're born to make our ways in this "Strong-Man's Country,"
While the God of the Sea stands on His waves and cheats the world's
narrow breadth.
At the empty edge of the world, spring sails fall—
I may be here in the Southeast, but my thoughts stay back in the
Northwest!

Commentary: Pao-t'o Mountain is a mountainous island east of Ning-
po just off the coast of Chekiang. The name derives from *pao-t'o*
or *pu-t'o-lo*, Potala (Potalaka), a mountain southeast of Malakūta in
India which is the reputed home of Avalokiteshvara, who becomes
Kuan-yin, the Goddess of Mercy, in China. Pao-t'o Mountain was
the center of a Kuan-yin cult. The lodgings mentioned in the preface
were probably at the temple dedicated to Kuan-yin where the Monk
Lu-shan lived. The "Rugged One" translates P'an-t'o. Lines 1 and
2 are concerned with the sun: six dragons are harnessed to it in
readiness to pull it across the sky, and the Golden Raven *(chin-wu)*
is a zoomorphic symbol of it. Lines 3 and 4 are concerned again
with the Nü-kua myth. When the goddess repaired Heaven, she
also replaced the pillar in the Northwest which Kung Kung had
butted down with the leg of a giant *ao*-turtle. To insure that the
other corners would stay up, she replaced the other three pillars
with giant *ao*-turtle legs as well. Here Kuan seems to be describing
the white glow which spreads across the sky before sunrise. The
ao-turtle's leg in this instance would be the one in the Southeast,
where the sun would come up at this time of the year. In line 8,

the Central Plain (Chung-yüan) refers to the Yellow River Valley, the center of power and politics and the heartland of the state. Lines 9 and 10 describe the action of waves as they dash against the rocks. In line 11 "ink flowers fresh" translates *mo-hua hsien*; "ink flowers" are the ink patterns which form on the surface of an inkstone. In the next line, the Dragon Maid (Lung-nü) is the daughter of the Dragon King who reigns over this watery realm, and in the line after that "Strong Man's Country" translates Chang-fu kuo. There is in the *Shan-hai ching* a reference to a fantastic country in the far west which is inhabited solely by people of male appearance who dress in gowns and caps and are armed with swords.[22] Kuan here characterizes the China of his own day as a Chang-fu kuo, a country dominated by a "masculine" military establishment. In line 14 the God of the Sea, T'ien Wu, can live beyond the narrow strictures of the inhabited world. "Empty edge of the world" translates *ch'ien-k'un k'ung-chi*; the character *chi* is inked over in the *Yüan-shih hsüan* text but is preserved in the text of the poem contained in the *Huang-Yüan feng-ya* (Airs and Odes of the August Yüan Dynasty).[23]

Poem 6 Song of Pick Rocks Mountain *(1317)*

Atop Pick Rocks Mountain the sunshine pales,
As below Pick Rocks mountain the river becomes flowing snow.
This wanderer could not bear to pass it by, though the water bears no
    trace,
And it's so hard to call up T'ai-pai's departed ghost!
I, too, do not stay in White Jade Hall,
Since the capital's wine is weak and Hsiang clouds linger long.
Here at New Pavilion in wind and rain, night brings me a dream.
Across a thousand years I long for him—each one breaks my heart!

Commentary: Pick Rocks Mountain (Ts'ai-shih shan [chi]) juts up in the middle of the Yangtze not far downstream from Nanking. It is named for the multi-colored stone people used to pick (*ts'ai*) or collect at the summit, and it is a place important in the lore concerning Li Po. Li's biography in the *New History of the T'ang* contains the most concise account of the events which seem to have inspired Kuan's poem: "Li Po was once present in attendance upon the Emperor. He was drunk and had Kao Li-shih remove his boots. Li-shih, a favorite of the emperor's, felt humiliated by this, and so he took a poem [which Li had written satirizing Yang Kuei-fei (Im-

perial Concubine Yang)] and showed it to her, thus provoking her
to anger. Whenever the emperor wanted to appoint Li to office,
Concubine Yang then always prevented it . . . . [Consequently, Li]
begged to be allowed to return to the mountains, and the emperor
gave him gold and let him go. Li Po then wandered to all parts of
the empire. Once when he was traveling by boat on a moonlit night
with Ts'ui Tsung-chih from Pick Rocks to Chin-ling [Nanking], he
wore a palace-style brocaded gown and sat in the boat as if there
were no one else there."[24] The "White Jade Hall" of line 5 is a
cliché for government offices at court. "Hsiang clouds" means clouds
over the Hsiang River, for which see the commentary to Poem 3.
New Pavilion (Hsin-t'ing) was situated upstream from Chin-ling and
was immortalized in Li Po's famous poem "The New Pavilion at
Chin-ling."[25] This poem was probably written soon after Poem 5,
because of the way it fits with Kuan's likely itinerary at the time
and because of the sentiments involved—"early postretirement."

Poem 7 The Grief of Parting *(1317)*

Alas, the grief of parting, oh!
In the open country at Ts'ang-wu spring shrubbery lies green,
And before Huang-ling Temple spring waters rise.
As sun sets, the skirt of the Hsiang flutters its emerald sheen;
The jade trees, soaring loftily, run their red tears.
Once again at Kai-hsia I hear Lady Yü weep—
Just as if it were first shock in the small round tent at Ch'u song's cease.
The fair lady stifled her tears and abandoned her hero,
But the blood from the sword didn't wash out the green from this
    countryside!
What is this thing called "Grief of Parting"?
It's the heart pounding with the ring of bronze.
Far better to hack down the bamboos and cut away the grass,
So to prevent people summing up one's life with:
"He's grown old with grief!"

Commentary: Ts'ang-wu in Hunan is the place where the sage-king
Shun is supposed to have died and where his two consorts drowned
in the Hsiang River, just south of Tung-t'ing Lake, while they were
trying to find him,[26] and Huang-ling Temple was situated at the foot
of Huang-ling Mountain on the shore of Tung-t'ing Lake where the
Hsiang enters it. Tradition has it that Shun's consorts are buried

on top of the mountain. In line 4, "skirt of the Hsiang" (Hsiang-*ch'ün*) is a pun on Hsiang-chün (Princess of the Hsiang)—that is, the princess (chün), who dwells in the waters of the Hsiang, is fluttering her own skirt (*ch'ün*). Instead of *yü-shu* (jade trees) in the next line, the texts preserved in *Huang-Yüan feng-ya* and in *Yüan-shih t'i-yao* (Essentials of Yüan Verse) have *hsiu-chu* (tall bamboos).[27] The "red tears" allude to the story that when Shun died his consorts wept so bitterly that their tears of blood stained the bamboo along the banks of the Hsiang, the descendants of which compose that species of speckled bamboo which is native to the region. Lines 6–9 allude to the defeat of Hsiang Yü (232–211) by Liu Pang, the first emperor of the Han Dynasty, at Kai-hsia in Anhwei. Surrounded by Liu's forces, Hsiang and his Lady Yü were in their tent when they heard Liu's men singing Ch'u songs (Hsiang was the King of Ch'u), a ruse to make Hsiang's troops think that Ch'u had already surrendered. Hsiang then got up and sang his own lament, said farewell to Lady Yü, and, with a few men, broke through the encirclement. He died the next day. It is assumed that Lady Yü committed suicide, perhaps by sword as is suggested here.[28] In line 12, the bamboo and grasses are symbols of parting and the grief which ensues. This poem, also set in the Tung-t'ing Lake region, is a farewell poem to an unknown woman, a woman Kuan seems to be leaving forever.

Poem 8 Reed-Floss Quilt (1318–1323)

When I was passing through Liang-shan Marsh, there was an old fisherman weaving reed-floss together to make a quilt. I admired its purity and offered to trade one made of silk for it. The old man said, "If you admire this pure thing, you will have to pay for it with a poem." I then composed this poem for him, and he actually refused the silk quilt!

> You have plucked reed-floss unsoiled by dust,
> So I shall just borrow your straw raincoat as mat for awhile
> And let the west wind flit across my dreams as autumn stretches
>   endlessly—
> As nocturnal moon begets its fragrance, the snow covering my
>   body.
> My hair and bones, following Heaven and Earth, have already
>   grown old,

But, in fame, I won't yield to the poor of antiquity or of modern
times.
Black damask silk isn't anything mandarin ducks covet,
And in the creaking sound of oars lies the promise of another
spring!

Commentary: Liang-shan Marsh lies to the southeast of Mount
Liang in Shantung. Since this is an autumn poem, it might have
been written as late as the autumn before Kuan's death. Ou-yang
Hsüan's stele inscription indicates that it was written after Kuan
settled at Hangchow.[29] The "snow" which appears in Line 4 is
actually moonlight, a compound image of substitution, and the
whole line is a piece of synaesthesia where light, fragrance, and
sense of touch (*cold* moonlight) fuse. Line 6 means that Kuan considers himself to be the equal of all the poor but noble scholars up
to his own time. Black damask silk (*ch'ing-ling*) quilts were presented to high officials during the Han dynasty.[30]

Poem 9 Feelings Aroused by the Autumn River (1317)

On a clear and limpid autumn river floats this big boat.
What I've been through should be unbearable, but I'm content with life.
Here the west wind is at my temples, and mountains and rivers remain
As setting sun floods the boat and wild geese call.
Some village brew's still left, though the "Prime Minister" is drunk—
The short lamp still shining on his feelings for the Jade Gate.
There's sure to be a homesick dream tonight,
When wind soughs in withering leaves and moon at second watch.

Commentary: The sentiments involved and the travel setting suggest that this poem was written during the first autumn of Kuan's
retirement. Line 3 is reminiscent of "the state is crushed, but mountain and river are still there," a line in Tu Fu's famous poem "Spring
Vista" (*Ch'un-wang*).[31] Tu's poem concerns the crisis of national
failure, whereas Kuan's deals with personal failure. In both cases
man and his endeavors fail while nature carries on unchanged. The
"Prime Minister" of line 5 is Kuan himself—a would-be prime minister who never was and never will be. The Jade Gate (*yü-men*) is
a cliché for the imperial palace. This line suggests that, though
drunk, he will continue to long for the career that is no longer his.
Line 8 follows the text in *Yüan-shih t'i-yao*;[32] The *Yüan-shih hsüan*
has "soughing of the wind as moon sets—the moon at second watch."

Poem 10 The Rush-Sword *(1317–1323)*

Three feet high and green as can be, ancient T'ai-o swords
Dance in the wind, cutting to pieces all the waves in the river.
At Long Bridge they cast reflections and scare the scaly dragons
As flowing water, without a sound, sharpens them day and night.
On the two banks, covered with mist, they beget an aura of war
And, at the fifth watch, strum the rain in harmony with fishermen's
    songs.
When autumn comes they only fear how cruel the west wind can be—
If it ruins their sharp points, oh, what a pity!

Commentary: The leaves of the rush-sword or calamus plant (*ch'ang-
p'u ts'ao* or *p'u-chien*) were put up at the sides of gates along with
the leaves of the mugwort plant (*ai-tzu*) on the day of the festival
of Tuan-yang (Upright Sun), the day of the Dragon Boat Festival
(fifth day of the fifth month). The leaf of the calamus resembles a
sword, and the leaf of the mugwort resembles a tiger, both fitting
shapes to avert misfortune. The mention of Long Bridge (Ch'ang-
ch'iao) in line 3 fixes the setting of this poem; it is at the bridge of
that name in I-hsing (Kiangsu) which spans the stream Ching-hsi
in the city itself. The bridge was also called the Chiao-ch'iao (Scaly
Dragon) Bridge because during the Chin dynasty (265–420) a scaly
dragon, which used to come out and devour people, lived in the
river beneath the bridge. A man named Chou Ch'u then went into
the river and beheaded it with a sword. This dragon's successors
are since kept at bay by the reflection of swords (the calamus leaves),
a constant reminder of what happened to their predecessor. The
poem was probably written on the occasion of one of the Dragon
Boat Festivals during Kuan's period of retirement, since I-hsing was.
not too far to the north of Hangchow. T'ai-o, legend has it, was the
name of a marvelous sword made by the swordsmith Kan Chiang
of Wu (third century B.C.) for the King of Ch'u.[33]

Poem 11 Triune Retreat *(1318–1323)*

Wind soughing in the thatched roof, here, amidst water and rocks
Where the mind's at peace all day long before forested mountain peaks,
Back from dreams, caught unaware the elixer's ready for the stonework,
I begin to realize, only when the chanting stops, that I'm leaning on the
    railing.

As medicine pestle pounds into the night, the mica's worked fast,
And now, with autumn gush in the stone bottle, the bloom on the well
  is cold.
Since all fish too can find delight in wandering about,
Why take up a fishing pole with a scheming mind?

Commentary: The Triune Retreat (San-i An) was built by Ko Ch'ang-keng during the early thirteenth century. The prominent poet-scholar Ch'en Wen-shu (1775–1854), a native of Ch'ien-t'ang and an ardent student of its lore, once wrote a poem on the Triune Retreat entitled "Paying a Visit to the Ruins of Pai-yü ch'an's [White Jade Toad's] Triune Retreat Built during the Sung on Pao-chia Mountain, Following the Rhyme Scheme of Kuan Suan-chai." Ch'en's preface to this poem, in part, states: "White Jade Toad was originally called Ko Ch'ang-keng, and his sobriquet was Hai-ch'iung [Master Sea-Jade]. He was profoundly learned in Confucianism and was an excellent calligrapher and painter . . . . During the Chia-ting era [1208–1224] he answered the Imperial Summons to be Master of Sacrifices at T'ai-i Kung [Shrine of Primordial Unity; i.e., on Heng-shan, the Sacred Mountain of the North]. It was after this that he built his retreat here. Ruins such as the Pi-chien ch'ih [Retiring from the Sword Pool] and Te-yüeh lou [Pavilion for Catching Moonlight] are also here. The retreat is at the foot of Pao-chia Mountain and to the right side of the Shan-ch'uan t'an [Altar to the Spirits of Mountain and Stream]." Pao-chia Mountain is several miles south of Hangchow and to the west of where Kuan's residence was. Ch'en's poem reads:

Here a thatched cottage was once built amidst water and clouds
Which pointed the way to green forests hidden among mountain peaks.
Cloud shadows follow me to stop on the painted roof beams,
As flecks of the river's gleam, like raindrops, wet the red railings.
By the side of the pool, silent and lonely, the pure spring is all dried
  up.
Outside the pavilion the verdant expanse spreads, and evening glow is
  cold.
There still remains the altar stone from a dynasty long ago,
And here, amidst the rustle of yellow leaves, I put down my fishing
  pole.[34]

The expression *san-i* (three-in-one, triune) is an important concept in the Taoist tradition. It occurs, for instance, in Ko Hung's (fl. c.

320) *Pao-p'u tzu nei-p'ien* (The Inner Chapters of the Master Who Embraces Simplicity): "The Way arises from Unity and is honored without peer. Each thing which dwells in Unity is the image of Heaven, Earth, and Man. This is the reason for the expression *san-i* (Triune)."[35] When Kuan visited the Triune Retreat, some eighty or ninety years after it was constructed, it was apparently still inhabited by a Taoist recluse-alchemist. I have been unable to identify him. In line 3, "ready for the stone-work" translates *lin ch'i*. I take *ch'i* to be the stonework (or brickwork) which serves as the foundation for the alchemist's stove, though it may also be the stonework of a well. The chanting of formulae accompanies the alchemical process, and *yün-mu* (Mother of Cloud) is muscovite $KH_2Al_2(SiO_4)_3$— the common light-colored mica.[36] In line 6 "stone bottle" refers to the alchemist's well, and "bloom on the well" translates *ching-hua*, the spatter from well water.[37] The last two lines involve several allusions. "Delight in wandering about " alludes to the *Chuang-tzu*: "See how the minnows come out and dart around where they please! That's what they really enjoy."[38] *Chi-hsin* (scheming mind) is also from the *Chuang-tzu*, which Burton Watson translates as "machine mind": "With a machine mind in your breast, you've spoiled what is pure and simple; and without the pure and the simple, the life of the spirit knows no rest."[39] "Scheming mind" also appears in the commentary to the biography of Kao Jou (174–263) in the *Wei-chih* by P'ei Sung-chih: "If a scheming mind sprouts inside you, then the seagulls will not come down."[40] This in turn alludes to a passage in the *Lieh-tzu*: "There was once a man who went on the sea who loved seagulls. Every day he went out and followed them, and they would flock to him in the hundreds. His father said, 'I've heard that the seagulls follow you about. You catch some, for I would amuse myself with them.' The next day when he went out to sea, the gulls danced about in the air but would not come down."[41]

Poem 12 At the Capital, Sent to a Friend *(1313)*

> Across the great vastness of the blue sea I send you words
> from afar,
> For who wouldn't break out in song for the sake of his native
> place!
> These ten years, old friend, have been a dream spanning
> three incarnations

But the myriad leagues between us are compressed into the
one inch of my heart!
With autumn waters, at night, I contemplate my sword
beneath the lamp;
In spring breezes, at times, I play my zither which hangs on
the wall.
Recently, I've become embarrassed that while hair still black
I've got people to call me "Young Member of the Academy"!

Commentary: This poem dates from the time Kuan was appointed
to the Han-lin Academy in early 1313. If the ten years of line 3 can
be taken literally, it is addressed to someone once very close to him
from whom he has been parted since about 1303 when he was
seventeen, someone from his "native place," which is probably
Yung-chou. There is no way to determine who this person might
have been. "A dream spanning three incarnations" is a cliché similar
to "it seems a lifetime" in English. The sword is a symbol of action
and service to the state, and the zither is a symbol of repose and
self-cultivation.

Poem 13 Longing for My Mother *(1313)*

Here at the edge of the world fragrant shrubs are scattered about too.
I may now have a grand salary, but, sad and lonely, what good is it to
me?
When I carefully compare the ten years of tears that have run down my
coat,
I find them less than the treadlike wrinkles spun by my kind mother!

Commentary: This poem appears to have been written at the same
time as Poem 12, and perhaps it was a companion piece to be sent
to his mother. The "grand salary" is that of *san-fu* (three large grain
measures), a cliché for the salary of a high state official. The text
of the last two lines follows that preserved in Ku K'uei-kuang's
Yüan-shih hsüan,[42] since it is far superior to the one contained in
Ku Ssu-li's *Yüan-shih hsüan*. Ku Ssu-li's version has *yüan hsia lei*
(tears that have actually run down) and *pu-chih* (don't know) instead
of *pu-ju* (less than). The poem as a whole is obviously inspired by
Meng Chiao's (751–814) "Wanderer's Song" (*Yu-tzu yin*):

> From the thread in the hand of a loving mother
> Comes the coat on the wanderer's back.

He was about to leave when she stitched it close—
So afraid he'd be slow to return.
Who'd dare say that a heart tender as a blade of grass
Could ever repay all the sunshine of the spring![43]

Poems 14–18 Five Poems Written on Fans
Painted by Ch'en Pei-shan (1313–1317)
Poem 14 (I)

Autumn sets singing an infinite number of drunken Ch'in-o's
And puts handle to a light breeze to tease the fan's gauze.
The bright moon is clear as jade in a sky like water,
As the cloudy air on this mountain stirs up delicate waves.

Commentary: Ch'en Pei-shan is Ch'en Hao, one of the "literary courtiers" mentioned in the preface to Poem 1, a person discussed briefly in Chapter One.[44] Ch'in-o was a famous female singer of antiquity.[45] Here the "drunken singers" are the autumn crickets.

Poem 15 (II)

A red sun like a ball of lead rises above the sea,
Where, in deep blue waters, lies a tiny P'eng-lai.
Last night the East Wind, strong as wine,
Roused peach blossoms to bloom all over the trees!

Poem 16 (III)

Kingfisher-green curtains hang low and save the midday shade,
And inside the jade-green bottle the water mark is deep.
An easterly breeze fends off heat from the mortal world—
Enticing pure coolness to nourish a heart set on the Way.

Poem 17 (IV)

The curtain full of bright moonlight has brought him to the railing
Where the canopy of the universe presents an exquisite night view.
He's ready to fly on his immortal's raft to somewhere near the Milky
  Way—
There to beckon the bronze bowl out of the dewy vapors of the sea.

Commentary: The "bronze bowl" is the sun, an expression borrowed from Li Ho's "Poem on the Ch'in Palace" (Ch'in-kung *shih*).[46]

Poem 18 (V)

One can find immortality without taking cinnabar.
Smiling, he points to rosy sunset clouds—always a home for him there.
As in three feet of snow on a clear morning in the mountains,
The disposition of this Man of the Way is just like the plum blossom!

Commentary: Cinnabar (*tan-sha* or *chu-sha*) was the key ingredient in elixirs of longevity and immortality.

Poem 19 The Hall of Great Peace on Mount Lu *(1317–1318?)*

On the mountain are pure breezes, and below the mountain it's mortal dust,
As over jade sands there flows water shallow as in springtime.
Who was it that, beyond the pines, knocked on the moon
And startled me out of my Nan-hua dream?

Commentary: The Hall of Great Peace (T'ai-p'ing Kung) on Mount Lu at the northern border of Kiangsi is famous for its peaks, grottoes, ravines, and magnificent scenic views. It was a Taoist center. This poem may have been written during Kuan's year of travel before he settled at Hangchow, though, of course, it may have been written in 1308 at the time he was between his military office and his arrival in Peking. It may also have been composed during a trip made after he took up residence at Hangchow. *Nan-hua chen ching* (The Classic of the Perfected Man of Nan-hua) is another name for the *Chuang-tzu*. To be "startled" out of a "Nan-hua dream" means to have had the spell of transcendence broken, to lose one's place in the mystical order of Nature.

Poem 20 Yüeh-yang Tower *(1317)*

The reflection stands alone, a Yüeh-yang as far away as the sky,
From which I peer down at Meng Marsh where vegetation stretches endlessly.
Since the ancient trees south of town are still there as before,
I'll have to ask the Immortal's servant boy if he might have come again.

Commentary: Yüeh-yang Tower was situated on the east shore of Tung-t'ing Lake and southwest of Pa-ling (modern Yüeh-yang). It

commanded magnificent views of the lake to the west and the
Yangtze which flows by in the distance to the north. Its fame grew
throughout the T'ang Dynasty due to the many visits to its summit
by poets who immortalized its views. One such poet was the "Immortal" mentioned here—Li Po, the "Immortal of Poetry." Meng
Marsh, also called Yün-meng tse (Cloud Dream Marsh), extended
both to the north and to the south of the Yangtze. The town mentioned in line 3 is Pa-ling, the administrative center of Yüeh-chou
(Hunan). Since there is no evidence that Kuan visited Tung-t'ing
Lake more than once, I suggest that all the poems set there were
written at the same time.

Poem 21 Inscribed in Lien-ch'uan's Calligraphy on his Screen Wall
(1313–1317)

With the dawn, my staff making light of this distance to the ends of the
    earth,
I stopped my feet in an easterly breeze at the home of a mountain
    recluse.
How comfortable are his rustic clothes, all worldly looks gone,
As he lives at ease never contaminated by any luxury!
"Oh son, oh child—why now so happy, now so sad?"
In lamp's dim glow the little curtains make me want to linger.
The mountain recluse already enjoys a springtime as gentle as can be—
A person like me just has to want to leave behind a new poem.

Commentary: I have been unable to identify the recluse, here referred to by the sobriquet Lien-ch'uan. A screen wall (*yin-pi*) was
often placed opposite the gate to a residence compound. This seems
to be a high official's poem that contains some amount of envy for
this life of rustic seclusion, thus I would date it to Kuan's years in
the Imperial Academy. Line 5 indicates that the recluse has time,
freed from official duties and worldly cares, to tend personally to
his children and to reflect upon the fickle emotions of childhood,
though it may also have had implications for Kuan, who was still
caught up in the world of officialdom.

Poem 22 Music for the Tartar Pipe, Made for Mr. Hsi-ying *(1317)*

Male thunder hating separation, female thunder growing old,
A sea of clouds plasters over the sands, the grassless lands

Where, though,——— dust doesn't enjoy breezes perfumed by purple
    sandalwoods,
In the three-inch high reeds the Cosmic Breath is a wonder,
The faint sound rattling on and on, never letting up to rest.
Goblins sobbing in their dreams or gibbons starving with hunger—
It's the powerful sound of a nine-holed flute made of snow-white steel.
As the flame grows cold in a butter-oil lamp, put out by the spring
    wind,
With nightfall the god's wife passes around a cup made from a human
    head;
Taken off upside down, thus filthy with gore, they drink its fresh blood.
Over the Purple Terraces clouds scatter, leaving the moon so lonely and
    remote.
Since few are those who take the road home, this song will last even
    longer!

Commentary: "Tartar Pipe" translates *pi-li*, a multi-holed vertical
flute whose piercing sound is associated with sad, mournful melo-
dies. Mr. Hsi-ying is A-li hsi-ying, a contemporary of Kuan's and
a renowned player of the *pi-li*.[47] This poem was probably written
at the same time as Lyric 79, during a visit Kuan made to A-li hsi-
ying's residence at Wu-ch'eng in Kiangsu sometime in 1317 (see
the commentary to Lyric 79). Line 1 describes the setting, the
different kinds of thunder, and alerts the reader that this is a poem
about separation. "When the spring thunder first begins, the kind
whose sound rolls out in thunderclaps is called 'male thunder'
[*hsiung-lei*]; this is dry ether [*kan-ch'i*]. The kind whose sound is
gentle and which does not occur in thunderclaps is called 'female
thunder'; this is wet ether [*shui-ch'i*]."[48] On another level, the kinds
of thunder describe the sounds of A-li hsi-ying's *pi-li*. In line 3, the
first character in the Chinese text in the *Yüan-shih hsüan* has been
inked out, and since this poem is not preserved elsewhere, it cannot
be supplied. "Cosmic Breath" translates *yüan-ch'i*, in this sense
interchangeable with *t'ien-ch'i*, the primordial life force or energy
which pervades and animates all things. Here it is manifested in
the wind which constantly blows across the barren wastes of Central
Asia. However, like all lines in this poem up through line 6, this
describes a feature of the *pi-li* playing as well. Line 4 is particularly
clever since it could also be translated as "in the three-inch reeded
[instrument] the Cosmic Breath is a wonder"; i.e., the player's wind
control is a wonder. "Butter-oil" in line 8 translates *su*, which is

made from mare's milk, and "god's wife" in the next line translates
shen-ch'i: a shamaness.

The cup made from a human head is an allusion to an account in
the *Shih-chi* where we find the Hsiung-nu in the third century B.C.
defeating their perennial enemies, the Yüeh-chih, and capturing
their king, out of whose skull they made a drinking vessel.[49] The
episode as described in Kuan's poem is savage and gruesome. In
line 11, Purple Terraces (*Tzu-t'ai*) is a term for the *Chinese* imperial
palaces. An allusion is involved here which seems to be the key to
the entire poem; it is to the third of Tu Fu's five poems entitled
"Feelings Aroused by Ancient Sites" (*Yung-huai ku-chi*), the third
being "The Bright Consort's Village" in which the couplet occurs:
"As soon as she left home, the Purple Terraces linked her to the
Northern Desert,/Where all that remains of her is the green grave-
mound facing the yellow dusk."[50] The "Bright Consort" (Chao-chün)
was Wang Ch'iang, a lady in the harem of Emperor Yüan of the
Han dynasty. She was given in marriage to the Khan of the Hsiung-
nu in 33 B.C., lived out the rest of her life with his people, and was
buried in the desert. Tu's poem apparently was a favorite of Kuan's,
for he alludes to it as well in Lyric 34. Now we know that Kuan's
poem is Chao-chün's song, and laments her fate. It is significant
that Kuan identifies with her and pities her, and that he does not
identify with the ancestors of his own heritage. The implication is
that he regards himself as having suffered her fate of being forced
to be part of a culture he seems to have loathed and perhaps even
feared.

In addition to the character missing in line 3, whole lines of this
poem may have been deleted by Ku Ssu-li, since there exists a
poem in twenty lines written by a contemporary of Kuan's, Chu
Fan (1286–1347), which echoes its rhyme-scheme but is eight lines
longer. Chu's poem is entitled "Song on the Drinking Vessel Made
from the Skull of the King of the Yüeh-chih, Following the Rhyme-
Scheme of Scholar Kuan":

The Khan, his precious sword cold glimmering snow,
Drinks his enemies' blood from the Yüeh-chih skull.
The Nirvana Perfected One departs from the Crimson Palace—[51]
At times the heady brew can make him drunk to his bones.
Nightly in the Yen-chih's[52] tent, the fragrance of grapes
Flutters against rosy sunset clouds in spring or ripples the autumn
    moonlight.

A Hsien Prince gets up to dance, and a Lu-li Prince sings;[53]
Drinking in turns, they happily shout, pairs of ears burning.
Their shadows before the lamp half fade away
As behind it green phosphorescence already flickers out.
The purpose of holding cups is really to sprinkle grievances in the
    heart,[54]
So why instead of this are they doing injury to their souls?
Bow-snakes[55] can still make one completely confused—
How could Chih Yao[56] be such a senseless lout!
In this way the skull surely will quickly rot,
Captured alive and by mistake fallen into enemy hands.
Since he could bear to use a singing arrow to have T'ou-man shot,
Alas, how could we hope he'd shirk from killing even this fallen king![57]
But in years to come, Han emissaries east of the river Jo
Would still use ladles to pour out libations in memory of the alliance.[58]

Poem 23 Yüeh-yang Tower (1317)

The west wind blows on me as I climb this tower,
The bright reflection in my sword dancing—the universe floating there!
Green hills confront this visitor who's grown far too thin,
A wanderer who longs for you with an infinite sadness.
Last night, when a fisherman's song made this end of the lake vibrate,
There was enough autumn here to fill ten Heavens and Earths!

Commentary: Line 2 is modeled on a line in Tu Fu's "Climbing Yüeh-yang Tower": "Wu and Ch'u lie to the east and south,/And the very universe floats here day and night."[59] That is, Tung-t'ing Lake is so large that it can float (reflect) the entire universe. Kuan's line is even more hyperbolic, since it is his sword that is doing the reflecting! In the last line, it is likely that *ch'iu* (autumn) is a pun for *ch'ou* (sorrow).

Poem 24 At Tang-t'u Prefecture There Is a "Remove Boots Pavilion" Which Was So Named Because the Banished Immortal Was Once at Colored Rocks. Therefore, I Painted a Picture of It and Praised Him in This Poem (1317)

    With brocaded gown, oh, and black cap,
    A spirit pure, oh, his manner unconstrained,
    Vanquishing, oh, all things in existence,
    He commands, oh, the eight ends of the earth!

I long for this man of ages past, oh, Li T'ai-pai!
Who caused you, someone at the Imperial Academy in the
    morning,
To be at Pick Rocks on the same evening?
Wasn't it that favorite of the Emperor in the T'ien-pao Era?
But what did you, sir, ever have to do with either joy or gloom!

Commentary: Poems 24 and 25 are actually shortened versions of
two *tsan* (eulogies) written by the Southern Sung literatus and
statesman Mou Tzu-ts'ai (*chin-shih* of 1223) who was once prefect
of T'ang-t'u in Anhwei. The complete versions of the two *tsan* are
quoted in Chou Mi's (1232–1298) *Ch'i-tung yeh-yü* (Rustic Remarks
from East of Ch'i). Whereas they are exactly like Poems 24 and 25
up through line 9, there are an additional seven lines in each. The
rest of the first is:

He rudely brought your poem to light and gradually turned the court
    against you.
Whenever I look at my "Remove Boots Picture,"
I never fail to hate the attitude and behavior of the petty man
And be pained at the unconventionality and frankness of the superior
    man.
You have a lofty presence, oh, you're a scintillating dragon that cannot
    be bridled.
You laugh at wealth and nobility as if they were worn-out shoes, oh,
And when did you even feel happy or sad about success and failure![60]

We do not know how Poems 24 and 25 became part of Ku Ssu-li's
selection of Kuan's poetry. The most likely explanation is that they
were included in Kuan's now lost collected works to which Ku had
access. I have been able to find only Poem 24 in the *Yü-ting li-tai
t'i-hua shih-lei* (Collection of Poems Inscribed on Paintings by Category, Authorized by His Majesty), published in 1677, twenty-five
years before Ku's selection appeared in the *Yüan-shih hsüan*. There
it is also attributed to Kuan.[61] I think that Kuan had acquired Mou's
original paintings and so admired them that he copied truncated
versions of the *tsan* on them into his own collected works, where
they were found centuries later. He would have done this, in my
estimation, during the early period of his retirement when he would
have closely identified with Li Po and (in Poem 25) with Huang
T'ing-chien, men of "worth" hounded from office by "petty" men.

The "favorite" of the T'ien-pao era is, of course, Kao Li-shih, who exercised great power during the reign of Hsüan-tsung; see the commentary to Poem 6. The "oh's" in the translations of Poems 24 and 25 correspond to the *hsi* characters in the Chinese texts. I have included them in order to preserve something of the rhythm of the originals.

Poem 25 Shan-ku Had Been Prefect of Tang-t'u for Just Nine Days When He Was Slandered and Banished to I-chou. Therefore, I Have Painted a "Picture of Him Rowing Back" and Have Added to it This Poem *(1317)*

With turban, oh, and rustic clothes,
A portly figure, oh, his spirit aloof,
He soars alone, oh, so elegant and refined,
Spurning in contempt, oh, salary and rank.
I long for this man of ages past, oh, Huang Shan-ku!
What caused you, after six years in Po-tao,
To have but nine days in Ku-shu?
Wasn't it that political clique during the Shao and the Fu?
But what did you, sir, ever have to do with either glory or disgrace!

Commentary: Shan-ku was the sobriquet of Huang T'ing-chien, the great poet, painter, and calligrapher of the Northern Sung. From Tang-t'u in Anhwei to I-chou, far to the southwest in Kwangsi, is a tremendous distance. Huang was a conservative who opposed the reform policies which had first been introduced by Wang An-shih (1021–1086) and which were later continued by such men as Chang Ch'un and Ts'ai Pien. Chang and Ts'ai formed a clique which dominated court politics from the Shao-sheng (1094–1097) to the Yüan-fu (1098–1100) eras (that political clique of the Shao and the Fu), and they actively persecuted such conservatives as Huang. The six years mentioned in line 6 refer to the time Huang spent in banishment at various places in the hinterlands of Szechuan, Kweichow, and Yun-nan. Ku-shu was the administrative center for Tang-t'u District; to be prefect there would have been comfortable and rewarding, especially after having lived in such places as Po-tao at the juncture of the three southwestern provinces. However, his enemies had him dismissed and sent back into exile where he died a few years later.[62]

Poem 26 On First Arriving in the South, I Spend the Summer
         Resting on Phoenix Mountain *(1318)*

The path ends in verdant moss—that's as far as one can go—
Where spray from the spring, fine as hair, forms a dense jadelike mist.
As dragons sport in the sea nearby, my cloudy window becomes moist,
And since mosquitoes fear this mountain chill, my fiber net stays empty.
At peace on a high pillow and unaware that autumn waters rise,
Opening the door, I suddenly see evening sails heading east.
The infinite splendors of Nature had made me completely forget—
To the north, the distance there is only the inch of red in my heart!

Commentary: Phoenix Mountain, between West Lake and the
Ch'ien-t'ang River south of Hangchow, is the site of Kuan's two
residences during his retirement.[63] Ships heading east down the
Ch'ien-t'ang River would be going out to sea, and perhaps north
toward Peking. It is Kuan's realization of this which triggers the
thought of the last couplet. As much as a year and a half after his
resignation, his heart is still in Peking. The poem can be dated to
the end of Kuan's first summer at Hangchow in 1318.

Poem 27 Palace Song *(1313?)*

Nothing to do with wind, this tinkling—she makes jade pendants and
     bracelets ring,
As, jade-fair herself, she keeps the tryst up on the hill at the lake.
An attendant reports: "His Majesty summons you!"
Beneath the moon—lightly, lightly—she tidies up her verdant locks.

Commentary: Although it is possible that this is a mere literary
exercise which could have been written at almost any time, the fact
that it is a "palace song" suggests that Kuan wrote it while he was
associated with palaces. There is even the possibility that it is an
allegory of some aspect of Kuan's own relationship with the emperor. If so, then it may date from 1313, when Kuan received the
emperor's favor and was appointed to the Imperial Academy.

Poem 28 Tiger Run Spring *(1318–1324)*

The spring, the spring, the spring
Randomly spews precious pearls, each one of them round.

It's jade axes chipping out the essence from witless stones,
Golden hooks snatching up saliva from an ancient dragon!

Commentary: For the background to this poem, see Biographical
Appendix II at the end of Chapter One. Tiger Run Spring (Hu-p'ao
ch'üan) is on Ta-tz'u shan (Hill of Great Kindness) near West Lake.
The "precious pearls" are bubbles, and the "jade axes" probably
refer to the jade-green color of the water in agitation. "Essence
from witless stones" translates *wan-shih sui*. *Shih-sui* is also a term
for chalcedony, the crystalline veins in rocks. Stones, of course, are
dumb and witless, but since the spring lies within the precincts of
a Buddhist temple (Tiger Run Temple), this probably involves an
allusion to the common Buddhist saying: *wan-shih tien-t'ou* ([moved
by the recitation of the sutras even] the witless stones nodded their
heads). The "golden hooks" probably refers to the flecks of sunlight
in the water; *lung-hsien* (dragon saliva) also means ambergris. The
spring, like all bodies of water, is the dwelling place of a dragon.
Its "saliva" here is a conceit for the froth on top.

Poem 29 Farewell to the World *(1324)*

"Cave Blossom and Secluded Shrub, make good marriages for
  yourselves!"
I myself deceived others for forty years.
As of this day, I'll have nothing to do with either the living or the dead,
And the moon in the sky over the sea will remain just as round!

Commentary: For the background of this poem, see Chapter One.[64]
The names of Kuan's two concubines deserve some attention. Cave
Blossom (*Tung-hua*) might also suggest the meaning "Blossom in
the Bridal Chamber" (*tung-fang hua*), and Secluded Shrub (*Yu-ts'ao*) might suggest "Shrub in the Secluded Boudoir" (*yu-kuei ts'ao*).
Line 3 contains an allusion to a passage in the *Lieh-tzu*: "Yang Chu
said, 'an ancient saying goes: "We should pity the living and ignore
the dead." ' "[65]

Poem 30 A Poem Presented to Taoist Master Yü Hsing-chien *(1318–1324)*

Living in seclusion and escaping the mortal frame,
Elixir ready, you nourish your vital energy.

Spirit so pure it moves gods and demons,
And your angry shout is able to make wind storm and thunder crash.
When a crane takes off, it makes whirlwinds turn fast;
When a dragon comes back, it turns the air pungent with rain.
Sending off the Master, we sing short songs,
As a cool breeze fills the river pavilion.

Commentary: This poem is not preserved in any of the anthologies.
I discovered it in Juan Yüan's (1764–1849) monumental *Liang-che
chin-shih chih* (A Record of Inscriptions on Metal and Stone From
North and South of the Che River [i.e., from eastern Chekiang])
as part of an inscription taken from the T'ung-yüan kuan (Temple
Where the Ultimate Mystery is Unveiled) on Wu-shan, very near
where Kuan lived outside of Hangchow. The inscription is of Yüan
date and consists of three poems dedicated to the Taoist Master Yü
Hsing-chien.[66] The first, a five-syllable *lü-shih* (regulated verse), is
by Kuan; the second is a seven-syllable *lü-shih* by Yü Chi; and the
third, also a seven-syllable *lü-shih*, is by Chang Chu. All three
poems were written when the Taoist Master left on a journey. In
Kuan's poem, the first couplet describes Master Yü's mode of existence and his practice of techniques to achieve longevity and ac-
quire special powers. The second couplet attributes marvelous
powers to him, powers which have brought on the thunderstorm
which seems to have appeared just at the moment of departure.
Quick to notice the coincidence between Master Yü's departure and
the advent of the storm, Kuan phrases his poem along the lines of
this correspondence. It is as if the master were going to ride a crane
(the boat's sails) and a dragon (the boat itself). The last couplet is
a description of the scene at hand, including a bit of tongue-in-cheek
humor in the announcement that their songs are "short," and they
want to get the send-off over before the storm actually arrives! Since
it is set somewhere along the Ch'ien-t'ang River, we can date it to
the time Kuan lived in retirement there.

Poem 31 On the Portrait of Lung Kuang-han, a Eulogy *(1318–1324)*

> There's a man who lives here whose name is Kuang-han
> And who has given himself the sobriquet "Centenarian."
> If he lives another 200 years,
> He'll be exactly 300 years old!

Commentary: Like Poem 30, this poem is not included in the anthologies; it is preserved only in Yang Yü's (1285–1361) *Shan-chü hsin-hua* (New Anecdotes from a Mountain Dwelling),[67] a notebook which contains a wealth of unusual information concerning Hangchow of the Yüan era (Yang was a native of that area). "There's a man who lives here" translates *yu k'o*, which literally means "there is a visitor." Lung Kuang-han was not a native of Hangchow but was from Kiangsi, so in spite of his long residence there he was still a *k'o*, a "guest" in the area. Although it is possible, I think it very unlikely that the phrase means "I had a visitor," i.e., that at his great age Lung paid a visit to Kuan. This piece is described as a *tsan* (eulogy), but following it Yang Yü notes that Kuan "used this to poke fun at him." It is just the kind of thing that one might write in jest to amuse an old man. I include a translation of it here merely to make our survey of Kuan's verse complete. With it, every scrap of verse (*shih*) known to have been written by Kuan has been accounted for. However, a great deal of Kuan's verse has undoubtedly been lost. Before we turn to a consideration of his lyrics, I would like to speculate a bit on what some of his lost poetry might have been like.

Kuan's collected *shih-wen*, classical verse and prose, was never printed. The preface to *Kuan-Kung wen-chi* (The Literary Works of Mr. Kuan) by Teng Wen-yüan (Biographical Appendix III at the end of Chapter One) seems to have been composed during 1318, the year Kuan came to live in Hangchow. The fact that Teng wrote a preface to it suggests that Kuan may have been preparing it for publication; for some reason this intention was never realized. Nevertheless, the collection seems to have survived in one or more manuscript copies at least up to the time Ku Ssu-li made his selection of verse from it for inclusion in the *Yüan-shih hsüan* at the end of the seventeenth century. There are several indications that Ku had access to Kuan's *shih-wen*. In the General Principles of Compilation section at the head of the first series of the *Yüan-shih hsüan*, Ku states that earlier anthologies of Yüan verse all suffered serious omissions because they tended to rely on other anthologies instead of directly on the individual works of the poets themselves (their *pieh-chi*). He then declares:

What is passed down to posterity in this collection in all cases is taken from the complete collected works of the poets involved. I do not dare merely limit myself to anthologies for the sources used.[68]

There is no reason to doubt that Ku applied the same principle to the compilation of the *erh-chi* (second series) in which Kuan's *shih* is found. We know that Ku went to great lengths to obtain access to the works of the Yüan poets he included in the *erh-chi*. For instance, it is recorded in his *nien-p'u* (chronological biography) that he even borrowed such works from the libraries of friends such as Chu I-tsun (1629–1709).[69] A copy of a *Suan-chai wen-chi* is known to have been kept in the Ch'ien-ch'ing t'ang (Acres of Books Hall), the famous library of the Huang clan of Nanking. Huang Yü-chi (1629–1691) includes its title and notes its author as Hsiao-yün-shih hai-ya in the catalogue he prepared for the library, the *Ch'ien-ch'ing t'ang shu-mu*.[70] If not obtainable elsewhere, Ku may have had access to this copy. Poems 1–27 are included in Ku's selection proper; Poems 28 and 29 are quoted in the introduction to the selection. Of the twenty-seven poems, all but two seem to have been composed *before* Teng Wen-yüan wrote his preface in 1318. Only Poems 8 and 26 seem to be of later date. We know that Poem 8, "Reed-Floss Quilt," was written after Kuan settled in Hangchow, and thus after Kuan had showed his works to Teng (which he had done upon his arrival there).[71] We can also prove that Poem 26, "On First Arriving in the South, I Spend the Summer Resting on Phoenix Mountain," was not included in Kuan's *shih-wen* from a statement by Lang Ying (1486–after 1566): "I used to have his [i.e., Kuan's] *chi* [collected works], but the *lü* [regulated verse] quoted above [referring to Poem 26] was not included in it."[72] It is therefore likely that the *Suan-chai shih-wen*, or *Suan-chai chi*, which survived into the Ch'ing era was the text that Teng Wen-yüan saw in 1318. This conclusion is supported by the fact that the massive collection of Yüan verse published the year before Ku's *erh-chi* appreared, the *Yü-hsüan Yüan-shih* (item K in the Finding List which appears at the end of this chapter), which contains fifteen *shih* by Kuan (the next largest selection after Ku's), includes only poems that appear in Ku's selection. Although it contains twelve fewer *shih* than Ku's, the distribution is the same and quite unlike that of any other anthology of Yüan verse containing examples of Kuan's poetry (compare columns K and L with the rest). This suggests that both anthologies were made from the same source. As an anthology prepared by an editorial board operating under the auspices of the K'ang-hsi emperor, it would surely have been assembled from the very best sources possible. It is, in fact, very likely that in preparing the selection of Kuan's verse, the commission used the copy of Kuan's collected works preserved in the Ch'ien-ch'ing t'ang, since that work would have been known to the editors from the catalogue of the library. The *Ch'ien-ch'ing t'ang shu-mu* was, after all, utilized as the basis for the *Ming i-wen chih* (Bibliographic Monograph in the Ming History), which had been prepared by another imperial editorial board not too many years earlier.[73]

We should remember that Ch'eng Chü-fu wrote his colophon to what he knew to be Kuan's collected works in 1313 when Kuan first became his colleague at the Imperial Academy. Since there are *shih* in both the *Yü-hsüan Yüan-shih* and Ku Ssu-li's selection in the *Yüan-shih hsüan* that certainly date from after 1313, we can conclude that Kuan continued to add *shih* to his collected works up to the time he presented them to Teng Wen-yüan in 1318. However, we have it from Ou-yang Hsüan's spirit-way stele inscription that Kuan continued to write both verse and prose throughout his retirement in Hangchow.[74] Either these writings were collected together separately from the earlier *shih-wen* or they were never brought together at all. All that appears to survive of this later period of 1318–1324 is Poems 8, 11, 26, 28, 29, 30, 31, and, of course, Kuan's preface to *Yang-ch'un pai-hsüeh*, which is translated and discussed in the following chapter. Except for this preface, the preface to his edition of the *Classic of Filial Piety*, and the little prefaces to some of his *shih*, nothing of Kuan's extensive writings in prose seem to have survived.[75] One suspects that after Kuan settled in Hangchow he concentrated largely on the writing of lyrics and relegated the writing of *shih* to occasional verse, such as Poems 30 and 31, or to poems inspired by visits to scenic spots of some historical significance, such as Poem 11.

That we lack additional examples of his later *shih* is unfortunate, but, since so many lyrics date from this period, our understanding of him as a literary figure is not seriously impaired. It is the loss of works written prior to 1318 which creates difficulties for us. We do not know how representative the *Yüan-shih hsüan* is of his *shih* poems, and there is reason to suspect that it is not. Something of the "demonic quality" of his verse is visible in Poem 22, but there surely must have been more of this kind of verse, for his work as a whole was later characterized in just these terms.

It is also likely that Kuan wrote a considerable amount of patriotic verse—probably with strong Confucian undertones—during the

early years of his career. Poem 4, "Song on Painting a Dragon," is
of this kind, and the poem mentioned in Ch'eng Chü-fu's colophon,
"Seeing Younger Brother Off to Yung-chou,"[76] a "sincere piece of
moral advice," was probably of the same order. By way of contrast,
there is a hint of eroticism in Poems 2 and 27, and it is also likely
that Kuan wrote other such poems. Evidence for this conclusion
comes from Hsü Po-ling's (fl. c. 1465–1487) T'an ching-chün (Exquisite and Tasty Fare for the Silverfish):[77]

Suan-chai of the Yüan, Scholar Kuan Yün-shih, once composed a set of
Lan-fang liu nüeh-shih [Six Playful Poems for the Boudoir] which were
entitled: Liu-mei [Willow-Leaf Eyebrows], Hsing-yen [Star-Like Eyes],
T'an-k'ou [Sandalwood Mouth], Su-ju [Koumiss-White Breasts], Hsien-chih
[Slender Fingers] and Hsiang-kou [Fragrant Hooks]. "Fragrant Hooks"
refer to the [bound] feet. He got his idea for this from Tung-p'o's [Su Shih's]
Liu-i shih [Six Poems on Remembering (Her)], but the ones by Suan-chai
are just too gaudily erotic [t'ai yin-li].[78]

Unfortunately, Hsü then goes on to quote Su Shih's six poems
instead of those by Kuan. However, he may not have had access
to these poems supposedly by Kuan but may have been merely
referring to a passage in Li Chen's (1376–1452) Chien teng yü-hua
(Additional Stories to Tell after Trimming the Lamp).[79] One of the
tales in this collection is entitled Luan-luan chuan (Tale of a Lady
Named Phoenix). This concerns the story of the beauty Chao Luan-
luan and the talented young scholar Liu Ying, who are supposed
to have lived toward the end of the Yüan dynasty in Tung-p'ing,
Shantung.[80] After the usual obstacles are surmounted, the two manage to marry and settle down for a brief period of nuptial bliss. At
this time, Liu's cousin, who had been in Peking, returns home and
brings with him a copy of "Scholar Kuan's Six Playful Poems for the
Boudoir." These have the same titles as those listed by Hsü, except
that instead of "Star-Like Eyes" there is one entitled Yün-huan
(Cloud-Like Coiffure) which appears before "Willow-Leaf Eyebrows." Liu then borrows this copy of the poems, brings it home,
and looks it over with Luan-luan. He tries to write imitations, but,
before he can bring one off, Luan-luan always finishes one of her
own invention. The tale actually records "her" imitations of what
were supposed to be originals by Kuan, which again are not given.
The six by Luan-luan are:

1. Cloud-Like Coiffure

Fragrant clouds once in disheveled splendor, dampness not yet dry,
Now have become raven's feathers, cicada's wings—their cold gleam
  shining.
Toward the side she skews in a yellow gold phoenix,
And, toilette finished, her man looks at her and smiles!

2. Willow-Leaf Eyebrows

Curving, arching willow leaves pinched with sorrow at the edges,
The limpid pool of the caltrop mirror catches every knit in her brow.
This charming girl is impatient with her eyebrow pencil,
But the springtime mountains she brushes on still manage to come
  alive!

3. Sandalwood Mouth

She holds cup to mouth, slightly moves her cherry-red lips,
Coughs and makes the scent of jasmine dance lightly on the air.
So did I once see the mouth of this Fan Su from Po's house—[81]
Her teeth arrayed as melon seeds or studded as in a pomegranate!

4. Koumiss-White Breasts

Amidst scent of powder and moisture of sweat lie the tuning pegs of a
  jade zither
As thoughts of love induce the koumiss to melt into "white phoenix
  ointment."
After her bath, there where her lover fondles her
The coolness with its dewy sheen buds forth a purple grape!

5. Slender Fingers

Slender and graceful, soft jade tapers into spring scallions
Which had been grown inside fragrant and silken kingfisher-green
  sleeves.
Last night, on the strings of her lute,
Clearly, all of every nail showed its bright scarlet tint!

6. Fragrant Hooks

Spring clouds, ever so delicate, had enveloped her to her bamboo shoots
But now the evening moon, lovely as can be, reveals the beauty long
  obscured.
Her skirt, full of flocks of butterflies, is so long that where can one see
  them?
There, on the cross-bar of the swing when it comes down![82]

We have no way of ascertaining whether Li Chen invented this
reference to Kuan, or whether these poems really do have something to do with him. A number of Kuan's lyrics, Lyric 24, for
example, resemble these "boudoir poems," but that does not prove
that Kuan ever wrote anything as erotic as the poems in this story.
It may be that Li invented the entire episode and simply drew upon
Kuan's reputation as a romantic bon vivant to enhance the atmosphere of his narrative. In any event, this is one more indication
that Kuan enjoyed considerable fame as a poet in his own day—in
Peking and North China as well as in the Hangchow region—and
that his fame lasted well into the Ming era. It is a great pity that
we do not have more of his verse[83] upon which to build our estimation of him, but the lyrics do compensate for this in considerable
measure, and it is to them that we will now turn.

A. Chiang I, ed., *Huang-Yüan feng-ya* (SPTK). *Ch'ien-chi* 6 *chüan*,
     hou-chi 6 *chüan*; Kuan's *shih* is in the *ch'ien-chi*. Preface by
     Yü Chi is dated 1336.
B. Sun Yüan-li, ed., *Yüan-yin* (*Sung-fen shih ts'ung-k'an*). 12 *chüan*;
     reprint of the 1401 edition.
C. Sung Hsü, ed., *Yüan-shih t'i-yao* (*Ssu-k'u ch'üan-shu chen-pen*,
     third series). 14 *chüan*; preface to the original edition by Teng
     Lin is dated 1433.
D. Fu Kuan, ed., *Yüan-shih cheng-t'i* (*T'ang Sung Yüan Ming
     cheng-t'i shih* [*Cheng-t'i shih ssu-chung*]). 4 *chüan*; Fu's dates
     are 1444-1528. This is the Tao-kuang (1821–1850) re-engraved
     (traced) edition (*fu k'an-pen*) based on the 1506 woodblock
     edition.
E. Li Kun, ed., *Yüan i-p'u chi* (*Ssu-k'u ch'üan-shu chen-pen*, fourth
     series). 4 *chüan*; preface dated 1582.
F. P'an Shih-jen, ed., *Sung Yüan ssu-shih-san chia chi* (alternate

Finding List

	A	B	C	D	E	F	G	H	I	J	K	L	M	N	O
1.	1.4b	1.2a	9.23a			1.1a	11.10b			73.16b	26.1a	1b			
2.	1.4b	1.3a	7.23b			1.1b	11.11a			73.17a		2a	31.7b*		
3.	1.5a	1.3b			3.44b	1.2b	11.12a			73.17b		2b			
4.	1.5a							108.2b				2b			
5.	1.5a											3a			
6.	1.5b								6.14b	73.18a		3b			
7.		1.4a	9.23a			2.2b	11.12b			73.17b	3.5a	3b			
8.	1.5b	1.4a	10.22a	2.12b			11.13b		13.5a	73.18a			3b		4.6b
9.										73.18b	44.22b	4a			4.7a
10.				2.12b						73.18b	44.23a	4a			4.7a
11.												4b			4.7b
12.											44.23a	4b			4.7b
13.			14.4b								44.23a	4b	6.7b		
14.	1.5a		13.34a								4b	4b			2.16a
15.	1.5b										68.29a	5a			
16.	1.6a										68.29a	5a	30.8a**		
17.	1.6a										68.29a	5a			
18.	1.6a										68.29a	5a			
19.	1.6a										68.29b	5a	37.27b***		
20.											68.29b	5a			
21.												5b			
22.												5b			
23.								32.11b				5b			
24.											26.1b	6a			
25.												6a			
26.										73.18a	44.23b	6a			2.16a
27.											68.29b	6b			

*ts'e 31, ch'in-chü lei (bedding), 7b
**ts'e 30, shan lei (fans), 8a
***ts'e 37, hsien-kuan lei (Taoist temples), 27b

title *Sung Yüan ming-kung shih-chi*). Wood-block edition of 1615.

G. Ts'ao Hsüeh-ch'üan, ed., *Yüan-shih hsüan* (*Shih-ts'ang shih-erh-tai shih-hsüan*). 50 *chüan*; wood-block edition of 1630.

H. K'ang-hsi, nominal ed., *Yü-ting li-tai t'i-hua shih lei*. 120 *chüan*; wood-block edition of 1677.

I. Wu Ch'i, ed., *Sung Chin Yüan shih-yung*. 18 *chüan*; wood-block edition of 1678.

J. Ch'en Cho, ed., *Sung Yüan shih-hui*. 100 *chüan*; wood-block edition of 1683.

K. K'ang-hsi, nominal ed., *Yü-hsüan Yüan-shih* (*Yü-hsüan Sung Chin Yüan Ming ssu-ch'ao shih*). 1 + 80 + 2 *chüan*; wood-block edition of 1701.

L. Ku Ssu-li, ed., *Yüan-shih hsüan, erh-chi*. Wood-block edition of 1702.

M. K'ang-hsi, nominal ed., *P'ei-wen chai yung-wu shih-hsüan*. Wood-block edition of 1710.

N. Ku K'uei-kuang, ed., *Yüan-shih hsüan*. 6 *chüan* + *pu-i* (addenda). Wood-block edition of 1751.

O. Yao T'ing-ch'ien, ed., *Yüan-shih tzu-hsi*. 16 + 5 *chüan*; Japanese wood-block edition of 1858 (Yao was a mid-nineteenth century figure).

CHAPTER 4

Kuan as a Lyricist

I *Kuan's Place in the Yüan Lyric*

Some three generations of writers had been composing the *san-ch'ü*, the new form of lyric created during the Chin and the early Yüan, before Kuan turned his hand to it as a young man (about 1300). By Kuan's own day, this lyric form had become immensely popular among all classes of society; it had emerged long before from folk origins and the entertainment quarters and had become an important part of the literary repertoire of even such lofty literati as Yao Sui,[1] Kuan's Neo-Confucian mentor, while continuing to attract the attention of playwrights such as Kuan Han-ch'ing and Ma Chih-yüan.[2] There were few notable figures of the Yüan, literati *shih* poets and playwrights alike, who did not at least experiment with it. The writers represented in the *Ch'üan Yüan san-ch'ü*, for instance, came from almost every conceivable walk of life: from lofty officials (non-Chinese as well as Chinese) to figures clearly associated with the demimonde of tea houses, wine shops, brothels, and theaters. As such, the Yüan lyric reflects a broad spectrum of life and is a genre of considerable formal and expressive variety. Kuan's contribution to it is especially interesting, since he seems to have wandered the entire breadth of the social spectrum, and the thematic range of his lyrics consequently tends to be much broader than that of most other writers. Before undertaking a critical introduction to Kuan's own lyrics, an attempt will be made to determine what he thought of the lyric and what his contemporaries and later critics, both traditional and modern, thought of him as a lyricist. As well as helping to put Kuan's *san-ch'ü* in general and historical perspective, this should also indicate the kinds of things we should look for when we undertake our own critical survey of his lyrics in Part Two of this chapter.

Kuan is the author of one of the very few pieces of criticism of
the Yüan lyric which is actually of Yüan date.[3] This is his preface
to Yang Chao-ying's anthology of *san-ch'ü*, the *Yang-ch'un pai-hsüeh*
(White Snow of Sunny Spring):

Someone once said: "After Tung p'o [Su Shih] there is only Chia-hsüan
[Hsin Ch'i-chi (1140–1207)]." This criticism is too extreme! Actually, when
I came to the North, Hsü Tzu-fang [Hsü Yen (d. 1301)] had the reputation
of being *hua-ya* [polished and elegant] and Yang Hsi-an [Yang Kuo (1197–
1269)] the reputation of being *p'ing-shu* [well balanced and thoroughly
accomplished]. There are certainly people who realize this! Of those of a
nearer generation, Shu-chai [Lu Chih (1235–1300)] was *mei-fu* [attractive
and seductive] like a fairy goddess looking for a love affair [*hsün ch'un*].
How spontaneous and playful [*tzu-jan hsiao-ao*] he was! Feng Hai-su [Feng
Tzu-chen (1257–1327)] is *hao-la hao-lan* [intensely poignant and consummately evocative] and does not discriminate between the heartfelt affairs
of ancient and modern times [*pu tuan ku-chin hsin-shih*; i.e., he deals with
both with equal grace and ease]. He and Shu-weng [Lu Chih] cannot be
spoken of together with the same tongue [i.e., they are so different]. As
for Kuan Han-ch'ing [c. 1225 – c. 1307] and Yü Chi-fu [fl. c. 1251], their
diction [*tsao-yü*] is *yao-chiao* [attractive and charming]; like a young beauty
about to drink a cup of wine, its allure is more than one can bear! I have
studied the lyric [*tz'u*] since I was a youth, and, in the case of each of these
masters, I have realized that their respective depths of expression have
been like this. In recent years, I have been employed in the Bureau of
State Historiography. Gradually losing vigor and growing old, I could not
keep up with the front ranks of these other writers. I am ashamed of myself.
Yang Chao-ying of the Tan-chai [Placid Studio] has made a selection of the
lyrics (*tz'u*) of 100 authors and has called it the "White Snow of Sunny
Spring." He has therefore asked me to write a preface to it. Alas! The
echoes of the "White Snow of Sunny Spring" have been lost for a very long
time![4] Nevertheless, when I made a critical appraisal of the lyrics of the
writers represented in this anthology, I could not help but think that these
were "White Snow of Sunny Spring" songs too! A visitor once asked me:
"Those whom you have criticized do not account for all the writers represented in the anthology, so what about the rest?" I replied: "In the
western mountains when morning comes, there is such invigorating air."
The visitor laughed, and so did Tan-chai. This is a preface by Kuan Yün-
shih of the Suan-chai.[5]

It appears that both Yang Chao-ying, in calling his anthology
"White Snow of Sunny Spring," and Kuan, in bringing up the title

and commenting upon its historical connotations, want the reader to be aware of the ancient links the *san-ch'ü*, as a form of song-verse or lyric, has with the lyrical tradition. The fact that Kuan here refers to the Yüan lyric by the term *tz'u*, begins his survey of important lyricists with Su Shih and Hsin Ch'i-chi, and then goes on to say that various Yüan lyricists are the worthy successors of these Sung writers all suggest that he thought the lyrics of his own day were in the same tradition as those of the Sung and the ancient ballads (*yüeh-fu*). People of the Yüan period actually never referred to the *san-ch'ü* as *san-ch'ü* (a term invented later during the Ming to distinguish between the lyrics of the dramas, *ch'ü*, and the lyrics which were written independently and which circulated freely outside the dramas, *san-ch'ü*), but as either *tz'u* or *yüeh-fu*.[6]

This preface also suggests a few things about Kuan himself as a lyricist. First, he declares that he has been a serious student of this form of literature from his youth and that he has read widely and discriminatingly not only among the lyricists prominent in his own day but among the Sung lyricists as well. This assertion is supported in part by Teng Tzu-chin in his preface to Yang's other anthology of Yüan lyrics, the *Ch'ao-yeh hsin-sheng t'ai-p'ing yüeh-fu* (New Sounds of Court and Country: Ballads of the Age of Great Peace, 1351), in which he states that: "Mr. Kuan often gave his criticisms of contemporary writers of *tz'u*, and he considered those by Feng Hai-su to be *hao-la hao-lan*—this is what he really revered."[7] The translation of *hao-la hao-lan* as "intensely poignant and consummately evocative" is prompted by a comment of Chu Tung-jun on Kuan's preface in the *Chung-kuo wen-hsüeh p'i-p'ing shih ta-kang* (An Outline History of Chinese Literary Criticism):

As far as the *ching* [expressive qualities] indicated by the terms *p'ing-shu* or *wu-mei* [charming and attractive] are concerned, these can both already be found in the *shih* and the *tz'u*, but as for *hao-la hao-lan*, it is the *ch'ü-tzu* [i.e., the *san-ch'ü* and the *ch'ü* of the dramas] which are first capable of expressing these qualities. When one is so *yü-po ch'a-ch'i* [extremely depressed and hopelessly disappointed] and so *i-sai* [despondent] that it defies articulation in mere speech and can only be given vent to in song, this *ching-chieh* [realm] is called *hao-la*. When the myriad phenomena of existence in all their awe-inspiring magnificence [*wan-shih wan-hsiang sen-jen pi-chü*] inspire indescribable feelings and provoke limitless conceptions, and these feelings and conceptions are expressed in song, this is *hao-lan*.

These critical terms invented by Suan-chai are really quite capable of provoking inspiration [*chen yao* (literally) "be a shot in the arm"] for later
writers![8]

We might expect, therefore, to find among those of Kuan's lyrics
which are primarily personal expressions some of these *hao-la hao-
lan* qualities. It is also probably more than coincidence that later
traditional critics of the *ch'ü* who often characterized writers as
either *hao-fang* (poignantly emotional and free in style) or *ch'ing-
li* (aesthetically charming)[9] usually placed Kuan with the *hao-fang*
lyricists. The same character *hao* appears in *hao*-la and *hao*-fang.

So little contemporary criticism was written about Yüan lyricists
that it is not surprising that almost nothing was said about Kuan.
However, the fact that his lyrics occupy a prominent place in Yang
Chao-ying's two anthologies and that Yang asked him to write a
preface to one of them does indicate the high esteem Yang had for
him as a master of the form. Chang K'o-chiu's praise for his friend
was, of course, profuse.[10] A statement in Ch'eng Chü-fu's colophon
to *Suan-chai shih-wen* (Appendix IV, Chapter One) might also refer
to Kuan's *san-ch'ü*: "His five and seven syllable ancient-style verse
and his *ch'ang-tuan chü* effect a profound attainment in the fusion
of emotion and scene." It may be that the term *ch'ang-tuan chü*,
which literally means "lines of unequal length," merely refers to
the ancient ballad form, the *yüeh-fu*, examples of which would have
been appropriately included in a writer's *shih-wen*, and not to the
contemporary lyrics of the day which would not have been so included. However, it is not impossible that Kuan did include them,
for there is the statement in Ou-yang Hsüan's inscription: "There
are   in   circulation   today   [1349]   several   *chüan*   of   his
writings . . .including *tz'u*." Here *tz'u* surely refers to *san-ch'ü*.
However, Ou-yang's statement is ambiguous. We do not know
whether the *chüan* he mentions were all included in Kuan's collected writings or not. The version of Kuan's *shih-wen* which Ch'eng
saw was in manuscript form, and it is possible that Kuan appended
his *san-ch'ü* to it, as the *tz'u* of Sung writers were sometimes appended to their *shih-wen*.[11] The only other critical reference to
Kuan's lyrics made during the Yüan that has come to light is contained in the passage from the *Lo-chiao ssu-yü* cited in Chapter
One, in which Yao Tung-shou states that he regards them as *chün-
i* (spirited and free), a characterization much in keeping with later

critics who say that they are *hao-fang.*[12]

We shall next consider the criticism of Kuan's lyrics which appears in the *T'ai-ho cheng-yin p'u* (Handbook on the Orthodox Music of Supreme Harmony), preface dated 1398, by Chu Ch'üan (1378–1448), Prince Hsien of Ning, the sixteenth son of Chu Yüan-chang, the founder of the Ming Dynasty. In the second section of Chu's work there appears a *Ku-chin ch'ün-ying yüeh-fu ko-shih* (Styles of Lyrics by All the Noble Writers of Earlier and Later Times), and there he says of Kuan's lyrics: "The *tz'u* of Kuan Suan-chai is like a heavenly horse which has cast off its bridle."[13] This should remind us of the statement by Ch'en Chi concerning Kuan's calligraphy: "Mr. Suan-chai was like a wild goose in splendid isolation or a magnificent steed running free beyond the reach of harpoon-arrow or of bridle."[14] While it is possible that Chu Ch'üan may have been aware of this statement by Ch'en, it is far more likely that he coined the characterization himself, with the following ideas in mind: The heavenly horse (*t'ien-ma*) suggests great and sustained strength because these horses came from Ferghana in Central Asia (remember that Kuan was a Central Asian), could "sweat blood" and could gallop a thousand *li* in a day. "Cast off the bridle" (*t'o chi*) suggests escape from the snares and entanglements of the mundane world. Taken together, the entire characterization seems to signify unrestrained power, a free style unencumbered by close adherance to the rules of versification, and a lack of self-restraint in emotional expression.

Kuan may have been a free stylist, but Chu still admired his technical skill at fitting lyrics to melodic patterns enough to include no less than five examples of his lyrics as models in his *Yin-lü kung-tiao* (Handbook of Prosody and Musical Modes), part six of the *T'ai-ho cheng-yin p'u*: Lyric 40 to represent *Ch'ing-chiang yin* (Clear River Song),[15] VIII.1 to represent *Tsui ch'un-feng* (Intoxicating Spring Breeze),[16] VIII.2 to represent *Chien chin ssu-k'uai yü* (Four Pieces of Jade, with Hidden Gold),[17] VIII.3 to represent *Chien tzu mu-lan-hua* (Magnolia Blossoms, with Syllables Deleted),[18] and VII.4 to represent Yüan-yang sha (Mandarin Duck Coda).[19] Chu seems to have admired Kuan's lyrics as much for their technical virtuosity as for their expressive qualities. Although he does not place Kuan among the twelve writers he considers to be of the very highest quality,[20] he does place him at the head of the seventy writers he places in the second rank.

Wang Shih-chen (1526–1590), in his *Ch'ü-tsao* (Literary Elegance of the *Ch'ü*), also mentions Kuan and places him in the highest rank of *ch'ü* writers, in fact, right at the top of the list:

Various masters such as Kuan Suan-chai, Ma Tung-li [Ma Chih-yüan], Wang Shih-fu, Kuan Han-ch'ing, Chang K'o-chiu, Ch'iao Meng-fu [Ch'iao Chi], Cheng Te-hui [Cheng Kuang-tsu], Kung Ta-yung [Kung T'ien-t'ing] and Pai Jen-fu [Pai P'u] all surely had *ts'ai-ch'ing* [great talent] and all took delight in metrical composition [*sheng-lü*]. In consequence of this, they were the very best of their age.[21]

It is significant that Wang includes in this list writers who are not known to have written dramas, for instance, Kuan and Chang K'o-chiu. He was later censured for this by Li Tiao-yüan (*chin-shih* of 1763) in his *Yü-ts'un ch'ü-hua* (Yü-ts'un's Talks on the *Ch'ü*). After quoting the above passage by Wang, Li comments:

Kuan Suan-chai, Chang K'o-chiu and Kung Ta-yung were only skillful at *hsiao-ling* [i.e., they only wrote *san-ch'ü* but not dramas], and thus fell far short of Ma, Wang, Ch'iao, Cheng and Pai. They cannot be spoken of as if they were their equals.[22]

Besides taking too narrow a view of the *ch'ü*, Li has also made a mistake concerning Kung T'ien-t'ing, who in fact authored several dramas.[23] Wang Shih-chen was not unique in discussing playwright-lyricists and lyricists together; Chu Ch'üan did likewise in the *T'ai-ho cheng-yin p'u*.

Modern historians of Chinese drama do not usually think of Kuan in connection with drama, and they regard him strictly apart from the dramatists as a writer of *san-ch'ü*, but this sharp distinction between the drama and the *san-ch'ü* was not so carefully maintained in earlier times. People then seemed to regard the two as subgenres within the larger *ch'ü* genre as such. For instance, Kuan's and Chang K'o-chiu's lyrics seem to have had a lasting influence on the later tradition of dramaturgy, even down into the middle Ch'ing era. This is attested to by the important literary figure Wang Shih-chen (1634–1711)—not to be confused with the Ming figure whose name is romanized in the same way—in an epitaph for Chao Chin-mei (1621–1693), who, among other things, was a writer of *ch'uan-ch'i* (dramatic romances; i.e., the fully developed Southern Drama):

His various *ch'uan-ch'i,* such as *Yao-t'ai meng* [Dream of the Jasper Terrace) and *Li ti ch'eng fo* [Becoming a Buddha in an Instant], are, in the opinion of connoisseurs, not inferior to the works of Chang Hsiao-shan and Kuan Suan-chai.[24]

We noted the possible influence Kuan might have had on the development of the Southern Drama in Chapter One;[25] this now seems to be more than just a mere possibility.

Most modern surveys of Chinese Literature which touch on Yüan *san-ch'ü* at all often have something to say about Kuan. Among those twentieth-century critics and historians of the *san-ch'ü* whose remarks provide some special insight into the essential stylistic characteristics of Kuan's lyrics is the scholar Jen Na. Jen includes in his *San-ch'ü ts'ung-k'an* (A Collectanea of Works Concerned with the *San-ch'ü*), his edition of Kuan's and Hsü Tsai-ssu's lyrics, the *Suan-t'ien yüeh-fu.* His preface to this collection is factual and informative, and there are several things worth noting in connection with Kuan in another work by Jen, his *Ch'ü-hsieh* (Congenial Chats about the Ch'ü). For instance, he states that Lyric 23 is his favorite piece in the entire *Yang-ch'un pai-hsüeh* and that "the sound and feeling of its conclusion is so painfully sad [*ch'i-ch'u*] that it soaks right into one's heart and spleen [i.e., it "hits one right in the guts"]."[26] Jen also regards this lyric as the very best in Kuan's entire oeuvre.[27] However, he has mixed feelings about Lyric 1: "The twists of the plot [*p'u-p'ai chuan-che*] and the peaks of feeling at the turnings in emotional expression [*shen-li ch'i-shih*] coincide perfectly throughout." He immediately goes on to cite Chou Te-ch'ing's (fl. c. 1300–1325) critique of this lyric in Chou's *Tso tz'u shih-fa* (Ten Sets of Rules for Composing Lyrics):

Chou Te-ch'ing vigorously condemned it for having an excess of *ch'en-tzu* [extrametrical syllables]. The last line, in fact, has double the number of syllables that the original pattern entails. As far as the *san-ch'ü* is concerned, this really is something quite inappropriate, but even if we discuss it in terms of *ch'i-shih* [peaks of feeling], in the final analysis the last line would fail to be beautiful whether it contained fourteen syllables or not. In my opinion, although we can forgive it its excessive use of *ch'en-tzu,* what I am displeased with is that the word *shih* [events; in the third line] would have been such a difficult tone to sing [*chung-ya*] that there would have been no way to fix it up so that it could be saved [*pu-chiu*].[28]

Finally, Jen quotes Lyric 65 and says of it: "With a scant minimum of words, its *feng-ch'ü* [interest] is endless; any famous master would have been proud to have written it."[29] Evidently, although Jen could admire Kuan's dramatic and expressive qualities, he had reservations about him as a technical stylist.

Cheng Chen-to has strong words of praise for Kuan's lyrics. He thinks that they are reminiscent of the *tz'u* of Su Shih *and* Hsin Ch'i-chi, and in this respect he cites Lyric 40 as an example of unrestrained and exuberant expressiveness. However, Cheng also thinks that some of Kuan's lyrics are extremely *ch'ing-li wan-ni* [aesthetically charming and beautifully polished], and as an example of this he cites Lyrics 2, 55, and IV.3. He concludes his critique of Kuan by saying: "These pieces are good enough to rival the very best love songs of Kuan Han-ch'ing."[30]

Liu Ta-chieh also thinks that Kuan's lyrics cannot all be characterized by any single term. He cites Lyric 40 as an example of Kuan's *hao-fang p'iao-i* (poignantly emotional and free in style, and light-hearted) lyrics and Lyric 23 as an example of his *li-su sheng-tung* (earthiness and raw vitality). Lyrics such as these, he says, have exactly the same unadulterated feeling of expression as the lyrics of Kuan Han-ch'ing and Ma Chih-yüan and, as such, in style still belong to what he considers the "first period" of the *san-ch'ü*. Many other Kuan lyrics, however, consist of a mixture of raw exuberance and heightened refinement characteristic of the "second period." In this respect, he cites Lyrics 14 and 76.[31] These two lyrics, in his opinion, resemble in some ways the *kung-t'i shih* (palace-style verse) of the T'ang era, as well as certain *hsiao-ling* (short songs) in Sung *tz'u*. He does not say so, but here perhaps he has a writer such as Liu Yung (fl. c. 1034) in mind. Liu Ta-chieh finally closes his critique of Kuan's lyrics by commenting that "no matter what form of literature comes from the people, after it has gone through a long period of development at the hands of the literati, it inevitably results in something like this."[32] This suggests, and I concur, that we might look for a kind of dialectic between "popular" and "literati" elements within Kuan's lyrics. Liu implies that the interplay between these two dimensions—raw, earthy exuberance on the one hand, and refined sensibility and exquisite craftsmanship on the other—is what gives strength and beauty to much of Kuan's work.

II   *Critical Introduction to Kuan's Lyrics*

A. ALLUSION

I count eighty-eight different occasions in Kuan's lyrics where there seems to be allusion involved.[33] This is not at all excessive considering how many lyrics there are: seventy-nine *hsiao-ling* and nine *t'ao-shu* which consist of an additional forty-eight *hsiao-ling*. The total of all *hsiao-ling* is thus 127, and so the average is less than one allusion per lyric. This is a lower proportion than is the case even for many Yüan dramas, and this is surprising for a writer who wrote such highly allusive *shih* and was an erudite scholar. Equally surprising is the kind of allusions involved. All but a few are also native to Yüan drama.[34] This suggests that the majority of Kuan's lyrics were intended for basically the same kind of audience as were the dramas. He was not a scholar dabbling in the *san-ch'ü* and producing lyrics intended only for the amusement of other scholars, but a writer in the mainstream of the *ch'ü* form, a form dominated during the Yüan by nonliterati writers.

The contrast between the kinds of allusion used in the *shih* and in the *san-ch'ü* is particularly significant. Kuan's *shih* drew upon a great deal of T'ang verse. There are many improvisations on lines from poems by Li Po, Li Ho, Tu Fu, Li Shang-yin, and others, as well as from works such as the *Chuang-tzu*, the *Shan-hai ching*, the *Han-fei tzu*, some of the official histories, the *Ch'u-tz'u*, the *Lieh-tzu*, and so on, and often without a sense of the *locus classicus* many lines and even some whole passages become largely unintelligible. This rarely happens in the lyrics. Although many of these same sources provide allusions in the lyrics, many or perhaps even most of these allusions were to persons, things, and events which had entered the popular culture. Also, many allusions are so woven into the fabric of the lyrics that the lines are still intelligible without an awareness that allusion is involved. For instance, although the fifth line in Lyric 62 is an improvisation on a line in a *shih* by Han Yü, it is still perfectly intelligible as it stands. The same happens in Lyric V.7, where an allusion to Wang Hsi-chih's "Preface to the Orchid Pavilion Collection" occurs in the second line.

At times the lyrics go to very different sources for their allusions than do the *shih*; for example, to Sung *tz'u* and to contemporary drama. Lines 9–12 in Lyric 3, 7–9 in Lyric 26, the first line of Lyric 29, lines 3–4 in Lyric 53, and line 4 in Lyric 74 all derive from Sung *tz'u*. Lines 1–2 in Lyric V.4 are actually an allusion to Liu Yung's collected lyrics. Lines which seem to allude to dramas include line 9 in Lyric 2, line 2 in Lyric 11, possibly line 7 in Lyric 21, the first line in Lyric 32, while all of Lyric IX.2 may have been inspired by Pai P'u's drama "Madame Han Ts'ai-p'in Floats a Red Leaf on the Imperial Moat." Line 11 in Lyric 34 may have something to do with the dramas as well. It could have been inspired by Ma Chih-yüan's "Autumn in the Palace of Han" or perhaps by Pai P'u's "Dream of Ch'ien-t'ang," or even by both. One expression in the lyrics even alludes to marketplace entertainment; it occurs in the fifth line of Lyric 50.

Kuan's lyrics employ far more clichés than do the *shih*; for example, such expressions as "fish and geese"(letters), "flowers and willows" (singing girls or prostitutes), "clouds and rain" (love-making) occur throughout both the *hsiao-ling* and the *t'ao-shu*. On the other hand, there are very few scholarly allusions in the lyrics, those which could only be apprehended at sight by someone with a literati education. One such allusion occurs in line 5 in Lyric 44, and another possibly in lines 8–9 in Lyric 25. Some allusions which now appear obscure may not have been at the time; for instance, those to the *I-ching* (Classic of Changes) which, as a divination manual, enjoyed considerable popularity in its day.

In conclusion, it can be said that Kuan's use of allusion in the lyrics was varied, always functional, sometimes erudite, but very seldom obscure and never obtrusive or distracting.

B. IMAGERY

Imagery in Kuan's lyrics seems to be divided about equally between the compound and the simple types,[35] and this, too, is something that differs in comparison with the *shih*, where the imagery is overwhelmingly compound. Many of the lyrics are involved with simple and straightforward images which capture sensations and impressions of objective existence in a direct and immediate way. There is a fair amount of landscape in Kuan's lyrics, and it is here that simple imagery seems at its best, as, for example, in the lines:

> My thatched cottage's two or three rooms lie in green shade.
> There's a stream flowing behind the garden, a mountain
>   beyond the gate,
> And mountain peaches and wild apricots opening in infinite
>   bloom.
>
> (Lyric 66, lines 1–3)

In Kuan's many lyrics set in ladies' boudoirs, there is often a combination of simple landscape imagery and a straightforward depiction of the ladies themselves:

> There, in the garden filled with willow catkins scattered by the
>   east wind,
> A gentle rain just stopped, and swallows and orioles are at rest.
> Here, alone inside silken bedcurtains, I heave long sighs in vain.
> As spring scenery fades
> So his love wanes,
> And my fragrant heart grows afraid.
>
> (Lyric II.3)

Kuan's use of compound imagery varies considerably among the different types. Juxtaposition occurs, as in:

> On high, snowy fragrant orchids take over her cloud coiffure,
> Jade-white magic mugwort cupping raven locks from the
>   sides.
>
> (Lyric 22, lines 1–2)

> As up against Mount Wu, an emerald screen hung up
>   high . . . .
>
> (Lyric 63, line 3)

Comparison occurs as well:

> Just like a sprig of red almond blossoms peeping over a wall
> She lies beyond the reach of plucking hand.
>
> (Lyric 26, lines 7–8)

Substitution is also common:

> As on disk-like dimpled cheeks tarry traces of powdery frost.
>
> (Lyric 22, line 3)

Here "frost" substitutes for face powder.

Transference is very common in Kuan's lyrics. Some striking examples of it include: "and cool moonlight courses through the little garden" (Lyric 16, line 3), where the attributes of water are transferred to moonlight. Many instances of transference involve the description of objects in nature or inanimate objects in terms of human attributes and actions (i.e., personification—the "pathetic fallacy"). A most striking example is "as colorful trees wither, completely drunk on autumn frost" (Lyric 67, line 2) or "blouse sleeves become so wet and weighed down they begin to drown in my tear-filled eyes" (Lyric II.2, line 11). There are also some instances where this process is reversed, and aspects of natural objects are attributed to the person, as when a sad and lonely lady is made to say: "I'm a willow drooping kingfisher-green strands, a blossom dropping petals of rouge" (Lyric II.1, lines 1–2).

C. SYMBOLISM

The most common symbols in Kuan's lyrics involve wine, drinking, and drunkenness, all of which seem to symbolize freedom, emancipation from the snares and entanglements of the mundane world, and transcendence of the petty concerns which tie the individual to his fate. Many other writers in the Chinese tradition used these symbols, and Kuan like them borrowed this practice from T'ao Ch'ien (365–427), whose "Twenty Poems after Drinking Wine" provided a model of truly archetypal dimensions for the whole of the later tradition.[36] These symbols occur in no less than eleven of the lyrics: Lyrics 3, 6, 20, 40, 42, 48, 49, 64, 67, 68, and 69. Another symbol is the "safe and happy refuge" or "humble cottage" mentioned in Lyrics 41, 42, 48, and 72. These appear to be references to Kuan's own residence near Hangchow and signify his satisfaction with the simple joys of retirement. The reverse of this is the "jade hall" or "decorated hall," places where the rich and the powerful reside (in danger).

Ch'ü Yüan becomes a symbol in one of Kuan's lyrics, Lyric 71, where he is the archetypal worthy and upright minister who was slandered and ruined by petty men, and who attempted to justify his own existence by making the strongest possible protest, by way of suicide. This lyric is saturated with allusions which function as powerful and compelling symbols. In addition to Ch'ü himself, the

Ts'ang-lang River becomes a symbol for the erratic flow of human society and individual human fate. When the times are good and government is just, the just man serves, but when they are foul, the wise man knows that there is nothing he can do and so withdraws from office and tends to his own personal cultivation as best he can. Articulated in terms of symbols, this is actually a dialogue between different parts of Kuan's person. He is Ch'ü Yüan, and then he becomes the wily old fisherman who pokes fun at the would-be Chü Yüan and tells him he is a fool who would do far better to retire and find satisfaction in seclusion. Of course, nothing of this is new with Kuan, but the way he has woven it all together is remarkable. Lyric 71 is the most symbolic of all of Kuan's lyrics and is perhaps the most personal in the sense of being self-referential, autobiographical. It may be that the frequently encountered lonely lady pining away in her boudoir is also a symbol of personal frustration at his failure to achieve success in his official career, but since none of these lyrics can be dated, I prefer to treat them as dramatic pieces rather than as examples of personal expression operating through symbolism or allegory. Something more will be said about this in the last section of this chapter under "Expression."

D. DICTION

By comparison with his *shih*, Kuan's lyrics are far more denotative and straightforward. Lyric 22, in fact, is probably one of the best examples of explicit diction in the entire corpus of Yüan *san-ch'ü*; here words mean exactly what they say; we can take them at face value and need not search for implication and suggestion. This contrast between the *shih* and the *san-ch'ü* is especially apparent when we place Poem 2, "The Fair One," against any of Kuan's lyrics on the same theme, the lonely lady in her boudoir. This is a rather long poem, and so Lyric I will serve as an example. Poem 2 begins with a description of the lady in highly figurative language, but the lyric opens with a straightforward description of the physical setting, which is followed by a simple description of the lady and a depiction of her actions in equally unambiguous and direct language. The time of day is stated simply in the first line of Lyric I.1, but in the fourth line of Poem 2 an elaborate circumlocution is used, "a phoenix calls down the moon from over lonely hills," to announce the fact that it is almost dawn. The lyric uses a well-worn cliché, "blue phoenix letter" (for love letter) in the third line of I.1, but the poem mentions a letter in this way: She sends birds flying, gripping her chagrin in their beaks, over Long Gate Palace." The language of the lyric would, I imagine, have been immediately intelligible at the time it was chanted or sung, but the same could hardly be said for the poem. This may be a point so obvious that it is not worth mentioning, but it does indicate one basic difference between the *shih* and the *san-ch'ü* of the Yüan period. In this respect, Kuan's work in the two genres is typical. However, his expertise with the *shih* probably has something to do with the fact that some extremely connotative examples of diction appear from time to time in the lyrics. Particularly noteworthy is line 4 in Lyric 37: "Her kingfisher feathers stir up a breeze." The line that follows describes the lady's tears, and the significance of the first line becomes apparent: she is so shaking with sobs that she has set her kingfisher hair ornaments trembling, even to the extent that they fan up a breeze! The suggestion and hyperbole here would have graced any Late T'ang *shih*.

As a semiliterary, semivernacular genre, the *san-ch'ü* utilizes vocabulary drawn from both literary and vernacular Chinese.[37] It appears that the choice of expressions from the one or the other depends, in Kuan's lyrics, at least, upon the subject matter or theme and the kind of tone the lyricist wanted to project. The extensive use of vernacular expressions in Lyric 1 has already been noted by James Crump,[38] but why this particular lyric contains so much of the vernacular has not been made clear. Taken in isolation, Lyric 1 is in many respects ambiguous, but if one considers the possibility that originally it might have been linked to Lyric 2, as the first half of a lovesong narrated in the voice of a rejected lover, certain things seem to become clear. Although the second "half" is the far more vernacular of the two parts, even utilizing coarse slang from the pleasure quarters, the first half might be regarded as sharing with it a common tone, a tone essentially carried by the series of vernacular expressions which highlight almost every line. A similar thing happens in Lyric 4 where another unhappy fellow is having trouble with his girl. The vernacular expressions keep the narrative on a comic to ironic level: *t'a sheng-ti* (she's turned out to be), *ch'uai-che ko hsiu lien-erh* (shamefaced I . . .), *pai-pan-ti* (a hundred different ways), *ch'i-ti wo* (she makes me so angry . . .), and so on. On the other hand, a song-set such as Lyric VII with its lofty theme and setting (New Year's at the imperial palace) keeps the vernacular expressions to a bare minimum. Some of Kuan's *hsiao-ling* do not contain any vernacularisms at all: Lyric 13, 62, and 78, for example, but all of the *t'ao-shu* do, even such a noble one as Lyric VII. This might suggest that Kuan's *t'ao-shu* were always meant for some kind of public or semipublic performance, and thus were more inclined to the use of vernacular expressions so that they would be intelligible to the listening audience. The song-sets of Yüan times generally were written for performance,[39] and Kuan's were probably no exception. I have the impression that the closer the themes or motifs of the lyrics (both *hsiao-ling* and *t'ao-shu*) are to themes or motifs commonly occurring in the *shih* the less likely he is to use vernacular expressions, the corollary being that the newer the theme, the more the vernacularisms. The "newest" of Kuan's themes or subjects, as far as the tradition of Chinese poetry is concerned, appear in Lyrics 2 and 4, and it is in these that we find the most vernacularisms in his *hsiao-ling*; Lyric IV represents this phenomenon in the *t'ao-shu*.

As might be expected, lyrics which contain a considerable number of vernacular expressions also utilize a vernacular syntax; the fewer the vernacularisms, the more likely the syntax is to be literary. In those lyrics which contain no vernacular expressions at all, Lyric 78, for instance, the syntax is entirely that of the literary language; lines 2 and 3, in fact, resemble seven-syllable *shih* poetry and lines 5, 6, and 7 seem like five-syllable verse. The majority of lyrics, however, represent a mixture of syntactical patterns. There is no consistent proportion of the two, and the amount of vernacular syntax varies from a single morpheme to the entire text of the lyric. Lyric IV is probably the single most sustained piece of vernacular syntax in all of Kuan's work. Its tone is a mixture of irony and chagrin, and it is filled with slang expressions from beginning to end. The voice of the singing girl seems realistic and immediate, even now after six centuries.

E. EXPRESSION

The essential problem here is to determine when the voice of the lyrics is meant to be Kuan's own and when it is meant to be the voice of a deliberately assumed persona. In attempting to divide the lyrics into these two categories, some are found to fall easily into place; others do not. The most obvious kind of dramatic lyric is that in which the voice is that of a woman. Some employ first-person personal pronouns and some do not, but all have been translated as if they did. In the absence of pronouns, one has to decide, for example, between rendering a line as either "I feel so lonely" or "she feels so lonely." Thus, for the sake of consistency and clarity of dramatic values, I have chosen to use the first-person throughout. On the other hand, those lyrics in which the voice is obviously masculine are not all necessarily self-referential, and the "I" of the lyric, implied or not, does not always refer to the poet himself. There are examples of this in which the man's voice cannot be that of the poet. Lyrics 1 and 2, for instance, as the title states, were "written on behalf of someone," and Lyric 11 should be read as a dramatic situation inspired by a drama by Wang Shih-fu. Other lyrics are obvious examples of vigorous self-expression—Lyrics 25, 42, and 48–51, for example—and contain sentiments and ideas easily identifiable with Kuan as a person. To be sure, some lyrics are ambiguous, and one can never be sure how much, if any, of Kuan's real personality and real experience is contained in them. The commentaries will deal with this problem when it arises.

It would be fruitless to speculate on the amount of personal involvement Kuan had with the characters he presents in his dramatic lyrics. We know too little about his life to attempt to do so. The various personae are treated mostly with considerable sympathy, though occasionally with touches of irony and humor. The world they inhabit, the pleasure quarters of Hangchow and the West Lake, for the most part, appears familiar to Kuan; it is likely that he knew it well. It is conceivable that many of these dramatic lyrics, both short songs as well as song-sets, were written to be performed there by singers with whom he was acquainted and whom he may even have patronized. Such lyrics may also have been written originally for performance in the homes of friends and acquaintances and for presentation at dinner parties in his own home, later to become part of the popular repertoire of professional singers of the day.

The personality traits, feelings, values, and sensibilities that Kuan appears to express in the self-referential lyrics span a wide spectrum. For the most part, these lyrics appear to date from the post-1317 period of his life. They reveal his struggle for emancipation from the world of status, duty, and ambition as well as his eventual success in achieving happiness and release in the world of nature, music, poetry, wine, and human companionship. Here, he appears capable of both strong and sensitive feelings, and sincere in the friendship and love he felt for the men and women who sometimes figure in these lyrics. He thus emerges as an attractive and likable personality, and his struggles and successes in life and his reactions to them come across to us in a striking and immediate way. Rather than say any more about the formal and literary qualities of the lyrics, it would be better to let the lyrics speak for themselves. All extant lyrics which can be attributed to Kuan are translated in the following chapter. While a careful reading of all of them may fail to dispel all the shadows masking the poet's life, much more about him will emerge when one keeps in mind the biographical data presented in Chapter One and the classical verse translated in Chapter Three.

CHAPTER 5

Translation of Kuan's Lyrics

Lyric 1 Cheng-kung, Sai-hung ch'iu (Border Geese Autumn),
"Written on Behalf of Someone" in Two Verses (*CYSC*, p. 357)

Braving the west wind, tiny dots of migratory geese approach.
They move me to think of
Those events of the Southern Court that rend hearts forever.
Unrolling decorated note paper, I'd write a few lines that reveal
   my love,
But to no purpose it makes me
Halt the frost-tipped brush, struck witless for awhile.
Always before when inspired,
I could bring it off at once without the least flaw,
But now
Worn out with grief, I can just manage to write down the words
   "I love her."

Lyric 2

The first time I saw her I fell completely in love.
As the darling of my life,
With respect and devotion I made her my own.
In all these years have I ever tired of our affair!
Recently, all at once she's become stingy with her affection.
As excuse, she says it's
How strict her interfering "Willow Green" is
And how crazy her well-heeled "Uncle" is about her.
So I'm just a miserable Shuang Chien cast off by a pretty Su Ch'ing!

Commentary: The Southern Court (*Nan-ch'ao*) was located at the
city of Chien-k'ang (present-day Nanking). This was the site of the
successive capitals of the four Chinese states, the Sung, the Ch'i,
the Liang, and the Ch'en, which controlled South China during the
146

so-called Northern and Southern Dynasties or Six Dynasties Era (420–588). The heart-rending events (*shang hsin shih*) appears to be a reference to the many love affairs which are celebrated and lamented in the often voluptuous and extravagant "palace-style poems" of the times, many of which are preserved in the *Yü-t'ai hsin-yung* (New Poems from the Jade Terraces) compiled by Hsü Ling (507–583). Writing brushes are often made from the tips of animal tails which have white points. "Willow Green" (*liu-ch'ing*) was a slang expression meaning procuress, madame, or proprietress of a brothel.[1] "Well-heeled Uncle" translates *t'ung-man i-fu*, the patron of a kept woman.[2] The romance between Shuang Chien and Su Hsiao-ch'ing (Su Ch'ing) was often the subject of dramas, stories, and lyrics from the thirteenth century on. Su Ch'ing loved Shuang Chien, but her mother was greedy and married her off to a rich man, an archetypal situation that inspired scores of works.

Lyric 3 Cheng-kung, Hsiao liang-chou (Little Liang-chou), no title (*CYSC*, p. 357)

> Ruddy-faced black haired young lads
> All become dottering white-haired old men.
> Let flowers and willows be as fragrant as they like,
> They have no mind to enjoy them
> Nor do they bother themselves to chase after swallows and orioles!
> *Repeat*
> Got drunk at my neighbor's on the east and there I sang.
> So what if I get drunk again at my neighbor's on the west!
> When I'm drunk, I'm really drunk,
> And when I'm sober, I'm really sober,
> But if I were to get solidly drunk for one hundred years,
> It'd be thirty-six thousand times!

Commentary: Flowers and willows (*hua-liu*) is a cliché for prostitutes, and swallows and orioles (*yen-ying*) is an abbreviation of the expression *yen-lü ying-ch'ou* (swallow couple, oriole pair), a cliché for a "pair of happy lovers." The last four lines are derived from a *tz'u* by Su Shih, part of which is:

> All human affairs are fixed beforehand by fate—
> Who's to be weak and who's to be strong.
> So, making use of leisure time before growing old,

I might as well be a bit uninhibited.
In the course of one hundred years,
If solidly drunk as one can be,
It would be thirty-six thousand times![3]

Lines 8 and 9 in Kuan's lyric are particularly clever; *tsui ti ch'iang,
hsing ti ch'iang* can also be translated as "when drunk I'm strong,
and when sober I'm strong." Awareness of the allusion to Su Shih's
tz'u makes *ch'iang* into a pun.

Lyric 4 Cheng-kung, Hsiao liang-chou, no title (CYSC, p. 358).

With her peach blossom face and willowy waist
She's turned out to be utterly bewitching!
Finished with drinking, encouraged by wine, I'll meet her
    tonight.
We'll share a few words spoken in whispers,
Then, speechless, we'll be lost in each other's gaze!
Repeat
Shamefaced, I plead with her,
But she plays dumb and plays coy tricks a hundred different
    ways.
She makes me so angry that my heart starts to smolder,
Furious to no avail.
Could it be that in the Register of Predestined Lovers
Ours was secretly erased in a past incarnation!

Commentary: A common folk belief was that love-matches were
already determined in the man's and the woman's previous exis-
tences and written down by the Old Man beneath the Moon (*yüeh-
hsia lao-jen*) in the *yin-yüan pu* (Register of Predestined Lovers).

Lyric 5 Cheng-kung, Hsiao liang-chou, no title (CYSC, p. 358)

We embrace and hold each other with passion so intense
How can we ever bear to part!
It would be better to have never met at all.
My grief grows heavier and heavier
With the fear of how empty our painted pavilion will be!
Repeat
At the ferry landing among weeping willows I see him off.
Bent deep in prayer, I secretly beg the East Wind,

When he sets off and raises the sail high,
To fail to blow and move him not.
Let him stay but another night more—
Surely Heaven will allow me this!

Lyric 6 Cheng-kung, Hsiao liang-chou, "Spring" (CYSC, p. 358)

Borne on spring breezes and filling gardens, the scent of
    blossoming shrubs,
Horses tied among drooping willows,
Peach reds and willow greens reflected in the lake—
All these things are well worth enjoying,
But the sand's so warm it's put to sleep pairs of mandarin
    ducks.
Repeat
Whether clear or rainy, day or night,
It's as beautiful as Hsi Shih—in plain attire or all made up.
A girl fair as jade plucks the strings,
And another beauty sings a song.
Up in this room on my mountain by the lake,
Why shouldn't I get as drunk as I can!

Commentary: Lyrics 6–9 comprise a set of four songs on the seasons at the West Lake and appear to be a graphic reflection of his stay there. The two girls mentioned in Lyric 6 might well be his two concubines. Paired mandarin ducks (*yüan-yang*) are a symbol of conjugal (or not so conjugal) bliss. Line 5 is adopted from the first of Tu Fu's pair of "Quatrains."[4] Hsi Shih was a famous beauty (fifth century B.C.) of the state of Yüeh who was presented by the King of Yüeh as a present to his old enemy, the King of Wu, so that she might cause the latter's downfall. Her place in the Chinese tradition as the archetypal peerless beauty is much the same as that of Helen of Troy in the West. Her name is sometimes given as Hsi-tzu (Mistress West). Line 7 is derived from the second of two *shih* by Su Shih entitled "Drinking on the Lake, First Clear then it Rained," one couplet of which reads: "I like to compare West Lake to Mistress West;/They are always pretty whether unadorned or all made up."[5]

Lyric 7 Cheng-kung, Hsiao liang-chou, "Summer" (CYSC, p. 359)

Our painted boat was poled into the cool of willow shade,
But a flurry of reed-organ music and

Lotus pickers harmonizing on a lotus picker's song
Made sounds so sharp and penetrating
They woke this pair of bedded mandarin ducks!
Repeat
My beauty and I, a "man-of-talent," in our pleasure boat,
Mellow and merry with wine, laugh and drink more dramatine nectar,
Then row back late,
As the lake's gleam dances
Under the crescent of a new moon,
The scent of lotuses spreading for ten miles around.

Commentary: Dramatine nectar (*ch'iung-chiang*) is a cliché for an excellent wine of "transcendent" qualities.

Lyric 8 Cheng-kung, Hsiao liang-chou, "Autumn" (*CYSC*, p. 359)

Hibiscus blossoms mirrored in water and chrysanthemums
    glowing yellowly
Provide autumn splendor as far as eye can see,
As beneath withered lotus leaves egrets hide,
And the metal wind in fitful drifts
Makes the scent of cassia dance on air.
Repeat
Up Thunder Peak Pagoda path I climb high for the view
And look upon the Ch'ien-t'ang stretching out like the
    Yangtze.
The lake's waters grow still,
While the tide in the river surges;
At sky's edge there sets the moon,
Framed by two or three echelons of new wild geese.

Commentary: In traditional Chinese cosmology, metal is the element associated with autumn. Thunder Peak Pagoda (Lei-feng t'a) was atop Thunder Peak, south of Hang-chow between the West Lake and the Ch'ien-t'ang River; it commanded excellent views of both. The surge of the tide refers to the spectacular tidal bore in the Ch'ien-t'ang River.

Lyric 9 Cheng-kung, Hsiao liang-chou, "Winter" (*CYSC*, p. 360)

Vermilion clouds densely spread, envelop lofty peaks
And turn the chilly wind bitingly cold,

As the chips and flakes of the Milky Way sprinkle a vast sky.
The tips of plum trees freeze,
And snow packs the roads so it's hard to get through.
Repeat
Instantly the Six Bridges turn into silvery grottoes,
And the Nine Mile icy pines become powder and paint.
When the wine's all gone,
They see us off with reed-organ and song.
With our jade boat and silver oars
We're in a crystal palace!

Commentary: There were six bridges across various parts of the West Lake, and "Nine Mile Pines" (Chiu-li sung) was the name for a stretch of pines planted at one side of the West Lake.

Lyric 10 Cheng-kung, Hsiao liang-chou, no title (CYSC, p. 360)

Waiting for dusk to fall, I prayed to Heaven for help
And burned incense.
Since he left, my tears have flowed and flowed.
The passes and mountains keep him far away,
While I, abandoned, lie on a single pillow and sleep all alone!
Repeat
I beseech Azure Heaven to let us soon meet again,
But who knows what day, even what year that will be!
How I wish Heaven would have pity on me
And let me have my way.
If all the lovers in the world were united,
Wouldn't we be swept along and be united too!

Lyric 11 Cheng-kung, Tsui t'ai-p'ing
(Great Peace of Drunkeness), no title (*CYSC*, p. 360)

Out on the main street I beg,
And I keep myself alive in a dilapidated kiln.
After enduring it one spring after another,
How can I hope to find a wife,
To have Red Phoenix shine on my Lonely Star luck!
But even poor men like me ought to have marriage in their
fates,
So if I'm there where the embroidered ball falls I'll get a
spouse.
Because of all this, bearing my pain, I rap on the door.

Commentary: The mention of "dilapidated kiln" and the "embroidered ball" indicates that this lyric is concerned with the story of Lü Meng-cheng (946–1011) and his wife, Yüeh-o (Moon Goddess), as it occurs, for instance, in Wang Shih-fu's drama "Lü Meng-cheng Endures Wind and Snow in a Dilapidated Kiln" (*YCHWP*, No. 118). In Wang's play, Lü is a young and penniless student who lives in an abandoned kiln. One day he goes to the home of a rich man, Liu Chung-shih, where Liu's daughter is going to throw an embroidered ball to a group of suitors as a means to select a husband. Lü is present merely to write a congratulatory poem for the lucky man, but to everyone's surprise Yüeh-o throws the ball to him. She marries Lü, to her father's great displeasure, and lives with him in the kiln. Lü goes to the capital to seek an official career, and when years later he returns as a magistrate, he finds his wife living in the kiln and still loyal to him. "Red Phoenix" (Hung-luan) is the lucky star of love, and "Lonely Star" (Ku-ch'en) is the star of bad luck.

Lyric 12 Nan-lü, Chin-tzu ching (Scripture in Golden Letters), "Wounded by Spring" (*CYSC*, p. 361)

> With dawn, spring filled all things.
> Look—there in the west garden—the first bough in bloom!
> As incense warms red curtains and wine fills my cup,
> I think—
> Don't sing a song of heartbreak,
> Some sad story of love,
> Late at night when people are quiet!

Commentary: Lyrics 13–17 all seem to be written in the voices of lonely or abandoned ladies who lament their fates in their boudoirs.

Lyric 13 Nan-lü, Chin-tzu ching, "Spring Boudoir" (*CYSC*, p. 361)

> Glittering buds perfume the morning sun
> As a sparkling breeze floats across the little stream.
> As incense warms the golden censer and wine fills my cup,
> I marvel—
> Last night, after fragrance stole inside my bedcurtains
> And when I first fell asleep,
> I awoke from a dream of love with my man from the Jade Hall!

Commentary: "Love with my man from the Jade Hall" translates *yü-t'ang ch'un*. I take *yü-t'ang* to be a contraction of *yü-t'ang jen-wu* (A person from the Jade Hall), i.e., a high ranking official. *Ch'un* (spring) here means "love" or "love affair."

Lyric 14 Nan-lü, *Chin-tzu ching*, "Boudoir Emotions" (*CYSC*, p. 361)

Girls with moth eyebrows should be able to look after themselves,
But when he left, my tears fell like water poured.
"Don't sing the fourth line of 'Song of Kuan Pass'!"
Love
Wakens me from sad slumbers in the depths of night,
Where I'm so lonely and alone
With only the pallid moon at second watch.

Commentary: The third line seems to be a flashback to what she said when her man was about to leave her. The "Song of Kuan Pass" (*Yang-kuan ch'ü*) by Wang Wei (699–761) is probably the most famous song of parting in the entire Chinese tradition. Since it is a quatrain, to sing the fourth line would be to finish it; the parting would then take place. The girl, a professional singing girl with elaborately made up eyebrows like moth's wings, ought to be able to keep her emotions under control (*neng tzu-ch'ing*), but she cannot. The second watch was from nine to eleven P.M.

Lyric 15 Nan-lü, *Chin-tzu ching*, no title (*CYSC*, p. 361)

Tears spatter my gilded sleeves,
But they don't know on whose account I feel this way.
Though fragrant shrubs flourish everywhere, he hasn't returned.
I've waited
All spring long, and fish and geese were scarce.
I'm so upset
That grief weighs down my arched eyebrows.

Commentary: "Fish and Geese" is a cliché for letters. The ancient ballad (*yüeh-fu*), sometimes attributed to Ts'ai Yung (132–192), "Watering My Horse at a Spring at the Great Wall" narrates how someone receives a letter concealed inside a carp.[6] Su Wu (c. 143 – 60 B.C.), while a prisoner of the Hsiung-nu in the far north, caught a goose and tied a letter to its leg. When the goose migrated south to China, it was shot down, and the letter was discovered and delivered to the emperor, who then realized that Su was still alive. After the Hsiung-nu heard of this, they released Su.[7] "Arched eyebrows" translates *pa-tzu mei*, literally, "character eight eyebrows"; *pa* has a shape like a peaked arch.

Lyric 16 Nan-lü, Chin-tzu ching, no title (CYSC, p. 362)

> As notes of my purple flute begin to fade,
> Incense from the jade censer starts to thicken,
> And cool moonlight courses through the little garden.
> Since
> He left, quilt and pillow have been so lonely,
> Where I roam in ethereal dreams,
> My window screen covered with a snow of plum
>   blossoms brought by the wind.

Lyric 17 Nan-lü, Chin-tzu ching, no title (CYSC, p. 362)

> Though a light chill has settled on the kingfisher-green quilt,
> The easterly breeze warms my jade-fair fingers.
> As incense dies in the gold lion censer and moon turns around
>   on the curtains,
> I add
> To my moth eyebrows a new pale edge.
> The incense now goes completely out,
> But, leaning against the window, I find sadness far from finished!

Lyric 18 Nan-lü, chin-tzu ching, no title (CYSC, p. 362)

> At these Terraces of Ch'u clouds keep returning,
> All told, for two mornings then three.
> Here, amidst easterly breezes as languid as can be, is
>   her bright green flute,
> Flute,
> And with jeweled hairpins and golden hair ornaments,
> Her thrilling looks
> Make me burn with desire!

Commentary: In Sung Yü's (third century B.C.) preface to his *Kaot'ang fu* he relates how Wu-shan Nü (Lady of Shaman Mountain) visited a former king in a dream while he dozed below Kao-t'ang (a mountain in Ch'u). She shared his bed and upon leaving said: "When I reside on the sunny slope of Shaman Mountain, in the inaccessible reaches of the lofty peak, at dawn I am morning clouds, at evening moving rain, dawn after dawn, evening after evening— below Yang-t'ai [Sunny Terraces]."[8] The expression "dawn clouds and evening rain," or simply "clouds and rain," has become a euphemism for sexual intercourse, as have the terms Wu-shan, Kao-t'ang, Yang-t'ai, Ch'u-t'ai, etc.[9]

Lyric 19 Chung-lü, Shang hsiao-lou (Ascending the Little Tower), "Presented to an Actress" (*CYSC*, p. 363)

> I think you're absolutely stunning
> And you'll be on my mind for 1,000 years!
> But if you don't take advantage of the green spring of youth
> And make a fine match,
> How much longer can you afford to wait!
> Wait for a fool,
> Find a fourth-rate fellow,
> But let this Imperial Academician's wishes be fulfilled!

Commentary: This lyric seems to be written in Kuan's own voice, but we have no idea who the actress may have been. It probably dates from 1313–1317, the years Kuan held the office of *Han-lin hsüeh-shih*, since he could not have called himself an Imperial Academician before the fact, and it is unlikely he used the title after his resignation, though this cannot be ruled out as a possibility.

Lyric 20 Chung-lü, Hung-hsiu hsieh (Red Broidered Slippers), "Drink All You Can" (*CYSC*, p. 363)

> At East Village drunk, then at West Village the same thing again—
> I might be sober today, but tomorrow I'll need a pick-me-up.
> Only stop drinking when the sea runs dry and the rocks turn soft!
> Bringing along my dragon-slayer sword
> And my giant turtle-catcher hook,
> I'll meet up with some old friends and turn both things into drinks!

Commentary: The "art of slaying dragons" (*t'u lung chih chi*) is a cliché meaning a great skill or talent which is of no use to the world.

It derives from the story of Chu P'ing-man in the *Chuang-tzu*, who studied dragon-slaying for three years, and when he had learned how, he discovered there was no way of putting his skill to use. In the *Lieh-tzu* there occurs the story of the giant from Lung-po who caught six *ao* (giant turtles) at one go; *tiao ao* (catch *ao*'s) became a cliché to mean the performance of some great and heroic act and to achieve great prominence. Here, of course, these two expressions are used with ironic humor: "I'm going to turn these great *literary* skills of mine into a few drinks for me and my friends by using them to write lyrics in some wineshop and trading them for wine."

Lyric 21 Chung-lü, Hung hsiu-hsieh, "Autumn Thoughts" (*CYSC*, p. 363)

> Thinking back to that old ten-year affair
> Moves me to sadness again and to longing for her all night long.
> I'm so often reminded,
> When all is quiet by my little window late at night,
> How still the water was when the West wind idled.
> Then my autumn feelings were not deep enough to carry a poem,
> But now I find my red leaves have all withered away!

Commentary: "Autumn thoughts" (*ch'iu-huai*) signifies the grief felt at the passing of nature from the vitality and glory of summer through the brief splendor of autumn to the death and decay of winter—the cycle of seasons ripe with implications for the ironic brevity of the human condition. Tu Fu's set of eight poems entitled *Ch'iu-hsing* is perhaps the most famous example of this motif in the Chinese tradition. Here Kuan seems to say that ten years ago in the happy comfort of the love he felt for some woman his feelings were too weak to write an autumn poem, unable to appreciate the grief implicit in the season, and now it is too late. Mention of red leaves is probably an allusion to the story of Madame Han and Yü Yu, who wrote love poems to each other on red leaves (see the commentary to Lyric IX). The sense here seems to be: "Now I have no way to tell her of my love."

Lyric 22 Chung-lü, Hung-hsiu hsieh, no title (*CYSC*, p. 363)

> On high, snowy fragrant orchids take over her cloud coiffure,
> Jade-white magic mugwort cupping raven locks from the sides,

As on disk-like dimpled cheeks tarry traces of powdery frost.
In earlobes fashioned from ice and snow
Are little pierced holes filled with jade cream.
It's just those damned earrings that have damaged them so!

Commentary: Magic mugwort (*ling-chih*) is a marvelous plant which is supposed to confer immortality; here it is a conceit for the white orchids in the first line. In the last line, "damned" translates *yeh*, a Buddhist term for *karma*, the burden of sin; used adjectivelly, it would literally mean "sin-burdened."

Lyric 23 Chung-lü, Hung hsiu-hsieh, no title (*CYSC*, p. 363)

Cuddling, snuggling, we sit together at the cloudy window;
Embracing, hugging, we sing together on the moonlit pillow.
Listening, counting, saddening, fearing, already the fourth
watch is gone!
The fourth watch may be gone, but passion is far from
satisfied,
And passion unsatisfied, the night has passed as quickly as a
weaver's shuttle!
Oh Heaven!
Sneak in an extra watch—what harm would it do!

Commentary: The fourth watch lasts from one to three A.M.

Lyric 24 Chung-lü, Yang-ch'un ch'ü (Song of Sunny Springtime),
"Golden Lotuses" (*CYSC*, p. 364)

Her golden lotuses already a bit big,
She takes care to make them pretty, the more to show them off.
Now that we've met, I see she's not had much experience.
"Don't show them so!
The more kept hidden, the more love grows!"

Commentary: "Golden lotuses" is an expression for bound feet—the object of extreme (often fetishlike) interest. "A bit big" translates *hsieh-niang-ta*.[10] "She's not had much experience" translates *yen-p'i po*, which literally means "eyelids are thin"—an expression to describe the naive and ignorant.

Lyric 25 Chung-lü, Tsui kao ko kuo Hung-hsiu hsieh ("Rapt with
Wine Loftily Singing" followed by "Red Broidered Slippers"), no
title (*CYSC*, p. 364)

> When I see others saddled on horseback with their foreign
>   faces,
> I sigh to myself: Since this dirty world fouls all eyes,
> How would you "heroes" know a man of true worth?
> I could never lay my plaint before the likes of you!
> When the Yang Ether waxes, ice melts on the northern
>   shore,
> And when evening clouds gather, the sun sets on the western
>   mountains.
> Weather of the four seasons just goes around and around.
> Kan Lo of Ch'in came early into a rich salary,
> But Chiang Lü ascended the platform late,
> So, early or late, we're all pressed forward in the hands of
>   fate!

Commentary: Yang Ether (*yang-ch'i*) manifests the warmth of the
sun, etc. It is the life-sustaining force. This is an allusion to the
Classic of Changes, Ch'ien: "The concealed dragon refrains from
action; the Yang Ether remains submerged." The concealed dragon
is, of course, the man of worth who conceals himself when just
government is absent from the world.[11] Kan Lo was employed in
high office at the age of twelve by Lü Pu-wei (d. 235 B.C.), the
Prime Minister of Ch'in Shih-huang, and was rewarded very
highly.[12] Chiang Lü Wang (i.e., Lü Shang) worked for many years
in utter obscurity before King Wen of the Chou (father of King Wu
who overthrew the Shang in 1122 B.C.) discovered him and made
him his minister—this when Lü was already an old man.[13] "Ascend
the platform" (*teng t'an*) means to be appointed to high office. This
lyric may date from the period 1308–1313, the years in Peking
before Kuan received his appointment to the Imperial Academy.

Lyric 26 Chung-lü, Tsui kao ko kuo Hsi-ch'un lai ("Rapt with Wine
Loftily Singing" followed by "Arrival of Delightful Spring"), "On
Love" (*CYSC*, p. 365)

> Natural demeanor soft and tender,
> Winsome face demure,

When she looks at me, her sidelong glances glide to me
And kindle the pangs of my lovesickness.
Matchmaker bees and go-between butterflies fail to coax
    her,
Since swallows and orioles can't do as they please.
Just like a sprig of red almond blossoms peeping over a wall
She lies beyond the reach of plucking hand.
In vain I make myself believe
The wind and rain will be shy with these blossoms too!

Commentary: The bees and the butterflies suggest both the per-
sistence and profusion of the efforts made to win this girl away from
her present alliance (the mention of swallows and orioles in the sixth
line suggests that she is already "mated").[14] An allusion is probably
involved here to that peerless beauty and famous singing girl of the
T'ang, Ch'u Lien-hsiang, who was always pursued by bees and
butterflies whenever she went out because they were after her
scent.[15] The last four lines are derived from two *tz'u*—one by Chang
Pi (fl.c. 940) and one by Hsin Ch'i-chi.[16] Just as the actual blossoms
inevitably will be "plucked" by the wind and rain, so does the poet
realize that the girl will be had by someone else—perhaps someone
cruel. The fact that the last four lines are constructed out of earlier
lyrics suggests that this may be a composition that should be read
dramatically rather than as a statement of Kuan's own feelings and
experience. It is not impossible, of course, that Kuan could be
speaking in his own voice here.

Lyric 27 Yüeh-tiao, P'ing lan jen (Someone Leaning on the Railing),
            "On Love" (*CYSC*, p. 365)

Flower debts drag out my wine-sickness demon,
And who's that singing a heartbreak song of love?
I couldn't even bear my old troubles,
Now here's plenty of new ones!

Commentary: "Flower debts" (*hua-chai*) were debts incurred in the
pleasure quarters, and "wine-sickness demon" (*chiu-ping kuei*) is
an expression meaning to be always sick from overindulgence in
drink. The voice of the lyric seems to be that of a man, but since
Kuan was unquestionably wealthy, he would not have had any "flower debts"; thus, this expression should be read as dramatic invention.

Lyric 28 Yüeh-tiao, P'ing lan jen, no title (*CYSC*, p. 365)

> Yesterday we had joy, but today we've separation,
> And though my heart is full of grief, I've no place to make my plaint.
> I can only heave a long sigh,
> Since he who leaned on the railing is gone!

Commentary: Note the pun on the tune title: "Someone Leaning on the Railing."

Lyric 29 Yüeh-tiao, P'ing lan jen, no title (*CYSC*, p. 365)

> My song lies desolate in the shadow of the peach blossom fan,
> And my moth eyebrows are too ashamed to face mirror and
>   brush on emerald green—
> Because my dashing lover's passion has so cooled
> That I don't know what might happen next!

Commentary: The first line is derived from the fourth line of the following *tz'u* by Yen Chi-tao (c. 1041 – c. 1119):

> Gaily decorated sleeves intently hold the jade cup.
> In those days she loved to make her face flushed with wine,
> Dancing down the moon which shone into her room through
>   the willows,
> Singing away the breeze which lay in the shadow of her peach
>   blossom fan.
> Since they parted,
> She's remembered their meetings.
> "In how many dreams has my spirit been with you?
> Tonight I'll let the light from my silver lamp shine on and on,
> Still afraid our meetings will only be in dreams!"[17]

Lyric 30 Yüeh-tiao, P'ing lan jen, no title (*CYSC*, p. 365)

> New stains of love tears cover up the old.
> Since there's no one to tell my love troubles
>   to,
> At dusk I firmly shut my door
> And, under the quilt, keep myself warm all
>   alone.

Lyric 31 Yüeh-tiao, P'ing lan jen, no title (*CYSC*, p. 366)

> Too lazy to face the floral mirror, I'm loath to pick it up;
> Too grieved to attend to morning toilette, I'm not at all happy.
> Jade-fair and slender, my tender bamboo shoots once so sharp
> Now are too worn out to put on make-up!

Commentary: "Bamboo shoots" is a cliché for a lady's beautiful fingers.

Lyric 32 Yüeh-tiao, P'ing lan jen, no title (*CYSC*, p. 366)

> Carefully picking up a red leaf to express what's in my heart,
> I write love-longing all over it—why have I never been happy?
> To tell of sorrow, the mottled bamboo brush is sharp,
> But all it does is make my longing worse!

Commentary: For "red leaf," see the commentaries to Lyrics 21 and IX.2.

Lyric 33 Yüeh-tiao, P'ing lan jen, no title (*CYSC*, p. 366)

> Our meeting in the dream doubled my love for him,
> But when ended, it left behind much grief in this scented boudoir.
> To dream of him makes me sorrow-laden,
> So it would be better not to dream of him at all!

Lyric 34 Shuang-tiao, Ch'an-kung ch'ü (Toad Palace [Moon] Melody), "Autumn Boudoir" (*CYSC*, p. 366)

> Amidst new fragrance borne by bamboo breezes and a passing rain,
> On an ornamented zither with red strings
> I pluck notes at random—
> It's a woodgather's pipes startling the autumn,
> A fisherman's song making the evening ring,
> Or sparse bamboos rattling under a pale moon.
> I had tonight's music all prepared,
> So how could the moving clouds not stay at Kao-t'ang?
> The autumn river is larger than eye's reach,
> A view more than mind can comprehend,
> And when my girdle pendants returned in vain,
> This set the scene for lonely desolation!

Commentary: For Kao-t'ang, see the commentary to Lyric 18. Since the "moving clouds" (a variation of "moving rain") do not stay at Kao-t'ang, the line means that the lovers' rendezvous did not occur. Line eleven is borrowed from a line in the third of five poems by Tu Fu on "Feelings Aroused by Ancient Sites" entitled "The Bright Consort's Village" (see the commentary to Poem 22): "On moonlit nights her ghost, with girdle pendants, returns in vain." As such, this means that the singing girl who is the protagonist of this lyric is lamenting the fact that she has been discarded by an ill-advised lover (as Chao-chün was discarded by an ill-advised emperor). However, an allusion to Li Ho's "The Grave of Su Hsiao-hsiao" is a possibility, part of which goes:

> Grass as if her cushions,
> Pines as if her roof,
> Wind is her skirt,
> Water her girdle pendants.
> In her carriage with oil-silk sides
> She waits at dusk,
> The cold emerald candle's light wearily shining,
> Underneath the west grave-mound the wind blowing rain.[18]

In addition, Ma Chih-yüan's drama *Han-kung ch'iu* (Autumn in the Palace of Han), which dealt with the story of Chao-chün, was probably a popular drama in Kuan's own day, and Kuan may even have had that in mind when he composed the ending to this lyric—especially the last act which treats Chao-chün's sad end. Nevertheless, the story of Su Hsiao-hsiao, the famous singing girl of the T'ang, was a popular theme at the time as well. For instance, it was celebrated (mourned might be more appropriate) in Pai P'u's drama *Su Hsiao-hsiao yüeh-yeh Ch'ien-t'ang meng* (A Dream of Ch'ien-t'ang, Su Hsiao-hsiao on a Moonlit Night).[19] Perhaps Kuan is alluding to both motifs here: the singing girl is so heartbroken that she casts herself in the roles of both Chao-chün and Su Hsiao-hsiao!

Lyric 35 Shuang-tiao, Ch'an-kung ch'ü, no title (CYSC, p. 366)

> As soon as we met I lost myself over you,
> And, with dreams kept at bay by moving clouds,
> I find you really something to boast of in poetry!
> Out on the river the others go home,

While here in my house your powder pales
Against the boundless brightness of the moon.
Since leaving the West Lake wine shop,
You met this Lin Pu and entrusted your immortal blossoms to him,
You with your stockings heavy with frost flowers,
Enhanced by the bloom of youth.
Middle of the night and in love,
Your fragrance seeps out through the window's gauze!

Commentary: The only way I have been able to make sense of this lyric is to take it as a song addressed to a singing girl who seems to be named Mei-hua (Plum Blossom) and who is from a West Lake wine shop. The setting is Kuan's own residence. After other guests and singing girls have started back, the girl remains behind. This lyric is given the title "Plum Blossoms on Paper Curtains" in the *Yüeh-fu ch'ün-chu* (Collected Pearls from the Lyric Mode), an anthology of *san-ch'ü* compiled during the Ming, but no title appears in the original source for the lyric, the *Yang-ch'un pai-hsüeh*.[20] It is probably a later addition made by the unknown editor who tried to read the lyric as if it were addressed to plum blossoms painted or printed on paper curtains. I think this very unlikely as it would require a really tortuous interpretation of many of the lines. For "moving clouds," see the commentary to Lyric 18. Lin Pu (967–1028) was a famous recluse who made his home near the West Lake; he devoted himself to wine, poetry, and the raising of cranes and plum trees. Here, however, a different kind of "plum blossom" is involved with this latter-day Lin Pu. Instead of real plum blossom fragrance seeping *in* from outside, the scent of the girl Mei-hua seeps *out*, thus rivaling her namesake in nature!

Lyric 36 Shuang-tiao, Ch'an-kung ch'ü, "Enjoying West Lake"
(*CYSC*, p. 366)

If you ask, who has a West Lake in his heart?
It must be this Tung-p'o with his poetry and wine,
This Lin Pu with his purity and simple joy.
As moonlight pillows traces of ice
And dew congeals into lotus tears,
In her cloudy skirt she wakes from dreams,
Redolent with cold cassia scent as ancient as the moon.
Here's a Ch'ang-o who has no use for makeup and
    comb.

Her spring scenery spreads in glorious splendor,
And her autumn colors lie in jumbled profusion.
If you'd have a match for Hsi Shih,
How would this Mistress West do?

Commentary: Both Tung-p'o (Su Shih) and Lin Pu were famous
literary figures associated with the West Lake. Kuan apparently
thought of himself as a composite incarnation of both of them.
Ch'ang-o is the Goddess of the Moon, a popular cliché for a beautiful
woman. For Hsi Shih, see the commentary to Lyric 6. The last two
lines pun on the names of Mistress West and the West Lake.

Lyric 37 Shuang-tiao, Ch'an-kung ch'ü, no title (CYSC, p. 367)

Gossamer-shod, we tread the waves and take an evening stroll
   on bright mists,
While T'ai-hua clouds are so high
That beyond this sky there can be no sky at all!
Her kingfisher feathers stir up a breeze
And cold pearls shed tears of dew.
She always knows how to make me linger!
A jade-fair lilly trembling gracefully in bright moonlight,
She wafts a delicate scent which scatters and fills our lake boat.
Her person seems to have become a fairy maiden,
A blossom well deserving of my love.
With wine she fills my golden goblet,
As I cover this phoenix-patterned paper with a song!

Commentary: "Gossamer-shod, we tread the waves" translates *ling
po*, which literally means "gauze [stockings walking] on waves,"
i.e., what fairy maidens and goddesses can do since their feet are
so small and light. Here, of course, Kuan and his companion *seem*
to be doing this as their light craft skims the surface of the lake
through low-lying mist on a moonlit night. T'ai-hua is a name for
Hua-shan in Shensi, far to the north where the skies are often very
clear but with extremely high cloud cover. In line 4 the girl is
depicted as sobbing so much that it sets her kingfisher hair ornaments shaking, and this stirs up a breeze! In the next line she is
likened to those marvelous creatures who live in the South Seas,
chiao-jen (shark people), mermaids and mermen, who shed pearls
of dew.[21]

Lyric 38 Shuang-tiao, Ch'an-kung ch'ü, "Seeing Off Spring" (CYSC, p. 367)

If you ask where has the Lord of the East gone, he's gone to the
ends of the earth!
Here are setting sun and singing cuckoos,
Flowing water and peach blossoms,
Dim, dim distant mountains,
Thick, thick rosy sunset clouds.
Chasing willow catkins, where has He been blown?
Riding floating spider silk, to whose house has He been enticed?
Too listless to tune her lute,
She leans against the swing,
As the moon makes the window gauze gleam.

Commentary: The Lord of the East *(Tung-chün)* is the God of
Spring. The setting of this lyric is ambiguous, but I would like to
set it either at Kuan's own residence above the Ch'ien-t'ang River
(note the "flowing water" of line 3) or at a wine shop or restaurant
somewhere on the river. Perhaps it was composed at the same time
as Chang K'o-chiu's lyric "At a Banquet Provided by Scholar Suan-
chai."[22]

Lyric 39 Shuang-tiao, Ch'an-kung ch'ü, "For Ts'ao Hsiu-lien"
(CYSC, p. 367)

A warm breeze wafts and wakes the
    embankments
As stretches of ripples gleam.
Shimmering faintly and adorned in red,
Winsome manner light and supple,
Fragrant scent imperceptibly spreading,
Jade-green parasol held high—
Just let all the sightseers get a good look at you
And have all the gulls and egrets hide!
But the way of the world is fickle,
And I can but fear that with autumn's chill
Your empty chamber may grow desolate!

Commentary: This lyric is addressed to a singing girl, but other
than her name, Ts'ao Hsiu-lien (Embroidered Lotus), we know
nothing about her, except, of course, that she was a real beauty.

The lyric itself is an extraordinarily clever pun. Every line could be translated as if it were describing a real lotus in nature, the girl's namesake. Lines 7 and 8 tell us that the girl is so beautiful that she puts all others to such shame that they hide away. As addressed to the actual lotus, the sightseers would put the birds to flight as they attempted to view the lotuses. Now in her youth, this lotus attracts the attention of all, but with autumn (aging), this will end.

Lyric 40 Shuang-tiao, Ch'ing-chiang yin (Clear River Song), no title
(*CYSC*, p. 368)

> I've gone and spurned petty fame—how happy I am!
> A laugh beyond white clouds
> And a few close friends—
> What's to keep us from drinking as much as we can?
> My drunken sleeves dance and won't abide the way
>   the universe hems them in!

Lyric 41 Shuang-tiao, Ch'ing-chiang yin, no title (*CYSC*, p. 368)

> Fighting for rank and fame is like being in a cart
>   rolling out of control downhill.
> It's such a frightening danger, but who sees through it!
> Yesterday a minister in the Jade Hall,
> Today you might be struck with disaster.
> Can you compare with me who shuns wind and waves
>   and hides in a safe, happy nest!

Lyric 42 Shuang-tiao, Ch'ing-chiang yin, no title (*CYSC*, p. 368)

> I shun wind and waves and hide in a safe, happy nest.
> Here my universe is really vast!
> After sobering up, I'm drunk, and then again I'm sober.
> After lying down, well, I lie down again.
> Who has anything like this perfect leisure of mine!

Lyric 43 Shuang-tiao, Ch'ing-chiang yin, "Song for Plum Blossoms"
(*CYSC*, p. 368)

> Last night southern branches were first to burst their buds,
> Leaking the news of spring.

You're particularly becoming in the mingled lights of snow and moon,
And, although you don't provoke bees and butterflies to play,
At times your delicate fragrance finds its way into my dreams.

Lyric 44 Shuang-tiao, Ch'ing-chiang yin, "Song for Plum Blossoms" (*CYSC*, p. 369)

Ice-beauty, endowed by Heaven with such marvelous qualities,
You alone hold sway over this warm and balmy land.
Before beginning to bear fruit,
You first brew and blend the flavors of your mix.
Oh, please don't let her—in her painted pavilion—just play
    the flute thrice!

Commentary: The last line fuses two allusions. In Wang Wei's "Passing by the Mountain Tarn of Imperial Son-in-Law Ts'ui" there is the couplet: "In the painted pavilion there's a singing girl playing a flute,/While a tavern barmaid holds a golden goblet."[23] The second involves Wang Hui-chih (d. 388): "Wang Hui-chih was attending to a summons at the capital and moored his boat at Ch'ing-hsi. Huan I, who hitherto was unacquainted with Hui-chih, was passing nearby on the bank. . . .Hui-chih sent someone to say to [Huan] I, 'I've heard that you excel at playing the flute, so how about playing a tune for me.' At the time [Huan] I was an eminent official, but since he had heard of Hui-chih's reputation, he got down from his carriage, took a seat and played three tunes for him, and when he had finished, he got back into his carriage and left. Neither of the two had uttered a single word."[24] Therefore, Kuan seems to end this lyric by entreating the plum blossoms to help him get acquainted with a wine shop entertainer and not let the encounter pass briefly and in vain.

Lyric 45 Shuang-tiao, Ch'ing-chiang yin, "Song for Plum Blossoms" (*CYSC*, p. 369)

Your fragrant heart faces me, as if to speak in some charming way,
So I couldn't bear to pluck you, even with the utmost gentleness.
There, the stream's bridge with its pale and delicate mists,
Here, the thatched cottage with a clear, bright moon,
How many spring thoughts do these things harbor!

Commentary: "Fragrant heart" (*fang-hsin*) is here a *double-entendre* for the heart of the plum blossom as well as being a cliché for the feelings of a young woman in love, and "spring thoughts" (*ch'un-i*), as well as simply meaning thoughts about spring, is also a cliché meaning desire, longing, and thoughts of love.

Lyric 46 Shuang-tiao, Ch'ing-chiang yin, "Song for Plum Blossoms" (*CYSC*, p. 369)

> From your jade-fair complexion, clear and white, scent emanates,
> And there's no need to speak of the crystalline quality of your spirit!
> As a breeze drifts into my little garden,
> With moon in halo and everyone quiet,
> How attractive are your sharp and slender shadows there across the window!

Lyric 47 Shuang-tiao, Ch'ing-chiang yin, "Loath to Part" (*CYSC*, p. 369)

> A jade-fair beauty's sounds of tear-filled parting gradually die away,
> And she stands speechless and wounded to her innermost thoughts.
> "Here in my now desolate Wu-ling,
> Both the delicate rains and the fragrant shrubs
> Have been carried off by him—he's taken spring away!"

Commentary: Wu-ling is an allusion to T'ao Ch'ien's (365–427) famous tale, *T'ao-hua yüan*, in which a fisherman follows a stream in Wu-ling (Hunan) to its source and there discovers a happy and secluded place where people have been living in peace and comfort, cut off and forgotten for hundreds of years. In this lyric the girl depicted finds her peaceful refuge, once their paradise, desolate after her man has gone. Since the first two lines seem to be cast in the form of a third-person narrative, I have refrained from translating them in the first person. The same thing occurs in Lyric 53, which has a similar first line.

Lyric 48 Shuang-tiao, Ch'ing-chiang yin, "Contentment" (*CYSC*, p. 369)

> A decorated hall is not as good as a safe and happy nest
> Which allows all of us to sit as we like.

At leisure, we recline and lift our heads to sing,
Getting drunk, we curl up and lie down.
Who cares if those slaves of advantage and fame laugh at us!

Lyric 49 Shuang-tiao, Ch'ing-chiang yin, "Contentment" (CYSC,
p. 369)

But just bring on the thing-in-the-cup!
Don't bother to talk about Li Po's immortality,
Nor mention Liu Ling's tomb.
No one wastes wine on the earth above his grave!

Commentary: The "thing-in-the-cup" (*pei-chung wu*) is, of course,
wine. Besides being the "Immortal of Poetry," Li Po is also the
"Immortal of the Wine Cup." Liu Ling (c. 221 – c. 300) was so fond
of wine that he had a quantity of it buried with him, though now
no one tends his grave and pours wine on it as a libation. Kuan may
have had a couplet from Li Ho's "Bring on the Wine" in mind here:
"I beg you to stay drunk for the rest of your days,/Since no one
wastes wine on the earth above Liu Ling's grave."[25]

Lyric 50 Shuang-tiao, Ch'ing-chiang yin, "Contentment" (CYSC,
p. 369)

Burning incense, swept floor and a door half shut
With a few books for idle pleasure—
I've seen through the illusory self
And eliminated all desire for rank and fame.
You'll never see me again sport with danger atop a high bamboo pole!

Commentary: To "sport with danger atop a high bamboo pole" is
still a feature of Chinese acrobatic entertainment. Here the expression is used to symbolize the foolhardy risks of official service.

Lyric 51 Shuang-tiao, Ch'ing-chiang yin, "Contentment" (CYSC,
p. 369)

Friends come by to keep me company,
In my thatched cottage there are a thousand books,
And, beneath the moon, a zither to play an occasional tune.
I've ended up with just these things to while away the time!

Commentary: Kuan may have had a couplet in T'ao Ch'ien's "A Reply to Secretary Kuo" in mind here: "I have renounced the world to have my leisure/And occupy myself with lute and books."[26]

Lyric 52 Shuang-tiao, Ch'ing-chiang yin, "Loath to Part" (*CYSC,* p. 370)

> Framed by the window, this moon-goddess is stunningly beautiful,
> And it's been a fine night well worth a thousand pieces of gold!
> Now it's a handful of tender love
> For a few things said about the approaching dawn,
> All while this young scholar finds it difficult to stay his horse!

Commentary: I-chü (handful) more literally is "scoopful," i.e., what the two hands cupped together can hold. The cliché *i-chü lei* (a scoopful of tears) often occurs in poems and lyrics about parting. Lines 3 and 4 are *i-chü k'o-lien ch'ing/chi-chü lin-ming hua;* I take this to be an exchange between the girl's parting tears and the "young scholar's" words to the effect that "it's almost dawn, and I've got to go." The horse, of course, has been tethered outside all night long and is impatient to go home. There is no way of knowing if this lyric has some autobiographical import.

Lyric 53 Shuang-tiao, Ch'ing-chiang yin, "Loath to Part" (*CYSC,* p. 370)

> A jade-fair beauty's sounds of tear-filled parting gradually die away,
> Standing there so long her stockings grown cold.
> "Since there's no place now to entrust my love-filled heart,
> I'll turn my back on the swing—
> Oh, how I've been seduced by the pear blossoms and the moon!"

Commentary: Lines 3 and 4 are modeled on lines in a *tz'u* by Yen Chi-tao: "There's no place she can talk about her love,/So she turns her face away from the swing."[27] Yen in turn has borrowed the second of these two lines from a poem by Li Shang-yin. Professor James J. Y. Liu thinks that the girl turns away from the swing to signify that she has no further use for it, "a symbol of youthful gaiety."[28]

Lyric 54 Shuang-tiao, Ch'ing-chiang yin, "Loath to Part" (*CYSC,*
p. 370)

> With clouds over the Hsiang and rain in Ch'u, the way
>   back will be dark and lonely.
> This always breaks my heart.
> Amidst river sounds stirred up by evening waves
> And tree reflections held over by the afterglow of sunset,
> His orchid boat takes my sorrow and loads it all on board!

Commentary: "Orchid boat" (*lan-chou*) is a fanciful term for any
craft.

Lyric 55 Shuang-tiao, Ch'ing-chiang yin, no title (*CYSC,* p. 370)

> If you ever come across him,
> Pass on this true message—
> It's not that I won't write a letter,
> Nor is it that I'm at a loss for anything to say,
> It's just that I've gone all over Ch'ing-chiang,
>   but couldn't buy a piece of paper the size
>   of the sky!

Commentary: Ch'ing-chiang (p'u) in Kiangsu, near modern Chen-
chiang, was a bustling commercial town then, situated as it was
where the Grand Canal crosses the Yangtze. The voice of this lyric
is ambiguous; it could just as well have been translated in the voice
of a man—as his message for "the girl he left behind."

Lyric 56 Shuang-tiao, Ch'ing-chiang yin, no title (*CYSC,* p. 370)

> At leisure, we sing the "Clear River Song,"
> Freeing ourselves from melancholy.
> Since wealth and honor are decided in Heaven
> And life and death derive from fate,
> I'll let myself go and chat, laugh, drink with my friends!

Commentary: Lyrics 56–59 are "linked songs" (*lien-so t'i*), i.e., the
last line of one is repeated as the first line of the next.

Lyric 57 Shuang-tiao, Ch'ing-chiang yin, no title (*CYSC,* p. 371)

I'll let myself go and chat, laugh, drink with my friends!
Playing a tune on a gem-studded lute,
I can produce a great many sounds.
Keeping away from people clever in the ways of the world,
I lean against the screen and, in quietude, examine my own heart.

Lyric 58 Shuang-tiao, Ch'ing-chiang yin, no title (CYSC, p. 371)

I lean against the screen and, in quietude, examine my own heart.
The myriad affairs of existence are all fixed beforehand,
And failure and success each has its own time,
So, in meeting and in parting, be not an arrogant nor a
    parsimonious man.
If one stands in loyalty and in sincerity, step by step, the road
    ahead will be secure.

Commentary: Line 4 contains an allusion to a passage in the *Analects* of Confucius: "Though one has talents as admirable as the Duke of Chou, yet if he is arrogant and parsimonious these other things are not worth regarding."[29] *Chung* (loyalty) and *ch'eng* (sincerity) are the two cardinal virtues of Neo-Confucianism.

Lyric 59 Shuang-tiao, Ch'ing-chiang yin, no title (CYSC, p. 371)

If one stands in loyalty and in sincerity, step by step, the
    road ahead will be secure.
I encourage you to be diligent and prudent
And exhort you, moreover, to be patient.
Little by little, things will follow each other as they should,
And, in the end, good news will be the certain result!

Commentary: Lyrics 56–59 were obviously written while Kuan was still firmly committed to Confucianism, thus dating from before 1315–1316. If they are addressed to himself, they would be earlier, perhaps from the period 1308–1313, when he was in Peking but before his appointment to the Imperial Academy.

Lyric 60 Shuang-tiao, Ch'ing-chiang yin, "Beginning of Spring, in Which the First Character of Each Line Is One of the Five Elements, Metal, Wood, Water, Fire, Earth, and Each Line Contains the Character Ch'un (Spring)" (CYSC, p. 371)

Shadows cast by honeysuckles which tremble, spring swallows slanting
    away,
Branch tips of trees sprouting spring leaves,
Ponds that spring has begun to ripple,
The time for fires when spring first makes them hot—
The Earthen Ox has brought all these with him and Spring has arrived!

Commentary: Metal occurs in the word for "honeysuckle" (*chin-ch'ai*, metal/golden hairpin), so called because of its shape; wood occurs in the expression "branch tips of trees" (*mu-miao*); water occurs in the term for "ponds" (*shui-t'ang*); fire occurs in the expression "time of fires" (*huo-hou*), i.e., when the Kitchen God (*Tsao-chün*) returns at the New Year; earth occurs in the term "Earthen Ox" (*t'u-niu*). Earthen images in the shape of an ox were sacrificed to send off the cold ether (*ch'i*) of winter and to welcome spring at the "Beginning of Spring Festival" (*Li-ch'un*), a movable festival which occurs during the first lunar month of the year.

Lyric 61 Shuang-tiao, Shou-yang ch'ü (Song of Shou-yang), no title
    (*CYSC*, p. 371)

Carrying a spring picnic,
I ask her the way to a wine shop.
From the shade of a green willow, just like a picture unrolling,
She comes down off her swing, prettier than a flower,
Perspiration soaking her silk handkerchief through and
    through!

Commentary: "Carrying a spring picnic" translates *tan ch'un-sheng*, a variation of the expression *ch'un-sheng tan-tzu* (a shoulder-pole basket packed for a spring outing).[30] This lyric is also attributed to Chang K'o-chiu.[31]

Lyric 62 Shuang-tiao, Shou-yang ch'ü, no title (*CYSC*, p. 371)

Amidst the jade-greens of pine and fir
And the scent of white jasmines,
After a turn around the verandah, this old immortal leans on his
    staff.
Here in bright moonlight there's an evening breeze and the Precious
    Hall is cool,
As from the depths of the Jade Pool grow lotus blossoms 1,000 feet
    wide!

Commentary: "Old immortal" translates *lao-hsien*, a conventional term for an aged Taoist priest, though here Kuan is probably referring fancifully to himself. Precious Hall (*pao-tien*) is the main hall of a Taoist temple. The last line is an exaggeration of Han Yü's lines in a poem entitled "On Antiquity": "Lotuses in the Jade Well atop Mount T'ai,/When in bloom, are ten feet wide and big as boats."[32]

Lyric 63 Shuang-tiao, Shou-yang ch'ü, no title (*CYSC*, p. 372)

Fish blow the waves,
And wild geese settle on the sands,
As up against Mount Wu, an emerald screen hung up high,
I watch the tidal bore with its drummer's chorus of a billion drummers.
The jade-fair girl who rolled up the red blinds is pretty as a picture!

Commentary: The "fish" may be porpoises, which are known to inhabit the Ch'ien-t'ang estuary. Mount Wu (Wu-shan) is actually a mountain spur to the southwest of Hangchow which stretches from the West Lake to the Ch'ien-t'ang River. Kuan's summer residence nearby on Phoenix Mountain would have had a fine view of the river, in which the tidal bore is a spectacular sight, especially in autumn.

Lyric 65 Shuang-tiao, Shou-yang ch'ü, no title, (*CYSC*, p. 372)

The new autumn came
And he said good-bye.
Now, following the current of the Yangtze beneath the setting moon,
On and on his decorated boat sails east.
This will be my very first night of longing!

Lyric 66 Shuang-tiao, Shui hsien-tzu (Water Sprite), "A Home in the Country" (*CYSC*, p. 372)

My thatched cottage's two or three rooms lie in green shade.
There's a stream flowing behind the garden, a mountain beyond the gate,
And mountain peaches and wild apricots opening in infinite bloom.
Not to let spring's splendor pass before my eyes in vain,
I take half a day's perfect leisure from this fleeting life,

Invite the old man next door to join me
And have my servant boy bring over the cups.
Let me straightaway drink till the old pottery jug is dry!

Commentary: The fifth line is borrowed almost exactly from a quatrain by Li She (fl. c. 806) entitled "On the Crane Mountain
Temple": "Since I happened to pass by the bamboo garden and
meet monks talking,/I again took half a day's perfect leisure from
this fleeting life." Li's poem enjoyed considerable popularity in later
times. For example, this anecdote concerns it: "Once there were
several high ranking officials who met to spend their day off from
office. They went to the priest's quarters of a Buddhist temple to
relax and have a good time. After becoming mellow with wine, they
chanted a poem by someone in the past [the couplet from Li's
quatrain], and a priest overheard it and started laughing at them.
One of the officials asked, 'What are you laughing at, Master?' The
priest replied, 'You noble officials may have got half a day's leisure,
but this old priest will be busy for three days because of it—one
day preparing your lodgings, one day putting up with your happy
gathering, and one day cleaning up afterwards!' "[33] Kuan's allusion
to Li's poem here should be regarded as an attempt at humor, since
he has all the "perfect leisure" he could ever want now that he has
retired.

Lyric 67 Shuang-tiao, Shui hsien-tzu, "A Home in the Country"
(*CYSC*, p. 372)

Filling the forest, red leaves wildly flutter,
As colorful trees wither, completely drunk on autumn frost.
Deep green moss quietly rubbed away, I write a new poem
    there to see how it would look,
As wine brings a slight warmth to the stone tripod's chill.
My pottery jug is so deep it can wash away all sorrows and woes.
With clothes loosened up wide,
Things of no concern to me,
Let me straightaway drink till the old pottery jug is dry!

Lyric 68 Shuang-tiao, Shui hsien-tzu, "A Home in the Country"
(*CYSC*, p. 372)

This old rustic has no dreams of going to Ch'ang-an,
Since, with maidservant weaving and manservant plowing, I can be as
    idle as I like.

Silkworms are gathered and grain ripened, autumn's work done,
So we can avoid hunger and won't suffer from the cold.
Delighted at this bountiful year, I drink to heart's content, start to laugh
And shout to the boy, "Strain out the new brew!"
Then lean against my latticed window, face the guests and strum
"Let me straightaway drink till the old pottery jug is dry!"

Commentary: Ch'ang-an, the T'ang Dynasty capital, was used as a cliché for the national capital in post-T'ang times, wherever it was located.

Lyric 69 Shuang-tiao, Shui hsien-tzu, "A Home in the Country" (*CYSC*, p. 373)

My plain cotton robe and straw sandals bear the wind and cold,
While my thatched cottage, with its rustic study, has just two or
    three rooms.
Honor and wealth are but shadowy illusions,
And I look upon rank and fame as utterly commonplace things!
Let me wander as I might amidst the green waters and the blue hills,
Seek out a few close friends,
Strain out some village brew, drink several bowls and
Let me straightaway drink till the old pottery jug is dry!

Lyric 70 Shuang-tiao, Tien-ch'ien huan (Joy before the Palace), no title (*CYSC*, p. 373)

Oh, how wonderfully secluded!
In the spring breeze there are storied buildings everywhere!
For a time, my heart felt utter hopelessness,
Yet I opened myself completely to Heaven
And went back with Yüan-ming.
Perhaps cranes might resent me and mountain birds find me at fault,
But if they ask, "What fame have you?"
Suan-chai I am,
I am Suan-chai!

Commentary: Yüan-ming is the poet T'ao Ch'ien, the archetypal recluse in the Chinese tradition. Chang K'o-chiu composed two lyrics, apparently at the same time as this one by Kuan, which echoes its rhyme scheme:

At the fishing pier
We haven't roused the doubts of gulls for ten years.
White clouds come and go but green hills remain.
Before cups of wine we open up our feelings—
Though lacking the talent to save the world like I Yin and
    the Duke of Chou,
You violate the same rules against greed for wine as Liu Ling
    and Juan Chi
And you'll owe the same debts to poetry as Li Po and Tu Fu!
Suan-chai laughs at me,
I laugh at Suan-chai!

Shouting, "Come back,"
Wild apes on the West Lake mountains are sad,
For who knows, in the last twenty years, how many
    charming, dashing demons there have been!
Flowers fall and flowers bloom.
You look to a platform in the sky where they invest generals
And keep in your sleeve a plan, observed in the stars, to
    bring the country peace.
Then too, you have broken the snare of romantic infatuation!
Suan-chai laughs at me,
I laugh at Suan-chai![34]

Lyric 71 Shuang-tiao, Tien-ch'ien huan, no title (CYSC, p. 373)

The loyal minister of
King Huai of Ch'u drowned himself in the Mi-lo River.
When I finished reading "On Encountering Sorrow," I
    was filled with empty hopelessness,
Though he still shines together with the sun and moon.
You broken-hearted fellow, come on and laugh a while,
Laugh at yourself, you would-be Ch'ü Yüan!
Why don't you just let yourself go?
If the Ts'ang-lang waters soil you,
You go and soil the Ts'ang-lang waters!

Commentary: Ch'ü Yüan (fourth century B.C.), the author of "Li-sao" (On Encountering Sorrow), was the loyal minister of King Huai of Ch'u and an archetype of the upright official estranged from his sovereign by the slander of petty sychophants. "You would be Ch'ü Yüan" translates *ni ko san-lü ch'iang*, which literally means "you a *san-lü*." Ch'ü Yüan held the office of *san-lü tai-fu* (Grandee En-

trusted with the Affairs of the Three Branches of the Royal Family).[35]
In the "Yü-fü" (The Fisherman), another piece in the *Ch'u-tz'u*,
Ch'ü Yüan meets a fisherman who tells him to go along with the
ways of the world, to seek employment in good times and retire in
bad, quoting from the *Mencius*, "When the Ts'ang-lang's waters are
clear, I can wash my hatstrings in them;/When the Ts'ang-lang's
waters are muddy, I can wash my feet in them."[36]

Lyric 72 Shuang-tiao, Tien-ch'ien huan, no title (CYSC, p. 373)

I've come to realize and can say that
The fight for fame and the search for wealth are not really worth it!
When the west wind blows, it stirs my love for mountain forests,
So I shall spend what remains of my life this way—
Build a humble cottage by the side of white clouds,
Then keep a path for seeking fragrant blossoms,
And there while away the days and months, preserving my natural
     disposition.
Rank and fame have played tricks with me,
Now I'll play tricks with rank and fame!

Commentary: If we take the argument of this lyric literally, it would
appear to have been composed at the time Kuan decided to resign
his position in the Imperial Academy in 1317.

Lyric 73 Shuang-tiao, Tien-ch'ien huan, no title (CYSC, p. 373)

I fear that the west wind,
When evening fell, transported me up to the Great Cold
     Palace.
At this Jade Terrace it won't do to dally in dreams of some
     mortal boudoir.
Just when passion is getting intense,
I let my heart become one with fate,
And why should I bother to listen to any "Rainbow Skirt Song"!
"After another drink, have a yellow crane take me back!"
I've let an old mountain hermit get me drunk,
Now I'll get an old mountain hermit drunk!

Commentary: The Great Cold Palace (*Kuang han-kung*) is on the
moon, and the Jade Terrace (*Yü-t'ai*), in Heaven, is the dwelling

place of the immortals, hence it would not do to have a dream of mere earthly feminine beauty where the heavenly maidens are so much better! "Some mortal boudoir" translates *hsiang-lien*, which literally means "scent casket" (i.e., cosmetics box), a conventional synecdoche for a lady's boudoir. "Rainbow Skirt Song" is an abbreviation of *ni-shang yü-i ch'ü* (Rainbow Skirt and Feather Garment Song), a song supposedly heard by Emperor Ming of the T'ang (reigned 713–756) while journeying in dream to Heaven. This line means that Kuan did not let himself be distracted by the music, no matter now "heavenly" it was. The elaborate circumlocution here is worthy of Kuan's *shih* poetry. The lyric seems to be an account of an experience at an evening's entertainment, replete with singing girls and musicians in some high mountain retreat (high as the moon!) which belongs to a friend, the "old mountain hermit," whom I suspect to be Chang K'o-chiu, since this lyric seems to fit with Lyric 70 and the two lyrics by Chang which are translated in the commentary to it.

Lyric 74 Shuang-tiao, Tien-ch'ien huan, no title (CYSC, p. 374)

I'm afraid that when we met,
Afraid that when we met, once the songs were finished and the wine
    cups emptied
I came back drunk, and though it was a Sunny Terrace dream,
There's been no trace of clouds and rain.
Here in the moonlight of my room and in the breeze beneath my fan
My love for him weighs so heavily.
Oh, why couldn't it be as light as my hairpin phoenix!
In the dawning sunlight, I'm so frightfully thin
That I'm too embarrassed to face my mirror.

Commentary: For "Sunny Terrace" and "clouds and rain," see the commentary to Lyric 18. Here a singing girl meets her love at a party at which she performs and waits on guests, but he apparently ignores her and she has to return home alone. Line 5 is derived from the same *tz'u* by Yen Chi-tao as was the first line of Lyric 29.

Lyric 75 Shuang-tiao, Tien-ch'ien huan, no title (CYSC, p. 374)

I'm afraid that when autumn came,
Afraid that when autumn came, my autumn mood provoked an autumn
    longing.

Sweeping the steps clear of fallen leaves to where the west wind can't
  reach them,
I stand alone on the green moss
And watch the yellow flowers randomly blossom as they will.
Where is he?
He can never repay his debt of love to me.
Our morning clouds and evening rain
Have all turned into a Sunny Terrace merely of my dreams!

Commentary: For explanations of "Sunny Terrace" and "clouds and
rain," see the commentary to Lyric 18.

Lyric 76 Shuang-tiao, Tien-ch'ien huan, no title (CYSC, p. 374)

  Outside the curtain I hear
  The cry of a flower peddler brought intermittently by puffs of wind.
  Last night, after a gentle rain had washed the Steps to Heaven clean,
  In the little garden, a courtyard for idle pleasure,
  A light chill graced my kingfisher-green sleeves.
  Along paths tunneling through fragrant flowers
  We had twelve railings upon which to lean,
  There, amidst sparse shadows of apricot blossoms
  And the fresh gleam of the willows.

Commentary: "Cry of the flower peddler" (*mai hua sheng*) is also
the name of a tune in the *Shuang-tiao* mode; therefore, the first
two lines might also be translated as: "Outside the curtain I
hear/Someone singing 'Cry of the Flower Peddler' brought intermittently by puffs of wind." "Steps to Heaven" (*T'ien-chieh*) is a
constellation which forms part of Ursa Major; it is also called San-
t'ai hsing (The Three Terraces).

Lyric 77 Shuang-tiao, Tien-ch'ien huan, no title (CYSC, p. 374)

  Counting the days until he returns,
  My short comb is worn out by marking the green mossy wall,
  And the knife I keep in my skirt has cut the railing to pieces—
  All done because he went away!
  Above the west pavilion it's rare for geese to pass,
  So there's been no news.
  I've used up all my tears of longing to no avail.

From mountain ranges distant and waters far away
When will he return!

Commentary: For "geese," see the commentary to Lyric 15.

Lyric 78 Shuang-tiao, Tien-ch'ien huan, no title (CYSC, p. 375)

Nightfall starts the crows to caw
As willow branches blend with moonlight into verdant splendor.
The scent from my broidered slippers has stained the mossy path
On which I hesitate and scratch my head,
In failing lamplight my thin shadow lying there alone.
Blossoms fall and cause another year to flow away,
My spring gone, the season of my beauty squandered in vain.
This abandoned phoenix is vexed at something—
Passing geese have brought no letters!

Commentary: The fourth line is taken directly from the *Ching-nü* (Gentle Girl) poem in the *Classic of Poetry.*[37]

Lyric 79 Shuang-tiao, Tien-ch'ien huan, "Harmonizing on A-li hsi-ying's 'Lazy Cloud Refuge' " *(CYSC,* p. 375)

Here at Lazy Cloud Refuge
Who will help me take these Beauties of Shaman Mountain back
    to Sunny Terrace?
"The moonlight, why not just let it guide them!"
If he wants to remain a hermit, let him.
Covering the sky, constellations twinkle in multitudes
As I divide off a bit of mat to sit on.
"I've finished my 10,000 mile roc's journey and I'm broken,"
But he faces the misty rose-tinged clouds and laughs his scorn—
"Let the affairs of the world go to hell!"

Commentary: A-li hsi-ying left behind a set of three lyrics entitled "Lazy Cloud Refuge."[38] In the edition of Ch'iao Chi's lyrics published by Li O (1692–1752), the *Li O k'o Ch'iao Meng-fu hsiao-ling,* there is a colophon to Ch'iao's six lyrics on A-li hsi-ying's "Lazy Cloud Refuge" which states: "Hsi-ying excelled at playing the *pi-li* (tartar pipe). The Lazy Cloud Refuge in which he lived was in the northeast corner of Wu-ch'eng in Kiangsu overlooking the Yangtze,

a little more than half a *li* from the Shih-tzu lin (Lion's Grove) of
Ch'an Master T'ien-ju, Wei-tse. T'ien-ju once composed a 'Song for
the Pi-li' and presented it to him."[39] For "Sunny Terrace" and
"Shaman Mountain," see the commentary to Lyric 18. Here, after
spending the evening and most of the night, it is time for the girls
to go home. Kuan suggests that A-li hsi-ying and he accompany the
girls back, but A-li refuses and utters the third line of the lyric. The
fourth line is Kuan's comment on his host's behavior. "Roc's journey
of 10,000 miles" (*wan-li p'eng-ch'eng*) is a cliché for the years of
great promise in one's official career; it comes from the *Chuang-tzu*
(see the commentary to Poem 3). "Go to hell" translates *ts'o-t'o*,
which literally means "[let] slip and fall."

Lyric I Hsien-lü, "Boudoir Sorrows" (*CYSC*, pp. 375–76)

Lyric I.1 Tien-chiang-ch'un (Painting Red Lips)

> Flowers fall, dusk deepens
> And evening clouds all but gone,
> I intently watch for a blue phoenix letter,
> Incense smoldering in the jeweled animal censer.
> Again I've come to the sad hours in the day.

Lyric I.2 Hun chiang lung (River Churning Dragon)

> Love consoles my ennui.
> I lean sideways against the embroidered screen and just let it melt
>   my soul,
> My waist-sash as loose as can be
> And my spirit all wasted away.
> The kingfisher-green quilt, warmed no matter how much, stays cold,
> While my jade cup, can't be bothered to raise it, has been heated
>   countless times,
> And my phoenix hairpin, half askew, finds the cicada-wing hair buns
>   displeasing.

Lyric I.3 Chi-sheng ts'ao (Clinging Ivy)

> I've broken my jade hairpin
> And divided my precious mirror in half,
> Since this spring has again provoked last spring's chagrin.
> My teardrops are all shed but my grief knows no end,

This thin face no longer as pretty as it was then!
How many times have I thought of him and when will it ever cease?
Longing for him fills my heart and what year will it be over?

Lyric I.4 *Chin chan-erh* (Golden Cup)

When the wind forced itself inside my broidered silk quilt,
It scattered the clouds over our Ch'u Terrace,
Made the iron horses in the eaves tinkle
And shook, over idle steps, the emerald bamboos so that I couldn't bear
   to listen!
Now, filtering through the curtains, it makes shadows move
And incessantly brings me the water clock's sound.
Permeated by it, the flowers' breath freshens;
Played about by it, the moon's halo grows indistinct.

Lyric I.5 *Hou-t'ing hua* (Backyard Blossoms)

In the animal censer incense listlessly smolders
As atop the silver lampstand the light gradually goes out.
Inside silken bedcurtains I sleep in my clothes
While outside gauze curtains dawn colors grows distinct.
Thinking of my lover,
It's time to get up,
And I stamp my golden lotuses and rub my jade-fair bamboo shoots.

Lyric I.6 *Chuan sha* (Coda)

I've endured it till dawn.
But who ever came to see me!
Sleeping last night in my clothes, I've ruined the silk skirt with
   wrinkles,
My face all spoiled make-up and marks of tears shed in vain.
The sun is high but no one's in the garden,
And, closed in, door upon door,
Whom can I turn to with my frustration and chagrin?
So alone I face my caltrop mirror and tidy up the jumbled clouds of my
   coiffure,
But, just about to brush powder on this face grown thin,
And on the point of tending to comb and make-up, lovesickness arrives.
The breath of my sigh is so drawn out that it fogs up the mirror!

Commentary: "Blue phoenix letter" (*ch'ing-luan hsin*) is a cliché for
love letter. In Lyric I.3 there occurs an allusion to the story of Hsü

Ta-yen of the shortlived Ch'en Dynasty (557–589) and his wife, the
Princess of Lo-ch'ang and sister of the last ruler of the Ch'en, Hou-
chu (553–604). Hsü knew that when the tottering state of Ch'en
fell, his wife would be taken into some strongman's household;
therefore, he broke her mirror in half, and each of them took one
piece. He told his wife that if her love for him had not failed she
was to have her half sold in the marketplace on the fifteenth day
of the first month. Soon afterward Ch'en fell, and Hsü's wife was
taken into Yang Su's household. Later on, Hsü went to the marketplace at the appointed time and found an old man there with his
wife's half of the mirror for sale; he composed a poem on the spot:
"Mirror and wife both gone,/Now mirror's returned but she's not
here./There's no further trace of my Moon Goddess,/So the bright
moon's gleam lingers in vain." When Yang Su heard of this, he
summoned Hsü and restored his wife to him.[40] In Lyric I.4 the
character *feng* (wind) appears in every line, and in line 3 of this
lyric, "iron horses" (*t'ieh-ma*) are wind chimes. In Lyric I.5, for
"golden lotuses," see the commentary to Lyric 24, and "bamboo
shoots" is a well-worn conceit for a lady's fingers.

Lyric II Nan-lü, "Chagrin of Separation" (*CYSC*, pp. 376–78)

Lyric II.1 I-chih hua (A Twig of Blossoms)

I'm a willow drooping kingfisher-green strands,
A blossom dropping petals of rouge.
The velvet threads in my green window-silk are faint,
And the pearls of tears from my powdered face pelt it,
Forming spots like sprinkled bamboos.
The jeweled bracelets are loose on my icy wrists,
And my moth eyebrows are pale as distant mountains.
There's a saying, "A good match is full of obstacles,"
But who'd have thought so many thousands of troubles would crop up
    suddenly like this!

Lyric II.2 Liang-chou (Liang-chou)

I've cast my fortune so much with tortoise shell and coin, my jade-fair
    fingers are tainted with their smell,
And watching intently for goose-born letters, my gaze is cut off by
    cloudy mountains.

Who can ever get used to the pain of separation!
Recently, I'm too listless to strum my tiny silver zither,
Too languid to pluck my ornamented lute,
Too tired to finger the jade-green flute,
Too ashamed to peer into my bejeweled mirror.
Worn out by love-sickness, my face has grown frightfully thin,
And utterly sunk in depression, I've no idea how much sorrow there's
   been!
A floral ornament falls, but I can't be bothered to refix it to my scented
   cheek,
Blouse sleeves become so wet and weighed down they begin to drown
   in my tear-filled eyes,
Jade hairpin goes askew, but I'm too tired to put my cloudy coiffure
   back in order.
Recently,
When sitting,
I while away the time by composing a love letter,
But there's no fish or geese to deliver it for me!
I have 10,000 different kinds of loneliness and all are unbearable,
So what day will he return?

Lyric II.3 Ma yü-lang (Scolding the Fair Young Man)

Outside in the garden filled with willow catkins scattered by the east
   wind
A gentle rain just stopped as swallows and orioles begin to rest.
Alone inside my silken bedcurtains I keep heaving long sighs in vain.
As the spring scenery fades,
So his love waned,
And now my fragrant heart grows afraid.

Lyric II.4 Kan huang-en (Heartfelt Thanks for Imperial Favor)

Oh
Well, this love of mine has withered away,
This oriole's grown old, her blossom wilted.
Here's a curtain full of wind,
An April rain
And the chill of the fifth watch.
I'm just cast off, a lonely phoenix longing for her mate,
With extra room on my pillow and the quilt cold,
So out in the garden filled with pear blossoms
I'll sing the "Tea Picking Song"
And lean on the railing.

Lyric II.5 Ts'ai ch'a ko (Tea Picking Song)

> Looking off toward Ch'ang-an,
> I watch intently for his carved saddle,
> As, in evening glow, flowering shrubs and trees cover the
>   mountains
> Where heaped up mists in layers of jade arrest my distant gaze.
> Well, my heartless lover, where are you roaming the cloudy
>   mountains now?

Lyric II.6 Wei-sheng (Coda)

> With half a curtain of red sun this sad day now turns into evening,
> And my solitary lamp will burn far into the night.
> I don't at all resemble
> The way I looked then,
> Too listless to climb into my embroidered bed,
> No inclination to tend to comb and toilette
> And so thin and weak that my skirt is gradually bunching up!

Commentary: For "geese and fish letters" which appear in Lyric II.2, see the commentary to Lyric 15. The last line of Lyric II.4 is a pun on the song title "Someone Leaning on the Railing." Note that the next lyric, Lyric II.5, is actually composed to the tune "Tea Picking Song," an interesting ploy which heightens the dramatic realism of the song-set. In Lyric II.6, "bunches up" translates *tsan*, which normally means "hasten," "urge," or "hurry." Cheng Ch'ien suggests that *tsan* is here written for *tsuan*, "gather" or "bunch up," and comments: "Her waist is so thin that the span of her skirt must bunch up in order to conform with her figure."[41]

Lyric III Chung-lü, "Scenic Tour of the West Lake" (*CYSC*, pp. 378–81). This is a *nan-pei ho-tiao* (Medley of Southern and Northern Tunes)
Lyric III.1 Fen-tieh-erh (Butterflies), a northern tune

> Unportrayable on the light silk of a small fan,
> You're something that even the real P'eng-lai can't
>   surpass,
> Though you lack mountain and streams where 20,000 can
>   hold off a million.

Over there, embankments like inlaid gems link green
lowlands where there must be pavilions in the
hundreds!
I think to myself, "Tung-p'o
And Immortal Pu, who's there now to echo your poems?"

Lyric III.2 Hao-shih chin (A Marriage Is Near), a southern tune

Don't say how can the Phoenix Slope
Rival the glories of the Left Bank,
Since here are enough things to enjoy for an eternity,
Really, scenic spots as many as can be!
The mists envelop and the vapors enclose,
Forming emerald screens encircling the Six Bridges in
conch-shell shapes,
As blue-tinged cloudy mountains caress an azure sky
And water pure as pure-green jade buoys up golden waves!

Lyric III.3 Shih-liu hua (Pomegranate Blossoms), a northern tune

Now I see lotus pickers singing a lotus picker's song.
Really, this picturesque place surpasses all others!
Now there's that inverted image of a distant mountain plunged
into clear waves,
With its bright mists in links of kingfisher hue
And strange-shaped rocks thrusting precipitously.
Now I see sandgulls constantly dotting the lake's gleaming surface
As "Yi-yi and ya-ya"
The sounds of oars drift over.
Now I see this bashful beauty seated and shyly leaning on a
carved railing,
Just as if she were the Goddess of the Moon facing her Gem-
Studded Mirror!

Lyric III.4 Liao-ch'iao tung-feng (Chilly East Wind), a southern
tune

Why is it that
There's so much pleasure and enjoyment here?
With poetry friends and drinking companions singing along
And blossoms heavily made-up and the wine gorgeous,
Nothing can beat it for chasing away your troubles!
You can while away time in carefree delight

Or serenely sit and face the pure breeze and bright moon.
Whether it's a day in spring, summer, autumn, or winter,
To suit your mood, all the four seasons will do!

Lyric III.5 Tou an-ch'un (Squabbling Quails), a northern tune

As excited woodwinds and staccato strings make a noisy clamor
And orchid boats and painted barges form a tidy array,
There's a constant stream of delicate and dainty girls in
     powder and mascara,
Cloud after green-tinted cloud quivering all over in infinite
     number.
Really, this is an exquisite nest built by sifting the past and
     polishing the present!
If you don't believe me, take a look at
Its 10,000 wispy willows,
Its 10,000 red and ambrosial lotus blossoms!

Lyric III.6 P'u teng o (Moth Fluttering against the Lamp), a southern tune

As a fresh breeze brings the scent of marsh-orchids,
The moon bursts through mountain clouds
And provides a crystal-clear view of jade-green mist floating on the
     lake's sheen.
Clanging away, dawn bells ring out,
And apes make their "Wu-yeh-yeh" cries on the ancient ridges.
See the pairs and pairs of mandarin ducks sporting in the pure waves!
Way off in the distance, they look like fishing craft and angling skiffs,
Boats totally made of pure jade with hats of rain and coats of mist!

Lyric III.7 Shang hsiao-lou (Going Upstairs), a northern tune

How crowded and bustling it is over there,
And how dispersed and detached these few nests are!
Here I face bright mists,
Lean on blue mountains,
Steep myself in clear waves.
A fine rain just finished,
A thin mist just disappeared,
A gentle wind just stopped.
But really! Don't let me quote again, "Whether
     unadorned or all made up"!

Lyric III.8 P'u teng o (Moth Fluttering against the Lamp), a southern tune

Tier upon tier of storied buildings and decorated pavilions,
Cluster upon cluster of unusual flowers and exotic fruits,
Far in the distance, green sedges and rushes,
Spreading thickly, slopes of fragrant shrubs.
"Geh-deng geh-deng," with a clatter of hoofbeats,
In the dim distance, it seems as if Long Bridge is cantering across
    the waves!
Delicate and graceful, tiny flashes of green on the gold waves,
'Way off in the distance, look like fishing craft and angling skiffs,
Boats totally made of pure jade with hats of rain and coats of mist!

Lyric III.9 Wei-sheng (Coda)

In cloudy weather or bright, days endlessly are all filled with
    joy.
From ancient times till now, many have sung of your charms
Which, enhanced by snowy moon or wind-blown flowers, are
    pleasing in every way!

Commentary: Line 3 in Lyric III.1 alludes to the ancient state of Ch'in (present-day Shensi) which was blessed with natural strategic frontiers. For Tung-p'o and "Immortal Pu," see the commentary to Lyric 36. In Lyric III.2, Phoenix Slope (*Feng-huang p'o*) is a famous scenic spot near the West Lake. The Left Bank (Chiang-tso) refers to Chin-ling (Nanking), the site of various capitals of the Six Dynasties Era. The "Gem-Studded Mirror" (*pao-chien*) which appears in Lyric III.3 is an elaborate expression for the sun, but it could also here refer to the way the lake appears, as a beautiful mirror arrayed before the girl. Another possibility is that the lake and the girl are both so beautiful that they seem like the very sun and moon themselves. The last line of Lyric III.7 alludes to a poem by Su Shih; see the commentary to Lyric 6. Concerning the "Long Bridge" mentioned in Lyric III.8, an area at the southeast corner of the West Lake not far outside the Ch'ing-p'o men (Clear Waves Gate) of the old city wall was called Ch'ang-ch'iao (Long Bridge) into modern times, so it is likely that a bridge by that name was once there. The "clatter of hoofbeats," of course, is the water lapping at the bridge. Though the authorship of this song-set is in doubt,[42] both Jen Na and Sui Shu-sen attribute it to Kuan. The extremely sophisticated imagery is reminiscent of other lyrics by him, so I think the attribution is a likely one.

Lyric IV Ta-shih tiao, "Grievance" (*CYSC*, pp. 381–82)

Lyric IV.1 Hao Kuan-yin (Good Kuan-yin)

> Since first we met, we'd been a loving couple;
> Easy as can be, we became a pair of swallows, mated orioles.
> We used to sit together, shoulder to shoulder and holding hands,
> Like husband and wife, caring so for one another!

Lyric IV.2 Yao (Repeat) i.e., of *Hao Kuan-yin*)

I've asked around
And found out he's lately been crazy for song and drink;
Rumor has it
He's having an affair with some pretty young thing.
Cast off the old and love the new—there's always been that.
My hard-hearted man now doesn't think of his old sweetheart one bit!

Lyric IV.3 Wei (Coda)

> That heartless fellow's treated me so bad it's hard to bear,
> And when I think of him with that *ravishing*, that
>   *charming* thing at some drunken party,
> It's just so awful
> I can't stand it!

Lyric V Yüeh-tiao, "Remembering When We Parted" (*CYSC*, pp. 382–83)

Lyric V.1 Tou an-ch'un (Squabbling Quails)

> "My dear companion," I once wrote,
> "You have all the charms of a real beauty!
> You're slender and graceful,
> Attractive and fascinating,
> With a figure that is soft and tender,
> A heart honest and true.
> You're accomplished in all matters,

Well versed in all things.
Your marvelous dancing is most
  becoming,
Your clear singing even more beautiful."

Lyric V.2 *Tzu-hua-erh* (Violets)

We met unexpectedly
And fell immediately in love,
Then stayed constantly together.
Met last autumn,
We parted at the Double Five.
Wounded with sorrow,
We blended our tears and mixed in our sadness for the
  drink in our winecups.
When would we meet again?
Raising our eyes to the post-pavilion
And holding hands, we approached the parting of our ways.

Lyric V.3 *Chin chiao-yeh* (Golden Banana Leaves)

Before we even managed to finish "Song of Kuan Pass,"
The two words, "rank" and "fame," urged me to hurry on my way.
The saddest parting in all the world might be to leave one's native
  place,
But it will take more than an instant for me to forget my debt of
  love to her!

Lyric V.4 *T'iao-hsiao ling* (Poking Fun)

From Liu the Seventh's
Song Collection,
Arm in arm, we sing duets—it feels just like old times!
At a secret tryst, I've found my attractive and adorable beauty,
And, as if trees interlocking limbs or *chien* birds uniting wings,
We lie together asleep at a cloudy window, when I hear a cuckoo's cry
Which seems to have woken me out of a dawn dream elaborate in its
  illusion!

Lyric V.5 *T'u ssu-erh* (Bald Bonze)

I left the district city, sadly approached the Che River
And took up lodgings at Ch'ien-t'ang, heavy-hearted morning to night.

"Hurry, hurry!" The aura of travel about my whip urges me to go,
Spattered with pear blossoms
And pelted with rain
At Cold Food Time.

Lyric V.6 Sheng yao-wang (Sagely Medicine King)

The scenery here may be glorious,
But the fine days pass slowly.
The fragrant shrubs which stretch to the sky are just as thick and lush
      as can be,
And I'm here 10,000 miles away
From you at Chiu-i.
Those distant peaks, twelve in all, blurred by far-reaching mists,
Form a barrier to block my Wu-ling stream!

Lyric V.7 Wei (Coda)

Since parting from my jade-fair beauty, I remember it all in vain.
As did the ancients then, so do we look at the past now—
The evening rain? Clouds from Ch'u Terrace!
Peach Blossoms? The stream at Heavenly Grottoes!

Commentary: There are two hints that this song-set is not set in
Kuan's own day but during the Southern Sung dynasty. One is the
reference to Liu Yung's (fl. c. 1034) *Yüeh-chang chi* (Song Collection), a collection of *tz'u* written to Sung dynasty music which would
not have been sung in Kuan's day. The other hint occurs in Lyric
V.5 where the man leaves Chiu-i, a scenic mountainous region in
Hunan, and comes to take up office at Ch'ien-t'ang, that is, Hangchow, once the capital of the Southern Sung state. This suggests
that he used to serve in Chiu-i, but, being promoted to an office
at the capital, could not turn it down, since his desire for "rank"
and "fame" would not let him. The song-set should therefore be
read as a brief romantic drama set by the author in a bygone era.
In Lyric V.2, "Double Five" (*ch'ung-wu*) refers to the fifth day of
the fifth month, the day of the Dragon Boat Festival, which among
other things commemorates the suicide of Ch'ü Yüan. This is significant since the reason the man is leaving is to take up an official

post. The implication is that he should stay there with his girl and forget about it. In Lyric V.4 there occur three popular clichés. Trees with interlocking limbs (*lien-li*) and paired *chien* birds (the male and female had one wing and one eye each, so they united to fly) symbolize couples in love, though sometimes, such as here, they serve as more graphic metaphors. The cuckoo's cry is supposed to sound like *pu-ju kuei* (better go home). Its occurrence at this moment in the narrative is especially poignant. In Lyric V.5, Cold Food (*Hanshih*) is a festival which occurs on the third or fourth day of the fourth month. In the next lyric, the "Wu-ling stream" is a metaphorical one. T'ao Ch'ien's "Peach Blossom Spring" is placed in Wu-ling district (see the commentary to Lyric 47). In T'ao's account, a fisherman follows a stream to its source and finds a secluded utopia. As such, the "stream" in Kuan's lyric is the route back to the protagonist's lady love, a route blocked by the mountain barrier. The place where the lady is located, Chiu-i, is in the general area where the Peach Blossom Spring is supposed to have been. The second line in Lyric V.7, *ku yu chin chih shih hsi*, seems to be a paraphrase of a line in Wang Hsi-chih's (321–379) "Preface to the Orchid Pavilion Collection": "The way the future will look at our present is just the way we of the present look at the past."[43] That is, we look at things past in the same way as people did in antiquity and, considering the two lines that follow, express them in the same metaphors. The distraught lover sees evening rain and is reminded of the "Sunny Terrace" in Ch'u, of his moments of love with his beloved (see the commentary to Lyric 18). Then he sees the peach blossoms and is reminded of the following story: The Heavenly Grottoes (*T'ien-tung*) on T'ien-t'ai Mountain is the setting for the legend concerning Liu Ch'en and Juan Chao who are supposed to have lived sometime during the Eastern Han Dynasty (A.D. 25–220). They climbed T'ien-t'ai Mountain to gather herbs but lost their way. There they picked *peaches* at the mountain top, ate them, and drank water from the foot of the mountain. Later they met two women who entertained them for what seemed half a year, but when they made their way home, they discovered that seven generations had passed.[44] In the lyric, the protagonist likens himself to Liu and Juan. They were beguiled by the magic peaches and the fairy maidens, he by his craving for rank and fame, and, like them, he will not return until it is too late.

Lyric VI Yüeh-tiao, "My Delightful Companion" (*CYSC*, pp. 383–84)

Lyric VI.1 Tou an-ch'un (Squabbling Quails)

> My peerless beauty with her heavenly scent,
> Flesh of ice and bones of jade,
> Is a swallow chirping, an oriole warbling,
> A phoenix dancing to her mate's song.
> Moonlit nights and soft spring breezes mean
> Morning clouds and evening rain
> With my beautiful beloved,
> My pretty companion.
> But leaves fall and force autumn to return—
> They're flowers blooming which fill the roads!

Lyric VI.2 Chin chiao-yeh (Golden Banana Leaves)

> Seeing how her glances flirt with me,
> How could I ask for anything more!
> She says, "I've cast a brick but gained a gem!"
> But I say, "It's my profit from your misfortune!"

Lyric VI.3 T'ien-ching sha (Sand Clean as the Sky)

> Although we get along "like fish in water,"
> Hasn't every age been "short on truth and long on lies"!
> There might be idle gossip and superfluous chatter,
> But were I ever to let her down,
> I'd really have to be utterly immoral!

Lyric VI.4 Hsiao t'ao hung (The Little Peach is Red)

> Her intentions sincere and kind by nature above all else,
> There's nothing in the least to flaw her.
> At every chance, I seek her favors so we can care for one
>   another,
> And enjoy the pleasures of love.
> So when I visit, as soon as we meet we'll steal away for a tryst.
> She's a darling friend to be completely trusted,
> So all the tortuous love pangs she has caused me
> Won't at all be suffered in vain!

Lyric VI.5 Wei (Coda)

This patterned paper, sealed up and delivered, will be a Register of
   Predestined Lovers,
As this silk handkerchief, with her lingering scent, is a love pledge to
   me.
I always think how sweet will be her words when we meet,
And quickly forget my grief, here before the stars and beneath the
   moon!

Commentary: Line 3 in Lyric VI.1 refers to the lady's exquisite
singing. For "clouds and rain," see the commentary to Lyric 18. In
Lyric VI.3 the last line translates *tai-ku-li pu-hsin shen fo,* which
literally means: "I'd especially have to be someone who doesn't
believe in the Gods and in Buddha." For the "Register of Predestined Lovers" of Lyric VI.5, see the commentary to Lyric 4.

Lyric VII Shuang-tiao, New Year's Day at the Imperial Capital
                    (*CYSC*, pp. 384–85)

Lyric VII.1 Hsin-shui ling (New-Water Song)

Lush and abundant, an auspicious spirit inundates the whole land,
So let us celebrate the bountiful year and this time of universal peace.
The People are grateful,
And the State has no worries,
So let us look up with respect to the Imperial Capital
Where His Sagely Majesty has the Hundred Dieties to support Him!

Lyric VII.2 Chiao cheng p'a (Harmonizing Zither and Lute)

Our rivers and hills are blessed with riches,
And all in the world are joyfully obedient.
His Majesty is faithful and filial, generous and benevolent,
Outstanding in civil virtue as well as powerful in martial deeds
Whose accomplishments shake both Heaven and Earth!
The Army abides in happiness,
The People in contentment,
Since, relying on the Blessings of the Emperor, Army and
   People,
Together they find delight in this Earthly Paradise!

Lyric VII.3 Tien-ch'ien huan (Joy before the Palace)

Rivaling the eras of T'ang and Yü,
The *Chih-ta* Era of the Great Yüan Dynasty is without equal in ancient
  and modern times!
"Bridges which Span the Sea" face "Pillars which Support Heaven."
Arrayed in jade belts and golden tallies,
Here, blessed with wind and clouds, are our assembled dragons and
  tigers
With their marquisates of 10,000 households and salaries of a thousand
  bushels
Who shall spread glory throughout the world to last 10,000 years.
Three *Yang* combine in *T'ai*,
So may the five grains ripen when they should!

Lyric VII.4 Yüan-yang sha (Mandarin Duck Coda)

Gleaming spring dew from plum blossom boughs
Provides the taste of fragrant flavors in cups of peppered wine,
While the screens set out are made of mermaid silk,
The blinds rolled up of prawn whiskers.
Now we raise our voices and shout out,
"May Heaven Grant His Highness Long Life!"
Everyone then offers the most respectful prayer,
"May Your Virtue and Power Be Mighty!"
When all the officials receive the Dew of Imperial Favor,
With bows and posturings, they cry out at the tops of their voices,
"May You Our Illustrious and Sagely Ruler Live for Ten Thousand Ten
  Thousand Years!"

Commentary: The *chih-ta* era (Absolute Greatness) lasted from 1308
to 1311, so this song-set can be dated to the first day of 1309, 1310,
or 1311 in the Chinese calendar, but not to 1308, since Kuan still
held his military post of Myriarch Commander of Liang-huai until
after the first day of that year and would not have been in Peking
at that time. "Bridges which Span the Sea" and "Pillars which Support Heaven" are clichés much like "Pillar of the State" in English.
In the fifth line of Lyric VII.3 there is an allusion to the *Classic of
Changes*: "Clouds follow the dragon, wind follows the tiger. Thus
the sage arises, and all creatures follow him with their eyes."[45] Here
the "wind and clouds" refer to the grace emanating from a sagely
emperor; the "dragons and tigers" are men of heroic ability. *T'ai*

(Peace) is the eleventh hexagram in the *Classic of Changes* and consists of three upper broken (*yin*) lines and three lower unbroken (*yang*) lines. It is associated with the first month of the year. As such, the last two lines of Lyric VII.3 form a new year's salutation. The next lyric contains a reference to the fact that wine in which pepper was soaked is drunk at the new year. "Mermaids" translate *chiao* (shark people), for which see the commentary to Lyric 37. The screens are made of gauze as fine as that which fairy maidens and goddesses use for their stockings, and the bamboo blinds are so delicate they seem to be made of prawn whiskers.

Lyric VIII Shuang-tiao, no title (CYSC, pp. 385–86)

Lyric VIII.1 Tsui ch'un-feng (Intoxicating Spring Breeze)

> I'd be too embarrassed to paint on distant-mountain
>   eyebrows,
> Since it wouldn't suit these palace gowns.
> For no reason at all, I was summoned to this place of sorrow,
> The favor then granted all come to naught.
> I had to take the real self that I once had
> And immediately force it to be someone like this!

Lyric VIII.2 Chien chin ssu-k'uai yü (Four Pieces of Jade with Hidden Gold)

> From the first, my fated lover lacked courage,
> And I had the misfortune to have such pitiless parents.
> Truly, my family's wealth is an absolute misery,
> Since, for me, it's cruelly turned into an exile so far from him!

Lyric VIII.3 Chien-tzu mu-lan-hua (Magnolia Blossoms with Syllables Deleted)

> Right from the beginning, my sorrow has been a hundred-fold wound,
> And on top of that, now I've got to put up with autumn's splendor!
> Morning after morning I wait fixedly at the gate,
> Tremble at the approach of dusk,
> But what I really fear is that
> The sound of frontier horns will continue to linger!

Lyric VIII.4 Kao-kuo chin-chan-erh (Golden Goblet Passed High)

As I enter my orchid chamber,
It breaks my heart
To hear the blend of frontier geese honking and crickets chirping.
Aloes-and-musk incense is burned to the dregs,
And the silver lamp has gone completely out,
So I'm probably about to sleep a bit,
While outside my gauze-covered window a cool moon turns around the
   verandah.

Lyric VIII.5 Mai-hua sheng sha (Cry of the Flower Peddler Coda)

A swish of crimson curtains and, suddenly leaving my broidered bed
   drapes,
I find us together entering the nuptial chamber hand in hand,
But, on the point of telling him how much I love him, a dawn cock
   crows,
And, wakened out of my beautiful dream, I shed tears in ten thousand
   streams.
They all drip on top of the pillow.

Commentary: This song-set seems to concern a neglected palace
lady (the "palace-style gowns" [*kung-yang chuang*] of Lyric VIII.1)
who initially was granted the imperial favor of being selected by
the emperor but now languishes alone, the "favor come to naught."
Her situation is further complicated by the fact that she had fallen
in love before her "pitiless" (*hen-tu*) parents, seemingly motivated
by the rewards connected with their daughter's becoming a member
of the imperial household, presented her to the emperor. She implies, in Lyric VIII.2, that if her real love had approached her
parents before the imperial offer came, she would now be happily
married to him. The next lyric depicts her waiting at the gate to
her quarters for a summons from the emperor which never comes,
while still anxious for her "fated lover" who may be involved in the
fighting on the frontier (the lingering sounds of frontier horns). The
time of the song-set is autumn, something which emphasizes the
speeding on of another year and the passing of her youth; this is
the reason she is so upset about the autumn sounds of migratory
geese and crickets in Lyric VIII.4. The most poignant dimension
of her dilemma is saved for the last lyric, where she is tortured by
a dream of love which ends all too soon.

Lyric IX Nan-lü, "A Beautiful Lady in Love" (CYSC, pp. 1644-45)

Lyric IX.1 I-chih hua (A Bough of Blossoms)

Ginko leaves, yellow as duck's feet, withered and fallen,
Locust blossoms, purple as cockscombs, chilly and frail,
Red nutmegs, as if parrot's seeds, chewed to pieces,
And an emerald paulownia tree with branches for a phoenix to perch on
    and grow old.
I face the scene and sigh.
On the Yangtze here in Ch'u, wind-blown frost clips the wings of
    mandarin ducks,
While, as if at Wei City, willow-like mist envelops strands of kingfisher
    hue.
Stringing together yellow pieces of gold, chrysanthemum dew lies
    heavily,
Shattering green brocade, hibiscus blossoms rustle softly.

Lyric IX.2 Liang-chou (Liang-chou)

How lonely I sigh, my sad mood never ending.
How quickly I grieve, where did all that time go?
As if bursting out,
A spell of idle chagrin forces me to recall my old painful affair.
Though I've often expressed my grief on flowery note paper
And composed poetry on red leaves,
Which now have all become
Flying catkins on the wind,
Floating duckweed on the water,
I'm still painfully anxious I might snap these "Jade Interlocking Rings"
And am fearfully flustered I shall muddle this embroidered palindrome.
Wasted away to almost nothing, I face cosmetics and mirror box and
    listlessly brush on golden powder.
Gradually overtaken by sadness, here in my broidered boudoir I'm too
    tired to wield my needle.
Illness wearing me down, when plucking my embroidered zither I can't
    be bothered to set its golden bridges.
Thinking like this
And confronted by such things,
How very quickly, of the first three seasons of the year, two are gone.
Just now it's the beginning of the third, and soon it will be the first of
    the fourth.
Honking before the wind, a lonely goose
Starts in me a fit of sighing.

Lyric IX.3 Wei (Coda)

Goose, the song you're writing on the west wind seems to be in Ts'ang
    Chieh's script,
And, as you head toward the southern shore, it makes me sadder than
    anything Sung Yü wrote!
Precisely with spring, you went the other way,
And now, beating autumn, you're back again.
Much time has passed,
But little word has come from him.
You din on my ears,
Break my heart
And defeat my will!
Goose, you've stirred in me an infinite longing,
So why haven't you brought me at least a half-page letter from my lover!

Commentary: This song set is attributed to Chan Shih-yü (dates
unknown) in the *Ch'üan-Yüan san-ch'ü*, but its authorship is open
to debate.[46] It is attributed to Kuan in the original wood-block
edition published under the patronage of the Prince of Hui (*Hui-
fan pen*) of the *Tz'u-lin chai-yen* (Beauty Plucked from the Forest
of Lyrics) in 1525, and Jen Na includes it in his edition of Kuan's
lyrics in the *Suan-t'ien yüeh-fu*.[47] My feeling is that it could well
be by Kuan since the imagery in particular is reminiscent of many
of his lyrics. Lines 6 and 7 of Lyric IX.1 deserve comment. The
lady sees the mandarin ducks (symbolic of paired lovers) struggling
to take off from the river covered with whitecaps (the "wind-blown
frost") and the willows wrapped in mist which reminds her of Wang
Wei's famous poem of parting, the "Song of Yang Pass" (see the
commentary to Lyric 14), which is set at Wei City amidst willows
(symbolic of parting). The "strands of kingfisher hue" are, of course,
the willow branches in the scene before her. In the next lyric several
allusions occur. Line 6 alludes to the story of Madame Han and Yü
Yu, who are supposed to have lived during the reign of Emperor
Hsi (reigned 874–888) of the T'ang. Yü once happened to pick up
a red leaf out of the imperial moat and discovered a poem written
on it by a lady of the imperial household. Yü then wrote a poem
to the unknown lady on another leaf and put it into the upper part
of the moat so that it would float into the palace grounds, where
the lady found it. Later the emperor released some of his ladies
from service, Madame Han among them. She and Yü matched leaf-

poems, married, and lived happily ever after.[48] "Jade Interlocking Rings" is the name of a tune in the *ch'ü* repertoire, and "embroidered palindrome" (*chin hui-wen*) is an allusion to the story of the wife of Tou T'ou (mid-fourth century A.D.) who embroidered a palindrome in five colors to send to her estranged husband that so moved him that he took her back.[49] All of this means that although she has often written songs on paper and leaves and cast them on the waters of the river and to the wind she is still very careful how she is composing *this* lyric, i.e., the one by Kuan before us now. In the last lyric of this set, Ts'ang Chieh is the mythological hero who is supposed to have invented writing after observing the marks of birds on the banks of a river. Such writing would resemble the random pattern made by a goose bobbing up and down in the sky. Compositions attributed to Sung Yü (third century B.C.) are often concerned with the feelings of longing and separation. For "goose-borne" letter, see the commentary to Lyric 15.

Notes and References

Chapter One

1. The principal source for Kuan's biography is Ou-yang Hsüan (1283–1357), *Yüan ku han-lin hsüeh-shih chung-feng tai-fu chih chih-kao t'ung hsiu kuo-shih Kuan kung shen-tao pei* (Spirit-Way Stele Inscription of Mr. Kuan of the Yüan Dynasty, Former Member of the Imperial Academy, *Chung-feng* Grandee, Drafter of Imperial Edicts and Proclamations and Drafter of the History of the State), *KCWC*, 9.19b ff. This is translated in its entirety as Appendix I. Citations of the spirit-way stele inscription will be both to the original text and to the translation; this citation is *KCWC*, 9.22a, and Appendix I.13.
2. Francis W. Cleaves, "Chancellery Practice of the Mongols in the Thirteenth and Fourteenth Centuries," *HJAS*, 14 (1951), pp. 514–15.
3. *HYS*, 160.6926.3.
4. *MAC*, 13.12b.
5. *YSSTP*, 8342.46; *MWESC*, 92.1a.
6. *MAC*, 13.12b.
7. Francis W. Cleaves, "The Sino-Mongolian Inscription of 1362 in Memory of Prince Hindu," *HJAS* 12 (1949), p. 47, n. 52, and p. 104, n. 55.
8. *MAC*, 13.12b.
9. *MWESC*, 92.12b.
10. *MAC*, 13.12b.
11. The principal source for Arigh Qaya's biography is Yao Sui (1238–1313), *Hu-kuang hsing-sheng tso ch'eng-hsiang shen-tao pei* (Spirit-Way Stele Inscription of the Assistant Chief Administrator of the Left of Hu-kuang Province), *MAC*, 13.12a ff. The following biographical sketch is derived almost entirely from Yao's inscription; only when information is drawn from other sources will references be cited. Dates are sometimes supplied from *Hsü tzu-chih t'ung-chien* (Peking, 1958), Vol. 4.
12. See Francis W. Cleaves, "The Biography of Bayan of the Bārin in the *Yüan Shih*," *HJAS* 19 (1956), pp. 183–303.
13. The account of this recorded in *YS*, 128.6b–7a, has been translated

by A. C. Moule in "The Siege of Saianfu and the Murder of Achmach Bailo," *JNCBRAS* 59 (1927), pp. 11–12.

14. *YS*, 127.1b–2a; Cleaves, "Biography of Bayan," p. 209.

15. *YSSTP*, 8340.44; *YS*, 125.10b.

16. *YS*, 9.1–a.

17. *YS*, 128.11a, and *HYS*, 160.6927.1, for example.

18. *YS*, 14.6a–6b; *HYS*, 160.6927.1.

19. *YS*, 14.11a–11b.

20. See Appendix I.4.

21. *YSSTP*, 8342.46; *MWESC*, 92.6a; see also *YS*, 8.2a.

22. *MAC*, 13.18b.

23. *YS*, 127.4b; Cleaves, "Biography of Bayan," p. 219.

24. *HYS*, 160.6927.2; *MWESC*, 92.6b; *YSSTP*, 8342.46.

25. *MAC*, 13.18b.

26. *YSSTP*, 8342.46.

27. *MAC*, 13.18b.

28. This may have been merely a posthumously conferred title; there is no evidence that he ever actually held this office.

29. Qus Qaya's other titles and offices are listed in *YSSTP*, 8342.46, and in *MAC*, 13.18b.

30. Francis W. Cleaves explains this term in "Darugha and Gerege," *HJAS* 16 (1953), pp. 237–59.

31. *MAC*, 13.18b, gives this title as *hu-fu chien* Liang-huai *chün* (Supervisor of Military Prefectures in the Liang-huai Region, Who Holds the Tiger-Tally Badge of Office), and corresponds to an office once held by Arigh Qaya; namely, Supervisor of the Circuits (*lu*) of North China, i.e., the Huai-tung and Huai-hsi regions; see also *MWESC*, 92.1a–1b. In Kuan's spirit-way stele inscription (KCWC, 9.20b, and Appendix I.6) the title is Liang-huai *wan-hu-fu ta-lu-hua-ch'ih chen* Yung-chou (Garrison Commander and General of the Liang-huai Division with Headquarters at Yung-chou). It appears that the army which garrisoned Yung-chou (the center of the lower Hsiang River region) was originally composed in the days of the conquest of south China by troops recruited from the Liang-huai region by Arigh Qaya. The office of *wan-hu-fu* (literally "Myriarchy") of Liang-huai is the one Kuan inherited from his grandfather through his father. Now, a generation or two later, this army is still called the Liang-huai Myriarchy (Division).

32. *HYS*, 155.6917.3. In the stele inscription, he is identified as "the former Chief Administrator in the Central Chancellery." I have been unable to verify this in other sources, so it is likely that this is merely a posthumous title conferred upon him out of deference to the fact that his younger brother Hsi-hsien had once held this office.

33. A brief account in English of Lien Hsi-hsien's career can be found in L. C. Goodrich, "Westerners and Central Asians in Yüan China," *Oriente*

Poliano (Rome, 1957), p. 4 ff. The biographical sketch presented here, unless stated otherwise, derives entirely from his biography in *YS*, 126.4b–17b.

34. Lien Hsi-hsien's program included the establishment of a Chinese-style education system headed by Hsü Heng, the emancipation of Confucian scholars from slavery, and their registration as persons of privileged status, as well as the general implementation of strict standards of law and order.

35. See Hsü's biography in *YS*, 158.6b–21a, and Yao's biography in *YS*, 158.1a–6b.

36. In addition to their biographies in *YS*, see *Sung-Yüan hsüeh-an* (*Ssu-ch'ao hsüeh-an* ed.), 90.1689–1705.

37. This is discussed later in this chapter.

38. *KCWC*, 9.21a, and Appendix I.9. Yao, it should be remembered, composed Arigh Qaya's spirit-way stele inscription.

39. The account in *YS* which deals with this episode is translated in Ch'en and Goodrich, *Westerners and Central Asians in Yüan China under the Mongols* (Los Angeles, 1966), p. 245.

40. *HYS*, 32.23b; *YCHNP*, 8270.18.

41. *KCWC*, 9.20b, and Appendix I.6.

42. *HYS*, 32.6677.2–3; *YCHNP*, 8267.15.2.

43. *HYS*, 32.6677.3; *YCHNP*, 8262.10.2, has him transferred to this post in 1323. He would have been at least sixty at the time.

44. There is evidence that Kuan-chih-ko may have been something of a bonvivant with an eye for the ladies, if we can trust an entry in Hsia Po-ho's (late Yüan) *Ch'ing-lou chi* (Collection of Anecdotes about People of the Pleasure Quarters): "Chin shou-t'ou (Golden Gargoyle) was a famous courtesan from Hu-kuang [i.e., Wu-ch'ang]. Chief Administrator Kuan-chih-ko took her as his concubine, but when he died, she wandered from place to place in the Tung-t'ing Lake and Hsiang River region. Suan-chai [Kuan Yün-shih] once satirized her with a composition entitled 'An Old Crane Pecks for Food' " (*Ch'ing-lou chi* [*CKKT* ed.], p. 26). This may be spurious. Other sources indicate that Kuan-chih-ko outlived his son by at least two years (he still held office in 1326); this passage implies that Kuan wrote his satire *after* his father had died, and that would have been impossible. It also seems unlikely that Kuan would have satirized his own father's concubine, although, since we know nothing about his relationship with his father, this cannot be ruled out entirely.

45. *KCWC*, 9.20a, and Appendix I.5.

46. *KCWC*, 9.20a–20b, and Appendix I.5.

47. Another possible hero for Kuan is Hsi-hsien's younger brother, whose name is also romanized as Hsi-hsien, and who, as a *kuo-hsin shih* (Envoy Plenipotentiary) from Qubilai to the Sung during Bayan's southern campaign, was martyred in 1275 when Sung troops, mistakenly or perfid-

eously, attacked him and his guard; see *YS*, 127.8a, and Cleaves, "Biography of Bayan," p. 230.

48. In the stele inscription it is stated that Kuan's own daughter was "learned and knowledgeable and could write in an accomplished style." This might indicate that it was a tradition to educate the women in Kuan's family, something that may have begun with his mother.

49. *YS*, 126.5b; after Hsi-hsien's feat, everyone is supposed to have exclaimed: "What a combination of civil and military talent!"

50. As a grandson of the former Chief Administrator of Hu-kuang Province, Kuan would have had his first appointment somewhere in the province. This document is concerned with his misadventure in Chi-chou Commandery (Kiangsi) when he was about nineteen or twenty.

51. Preface to *Hsin-k'an ch'üan-hsiang Ch'eng-chai Hsiao-ching* (A New Edition of Ch'eng-chai's *Classic of Filial Piety, Completely Illustrated*, Peking, 1938, photolithographic reprint of the Yüan woodblock ed.).

52. *KCWC*, 9.20b, and Appendix I.6.

53. *Ibid*.

54. *Yao Sui nien-p'u* (Chronological Biography of Yao Sui) appended to *MAC*, 18b–19a.

55. *KCWC*, 9.20b-21a, and Appendix I.8.

56. *KCWC*, 9.21a, and Appendix I.8.

57. *YS*, 27.1a.

58. A treatment of this aspect of the work can be found in Yoshikawa Kōjirō, "Kan San-sai 'Kō-kyō chokkai' no zengo" (The Historical Context of Kuan Suan-chai's *Classic of Filial Piety with a Commentary in the Vernacular*), *Yoshikawa zenshū* (Tokyo, 1969), Vol. 15, pp. 319–32. For a study of the transmission of the work, see Hayashi Hideichi and Nagasawa Kikuya, "Gen-*kan hon* Sei-sai *Kō-kyō chokkai ni kan shite*" (Concerning the Yüan Edition of Ch'eng-chai's *Classic of Filial Piety with a Commentary in the Vernacular*), *Shoshigaku (Bibliography)*, Vol. 1, No. 5 (September 1933), pp. 411–13.

59. For Ayurbarwada's patronage of Neo-Confucianism, see John W. Dardess, *Conquerors and Confucians* (New York: Columbia University Press, 1973), pp. 35–37.

60. *Hsiao-ching (SSCCS* ed.), 5.1a.

61. *Hsiao-ching*, 6.4b.

62. Four characters are missing here.

63. *Li-chi (SSCCS* ed.), 51.16b.

64. Hsü's *Ta-hsüeh chih-chieh* is preserved in *chüan* 4 of *Lu-chai i-shu (SKCSCP* third series ed.); his *Chung-yung chih-chieh* (Doctrine of the Mean with a Vernacular Exegesis) is to be found in *chüan* 5.

65. See note 51.

66. See above, p. 22.

67. Yoshikawa points out that in the table of contents of the Ming

reprint edition of the *Lu-chai i-shu* there is listed a *Hsiao-ching chih-chieh* in *chüan* 3, followed by the note: "text missing." He also mentions the preface Ch'eng Chü-fu (1249–1318) wrote to a *Hsiao-ching chih-chieh* by a Mr. Ch'ien, which is preserved in Ch'eng's collected works, the *Ch'eng Hsüeh-lou wen-chi, chüan* 9. This too has not survived. See Yoshikawa, "Kuan's *Classic of Filial Piety*," *Zenshū*, Vol. 15, pp. 327–28.

68. *YS*, 24.2b.

69. The format closely resembles that of the vernacular historical tales published in illustrated editions by the Yü family from Chien-an, Fukien, during the Chih-chih era (1321–1323); see *Ch'üan-hsiang p'ing-hua wu-chung* (Five Completely Illustrated Vernacular Historical Tales, Peking, 1956).

70. Yoshikawa, *Zenshū*, Vol. 15, pp. 328–29.

71. A brief history of this faction and an outline of its ideology can be found in *Conquerors and Confucians*, pp. 328–29.

72. Ch'eng Chü-fu, *Ch'eng Hsüeh-lou wen-chi (Yüan-tai chen-pen chi-hui* ed.), 25.7a–7b, and Appendix IV; *KCWC*, 9.21a, and Appendix I.8.

73. *Ch'eng Hsüeh-lou wen-chi*, 25.7a–7b, and Appendix IV.

74. *KCWC*, 9.21a, and Appendix I.9.

75. *KCWC*, 9.19b, and Appendix I.1.

76. Teng Wen-yüan, *Pa-hsi chi (SKCSCP* third series ed.), A.55a–56a, and Appendix III.

77. See the preface to Poem 1 in Chapter Three. Although there is no evidence that Kuan knew Yü Chi at this time, we know from the circumstances surrounding Poem 30 that Kuan and Yü were acquainted later during Kuan's time of retirement at Hangchow, and, since Yü was a prominent Confucian educator who had enjoyed the patronage of Ayurbarwada, both before and after he became emperor, and was appointed to various scholarly posts by him (*YS*, 181.5a–5b), it is likely that they were acquainted during the period 1308–1317 as well.

78. Chahan figures in the preface to Poem 1; see the commentary to this poem in Chapter Three. A brief account of his life and literary career appears in Ch'en and Goodrich, *Westerners and Central Asians*, pp. 176–77.

79. See Poem 1 and Poems 14–18. Ch'en's biography is in *HYS*, 236.7049.2. He never held office under the Yüan but seems to have been well acquainted with many of the leading figures in government.

80. See Appendix I.8, III.1–3, and IV. Another acquaintance from the Imperial Academy and the Bureau of Historiography, Yüan Chüeh (1267–1327), highly praised Kuan's personal character and literary talent in a poem entitled "Sent to Reader-in-Waiting Kuan Suan-chai." See *Ch'ing-jung chü-shih chi (SPTK* ed.), 10.23b.

81. *YS*, 26.1b.

82. If we place Kuan's resignation in early 1317, this conflicts with Ou-

yang Hsüan's statement in the stele inscription that "after he resigned on the pretext of illness, he returned to the South and for more than ten years toured famous scenic places one after the other" (*KCWC*, 9.21b, and Appendix I.11). Since Kuan died on May 30, 1324, Ou-yang would have him resign as of the spring of 1314, just a little more than a year after he had taken up his post in the Imperial Academy. This can be shown to be in error. The evidence comes from Teng Wen-yüan's preface to Kuan's collected works. Teng states that it was after he had finished his appointment as *kuo-tzu ssu-yeh* (Vice-Director of Education) that he first met Kuan, and that shortly after that Kuan and he returned to the South (*Pa-hsi chi*, A.55a–55b, and Appendix III.1–2). Teng did not receive his appointment to the post of *kuo-shih yüan pien-hsiu kuan* (Editor in the Bureau of State Historiography) until 1317 (*HYS*, 206.7002.1), and it was then that Kuan and he "finally met." Teng filled this post only very briefly, for he was soon posted to Hangchow to become *chien* Chiang-nan Che-hsi *tao su-cheng lien-fang-ssu shih* (Supervisor of Branch Censorates of the Circuits of Che-hsi [i.e., Chekiang] in the South), this also in 1317. Teng's preface implies that it was Kuan who went to the South first, and this seems to corroborate the above assertion that Kuan resigned fairly early in 1317. It was therefore only seven years and a few months at most that Kuan lived after his resignation.

83. *KCWC*, 9.21a, and Appendix I.9.

84. *YS*, 24.28a–28b.

85. Kuan Yün-shih, preface to *Yang-ch'un pai-hsüeh*, la.

86. *KCWC*, 9.21a, and Appendix I.10.

87. *Ibid.* This is not entirely accurate since Ayurbarwada authorized the implementation of rules concerning dress and fixed sumptuary regulations during early 1315; however, Mongols and other non-Chinese were largely exempted from them (*YS*, 78.13a). If this authorization was made as a compromise response to Kuan's memorial, we can date the memorial to the end of 1314 or early 1315.

88. The man Kuan tutored as a child, Shidebala, became emperor in 1320 (Ying-tsung), at which time he gave his entire support to the Neo-Confucian faction at court and even permitted a purge of the non-Chinese financial ministers. The purge was halted in mid-course, and the financial ministers assassinated Shidebala and began their own counter-purge of the pro-Confucian forces. See *Conquerors and Confucians*, pp. 37–38. Dardess does make the point, however, that it had been Ayurbarwada's policy to play off the Neo-Confucian faction against the financial ministers in order to achieve a balance of interests in the Central Chancellery. Whatever the reasons, Kuan failed to receive the emperor's support.

89. Teng Tzu-chin, preface to *Ch'ao-yeh hsin-sheng t'ai-p'ing yüeh-fu* (Peking, 1955), p. 3.

90. Facsimiles of three seals appear at the end of Kuan's preface in the

Yüan woodblock edition: Ssu-yu t'ang, Shu-lan yeh-jen, and Ch'eng-chai. I assume that all three are Kuan's; Yang Tsung-han concludes that they are in his article "Hsiao-Yün-Shih Khaya," p. 95, n. 30.

91. *Wen-hsüan* (*SPPY* ed.), 43.2b. A complete translation of the letter by James R. Hightower appears in Cyril Birch, ed., *Anthology of Chinese Literature*, Vol. 1 (New York, 1965), pp. 162–66.

92. Preface to *Yang-ch'un pai-hsüeh*, 1b.

93. Recorded in Liu I-ch'ing, *Shih-shou hsin-yü* (New Specimens of Contemporary Anecdotes,) (*SPPY* ed.), CA.40a–40b.

94. By 1317 there was a heavy volume of shipping between points east and southeast of Peking and the mouth of the Yangtze. See H. F. Shurmann, *Economic Structure of the Yüan Dynasty* (Cambridge, Massachusetts, 1956), pp. 108–30. Poem 12, written soon after Kuan was appointed to the Imperial Academy, seems to suggest that either Kuan had originally come north by sea or at least that this poem to a friend who lives in the South was going to be delivered by sea.

95. It is possible that Kuan visited these places on other occasions, but since no mention is made of such a trip in the other sources, I assume that these poems must date from the time of his trip south after his resignation. The cynicism and disappointment readily apparent in some of them rule out the possibility that they date from *before* his assumption of office in Peking in 1308/9.

96. *KCWC*, 9.22a, and Appendix I.14.

97. *Ming shih-lu* (Taipei, 1962–1967), 32.7b.

98. *KCWC*, 9.22a, and Appendix I.14.

99. *Ibid.*

100. *KCWC*, 9.22a, and Appendix I.12.

101. T'ao Tsung-i, *Cho-keng lu* (*TSCC* ed.), 26.399. This is Poem 29.

102. *Hsi-hu yu-lan chih* (Peking, 1958), p. 86. The *Ch'ien-t'ang hsien-chih* (*WLCKTP* ed.) in the section entitled *Chi-hsien* (Recording the Cultural Heritage), 32a, states that Kuan had built a retreat on Lung-hua shan (Lung Shan or Wo-lung shan); this would have been several miles farther south. Ou-yang Hsüan in the stele inscription (*KCWC*, 9.21b, and Appendix I.12) says that his retreat was located on Pao-shan southeast of Feng-huang shan (Phoenix Mountain). The *Jen-ho hsien-chih* (*WLCKTP* ed.), 9.3b, agrees with the *Hsi-hu yu-lan chih*. In any event, the general location of the retreat is unquestioned.

103. *Jen-ho hsien-chih*, 9.3b.

104. *KCWC*, 9.21b, and Appendix I.11. See also Ku Ssu-li's biographical sketch of Kuan at the head of *Suan-chai chi* (*YSH*), 1b, and Appendix II; *Pa-hsi chi*, A.56a, and Appendix III.3; *Jen-ho hsien-chih*, 9.3b–4a; *Ch'ien-t'ang hsien-chih*, *Chi-hsien*, 32a.

105. The notices on Kuan in *Hsi-hu yu-lan chih*, *Jen-ho hsien-chih*, and *Ch'ien-t'ang hsien-chih* bear ample witness to this.

106. See *Suan-chai chi*, 1b, and Appendix II. The gentry see through his disguise at once and recognize him by name.

107. *Suan-chai chi*, 1b, and Appendix II.

108. There is a biographical sketch of Chang at the head of the section devoted to his lyrics in *CYSC*, I, p. 755.

109. *CYSC*, I, p. 830. This lyric has been preserved in five different sources; all except *Yao-shan t'ang wai-chi* (compiled by Chiang I-k'uei during the late Ming) have *Hsi-niao* (Stream Bird) instead of *Yu-ts'ao* (Secluded Shrub) in the eighteenth line, the first of four lines borrowed from Kuan's "A Valedictory Poem to the World" (Poem 29). The variant version in *Yao-shan t'ang wai-chi* is the preferred reading because it accords with the earliest known text of the lines as they are preserved in the *Cho-keng lu*; see above, note 101.

110. *Chiu-chia chi-chu Tu-shih* (Harvard–Yenching Institute Sinological Index Series Supplement No. 14), 22.2.3.

111. *KCWC*, 9.20b, and Appendix I.11.

112. *Suan-chai chi*, 1b, and Appendix II.

113. Poems 3, 8, 11, 19, and 21 all appear to date from his years in retirement and to some extent refer to Taoism; see also Lyrics 61 and 73.

114. *KCWC*, 9.19b, and Appendix I.1.

115. *KCWC*, 9.22a, and Appendix I.12.

116. See note 102 above.

117. *KCWC*, 9.21b, and Appendix I.12.

118. Ming-pen taught at his retreat called the Ssu-men, the "Gate of Death," where one passes from one incarnation to another, in the T'ien-mu (Eyes of Heaven) Mountains about fifteen miles to the northeast of Hangchow; see *Hsi-hu-yu-lan chih*, pp. 277–78.

119. His poetry is contained in *YSH* under the title *Chung-feng kuang-lu* in the *erh-chi* (second series).

120. *Hsi-hu yu-lan chih*, p. 278; see also Ch'en and Goodrich, *Westerners and Central Asians*, pp. 83–85.

121. *CYSC*, I, pp. 771, 776–77, 777–78, 795, 830, 888, 916.

122. *CYSC*, I, p. 771.

123. *CYSC*, I, pp. 776–77.

124. Note the statement in Ou-yang's inscription which alludes to Kuan's continuing interest in affairs of state (*KCWC*, 9.22a, and Appendix I.12).

125. *CYSC*, I, p. 795.

126. An entry in *Lu-kuei pu* (A Register of Ghosts) suggests that Yang Chü-erh may have been the author of the drama *Ch'in t'ai-shih tung-ch'uang shih fan* (Grand Preceptor Ch'in Plots a Crime beneath the Eastern Window, *YCHWP* No. 125), which is usually attributed to K'ung Wen-ch'ing.

127. *CYSC*, I, pp. 830–31.

128. *Ch'ing-lou chi*, p. 30.

129. See note 44 above.

130. See *CYSC*, I, p. 288.

131. *Ibid*, I, pp. 630–31.

132. *Ibid.*, II, pp. 1171–72.

133. *Ibid.*, II, p. 1175.

134. *Ibid.*, II, pp. 1297–98.

135. See note 89 above.

136. According to the *Ryō-Kin-Gen jin denki sakuin* (Index to Biographical Materials for Figures of the Liao, Chin and Yüan Dynasties, Kyoto, 1972), p. 197, Teng Wen-yüan had one son, Teng Yen. This may be the same person as Teng Tzu-chin, since Tzu-chin may be a *tzu* (personal name). For the origin of the Teng clan in Mien-chou and its subsequent move to Hangchow, see Teng Wen-yüan's biography in *HYS*, 206.7002.1.

137. See Jen Na's preface to *Suan-t'ien yüeh-fu* (*SCTK* ed.), 1a.

138. Yao T'ung-shou, *Lo-chiao ssu-yü* (*Pao-yen t'ang mi-chi* ed.), 24a–24b. Ch'en and Goodrich, *Westerners and Central Asians*, p. 179, romanizes this title as *Yüeh-chiao ssu-yü* (Private Chats from the Land of Music); this is incorrect. *Lo-chiao* is an allusion to the *Shih-shu* (Big Rats) poem in the *Shih-ching* (Classic of Poetry). See James Legge, *The Chinese Classics*, Vol. 4 (Hong Kong, 1960), p. 172, where the expression is translated as "happy borders." The contents of Yao's short work also argue against taking *lo-chiao* as *yüeh-chiao*; although this passage which deals with Yang Tzu and Kuan concerns music, much of the rest of the work does not.

139. *YS*, 210.12a. Ch'en and Goodrich, *Westerners and Central Asians*, p. 179, n. 476, refers to this episode in Yang's life as well, but has confused the *Chih-yüan* era of Qubilai's reign (1280–1294) with the era of the same name which occurs later during the reign of Toqon Temür (Hsün-ti) (1335–1340), thus misdating the expedition to Java.

140. *Lo-chiao ssu-yü*, 24b–25a.

141. Ch'en Chi, *I-pai chai kao wai-chi*, (*SPTK* third series ed.), 44b–45a.

142. T'ao Tsung-i, *Shu-shih hui-yao* (*TSCC* ed.), 7.17a.

143. An Ch'i, *Mo-yüan hui-kuan lu* (*Yüeh-ya t'ang ts'ung-shu* ed.), 2.47b; see also Yang, "Hsiao-Yün-Shih Khaya," pp. 98–99 and notes 50 and 51.

144. *Ming-shih* (Kaiming ed.), 126.7397.1 ff.

145. Yang, "Hsiao-Yün-Shih Khaya," p. 98, notes 48 and 49.

146. *Pei-chuan chi* (1893 ed.), 48.31a.

147. Wang K'o-yü, *Shan-hu wang hua-lu* (*Shih-yüan ts'ung-shu* ed.), 20.12b.

148. *YS*, 143.14b.

149. *YS*, 113.1a–1b.

150. *YS*, 113.7a.

151. *YS*, 42.16b.

152. *KCWC*, 9.22a, and Appendix I.14.

153. *HYS*, 32.6680.4.
154. *Ming shih-lu*, 32.7b.
155. *KCWC*, 9.22a, and Appendix I.14.
156. The expression "maid of Wu" (Wu-*chi*) occurs in several of Li Po's poems, "A Keepsake Poem Written in a Wine Shop in Chin-ling" and "With Wine before Me" (cf. *Li T'ai-pai chi* [*KHCPTS* ed.], 15.59 and 25.46, for example). These poems and Li's "Water Song" (*Shui-tiao ko*) are all romantic celebrations of wine, women, and song. Sa-tu-la implies here that Kuan has been able to create "something new."
157. Sa-tu-la, *Sa T'ien-hsi shih-chi* (Taipei, 1970), p. 42. Lu-kang, in Anhwei, was situated where a stream of that name enters the Yangtze.
158. Ou-yang Hsüan, *KCWC*, 9.19b–23a.
159. Ku Ssu-li, *YSH*, *erh-chi* (Second Series), *ping-chi* (Third Collection): *Suan-chai chi*, 1a–1b.
160. Teng Wen-yüan, *Pa-hsi chi* (*SKCSCP* third series ed.); the lacuna in line one of page A.55a has been amended by reference to tḥɘ *ch'ao-pen* (handwritten copy) of Yüan or early Ming date preserved in the National Central Library, Taiwan.
161. Ch'eng Chü-fu, *Ch'eng Hsüeh-lou wen-chi*, 25.7a–7b.
162. *Yüan tien-chang* (*Kōteibon Gentenshō keibu*, Vol. 2, Kyoto, 1970), pp. 533–34. By the time the directive was given to cashier the officers involved, Kuan had already become the Garrison Commander at Yung-chou.

Chapter Two

1. Western studies of Yüan *shih* poets have been almost exclusively concerned with painters who also happen to have written *shih*, and then mostly as biographical data. See, for example, Helga Kuntze-Schroff, *Das Leben und Dichtung des Ni Tsan* (Bombay, 1959). Chuang Shen, *Yüan-chi ssu hua-chia shih chiao-shih* (Poetry of Four Landscape Masters of the Late Yüan Period, Hong Kong, Centre of Asian Studies, University of Hong Kong, Occasional Papers and Monographs, No. 12) is typical of modern Chinese scholarship on the subject. One of the very few historical and critical surveys of Yüan *shih* is Yoshikawa Kōjirō, *Gen Min shi gaisetsu* (Introduction to Yüan and Ming Poetry, Tokyo, 1963).
2. An analysis of this dimension of the significance of the *Yüan-shih hsüan* appears in John D. Langlois, "Ku Ssu-li, the *Yüan-shih hsüan*, and Loyalism in Late Seventeenth-Century China," unpublished paper, October 1975.
3. Ku K'uei-kuang, ed., *Yüan-shih hsüan* (1751), and Shen Chün-te, ed., *Yüan-shih pai-i ch'ao* (also called the *Yüan-shih pieh-ts'ai chi*, 1764), for example.

4. Cf. my "Tradition and the Individual: Ming and Ch'ing Views of Yüan Poetry," *Journal of Oriental Studies* 15, No. 1 (January 1977), pp. 1–19, which also appears in a slightly different version in Ronald C. Miao, ed., *Studies in Chinese Poetry and Poetics*, Vol. I (Taipei, 1978).

5. From Li's biography in *Ming-shih*, 286.7794.1. High T'ang (*sheng-T'ang*) was the era of Li Po, Tu Fu, etc.

6. For instance, P'an Shih-jen's *Sung Yüan ssu-shih-san chia chi* (Poetry of Forty-three Masters of the Sung and the Yüan) was published in 1615 and has a lengthy preface by Yüan Chung-tao, the youngest of the Yüan brothers.

7. One entire section (*chüan* 6) of the *wai-p'ien* (Part II) of his *Shih-sou* (Thicket of Remarks on Poetry), comprising fifty-six items, is devoted to it.

8. Hu Ying-lin, *Shih-sou* (Taipei, 1973), *wai-p'ien*, 6.222.

9. This view becomes orthodox in the following century and extremely widespread in Ch'ing dynasty criticism, as we shall see in the following pages.

10. See Wang Shih-chen, *Ch'i-yen shih fan-li* (Principles for Selection of Seven-Syllabic Verse), *Ku-shih hsüan* (SPPY ed.), 3a, and Sung Lo, *Man-t'ang shuo shih* (*Ch'ing shih-hua* [I-wen yin-shu kuan] ed.), 1a–1b.

11. Sung Lo, preface to *YSH*, 2a.

12. Ku Ssu-li, *YSH*, *fan-li*, 1a.

13. Eighteenth-century pro-T'ang neo-archaists included such figures as Shen Te-ch'ien (1674–1769) and Weng Fang-kang (1733–1818); pro-Sung expressionists included such figures as Li O (1692–1753) and Chao I (1727–1814), as well as Yüan Mei.

14. Shen Chün-te, preface to *Yüan-shih pai-i ch'ao* (KHCPTS ed.), p. 1.

15. Usually in criticism, the two Li's of the T'ang refer to Li Ho and Li Shang-yin, but in this case we know that Yang was a close student of Li Po and Li Ho in the *yüeh-fu* form; see *Gen Min shi gaisetsu*, p. 96.

16. Ku Ssu-li, *Han-t'ing shih-hua* (*Ch'ing shih-hua* ed.), 2a–2b.

17. Kao Ping (1350–1423), whose *T'ang-shih p'in-hui* (A Classified Anthology of T'ang Verse) is one of the cornerstones of the Ming *fu-ku* (archaist) movement, makes this point in the *hsü-mu* (introduction) to a group of poets he calls *chieh-wu* ("successors" or "retracers"): "Alas! In the catastrophe of the T'ien-pao era [the rebellion of An Lu-shan] the ether of the Three Luminaries and the Five Sacred Mountains dispersed, and the character of the men of the day began to fall short of true excellence, thus the *wen-t'i* (form of literary art) began to change." See *T'ang-shih p'in-hui* (woodblock ed. of 1628–1644), *wu-yen ku-shih hsü-mu*, 10b. From Kao's critical remarks as a whole, it is obvious that we can take "began to change" to mean "began to decline": the decline of T'ang institutions after the *T'ien-*

pao era occasioned the decline of T'ang poetry, the corollary being that the prosperity and strength of institutions before the rebellion were the causes for the greatness of High T'ang verse.

18. Ku Ssu-li, *Han-t'ing shih-hua*, 2b.

19. This is an allusion to Tu Fu's famous line: "If my poetry doesn't startle people, I won't stop working at it till I die!" See *Chiu-chia chi-chu Tu-shih*, 409.30.2.

20. T'ao K'un-mou and T'ao K'un-ku apparently were neighbors of Ku K'uei-kuang in Hsi-shan District, and Ku published their *Yüan-shih tsung-lun* at the head of his short anthology of Yüan verse; the *Yüan-shih hsüan*, in 1751. The reference is to page 5b.

21. See Li Shang-yin's biography of Li Ho in *Li I-shan wen-chi* (*SPTK* ed.), 4.20b.

22. Ku K'uei-kuang, preface to *Yüan-shih hsüan*, 1b–2a.

23. James J. Y. Liu, *The Art of Chinese Poetry* (Chicago, 1962), p. 102.

24. James J. Y. Liu, *The Poetry of Li Shang-yin* (Chicago, 1967), p. 245.

25. Yoshikawa Kōjirō analyzes the expression *pei-wo* in his annotated translation of *K'u-han t'ing* (Icy Cold Pavilion); see *Genkyoku Kokukan tei* (*Yoshikawa zenshū*, Vol. 15), pp. 145–46.

26. In a study to be published soon, "Alternate Routes to Self-realization in Ming Theories of Poetry," I attempt to extract from the *Ts'ang-lang shih-hua* the qualities Yen yü attributes to the *shih* of the T'ang and the Sung eras.

27. Some earlier Yüan poets, still very much in the tradition of Sung dynasty philosophical verse, wrote a great deal of philosophical poetry. Liu Yin in particular is famous for this. For some examples in English translation, see Frederick W. Mote, "Confucian Eremetism in the Yuan Period," A. F. Wright, ed., *The Confucian Persuasion* (Stanford, California, 1960), pp. 215–16, 225–26, 227–28.

28. *The Poetry of Li Shang-yin*, p. 32.

Chapter Three

1. *Ch'eng Hsüeh-lou wen-chi*, 15.7b–8a.

2. *Li T'ai-pai chi*, 13.21.

3. See David Hawkes, *The Songs of the South* (Boston, 1962), p. 107.

4. See Wong Siu-kit, *The Genius of Li Po, A.D. 701–762* (Hong Kong, Centre of Asian Studies, University of Hong Kong, Occasional Papers and Monographs, No. 19), the section entitled "Woman and Moon in Li Po's Poetry," pp. 7–22.

5. *Li T'ai-pai chi*, 15.59.

6. Translation by James J. Y. Liu in *The Poetry of Li Shang-yin*, p. 52.

7. See *The Poetry of Li Shang-yin*, p. 66.

8. See *Wen-hsüan*, 16.6b.

9. Li Ho, *Li Ch'ang-chi ko-shih* (Shanghai, 1959), p. 67.
10. See Edward H. Schafer, *The Divine Woman: Dragon Ladies and Rain Maidens in T'ang Literature* (Berkeley, California, 1973), pp. 38–42, 57–70.
11. *Chuang-Tzu yin-te* (Harvard–Yenching Institute Sinological Index Series Supplement No. 20), p. 1.
12. *Chiu-chia chi-chu Tu-shih*, 21.1.17.
13. See *Shan-hai ching* (*SPPY* ed.), 16.5b–6a.
14. See *Chuang-Tzu yin-te*, p. 1.
15. Huang T'ing-chien, *Shan-ku ch'üan-chi* (*SPPY* ed.), 16.7a.
16. *Li Ch'ang-chi ko-shih*, p. 35.
17. *Chuang-Tzu yin-te*, p. 90.
18. See Chang Yen-yüan, *Li-tai ming-hua chi* (A Record of Paintings in Successive Dynasties) (*Hua-shih ts'ung-shu* ed.), 7.90.
19. See *YS*, 71.12b.
20. Hao Ching, *Ling-ch'uan chi* (*YSH* ed.), 18a.
21. See *Han-fei tzu* (*SPPY* ed.), 4.10a–10b.
22. See *Shan-hai ching*, 7.2b.
23. Chiang I, ed., *Huang-Yüan feng-ya* (*SPTK* ed.), 1.5b.
24. See *Hsin T'ang-shu* (Kaiming ed.), 202.4102.3.
25. *Li T'ai-pai ch'üan-chi*, 30.30.
26. See the commentary to Poem 3 and Schafer, *The Divine Woman*, pp. 61, 64, 66, 94, 101, 108–109.
27. Sung Hsü, ed., *Yüan-shih t'i-yao* (*SKCSCP* third series ed.), 3.10a–10b.
28. See *Shih-chi* (Kaiming ed.), 7.0032.2–3.
29. See *KCWC*, 9.21b, and Appendix I.11.
30. See *Han kuan-tien chih-i* (*SPPY* ed.), 3b.
31. *Chiu-chia chi-chu Tu-shih*, 296.9.1.
32. *Yüan-shih t'i-yao*, 10.22a.
33. See *The Songs of the South*, pp. 134, 149.
34. The preface and the text of Ch'en's poem are preserved in Ch'en Wen-shu, *Hu-shan huai-ku lu* (A Collection of Recollections Concerning Antiquities from the [West] Lake and [Surrounding] Mountains, *WLCKTP* ed.), 14b–15a.
35. See James Ware, trans., *Alchemy, Medicine, Religion in the China of A.D. 320: The Nei P'ien of Ko Hung (Pao-p'u tzu)* (Cambridge, Massachusetts, 1966), p. 301.
36. See Nathan Sivin, *Chinese Alchemy, Preliminary Studies* (Cambridge, Massachusetts, 1968), p. 294.
37. *Ibid.*, p. 186.
38. Burton Watson, trans., *The Complete Works of Chuang Tzu* (New York, 1968), p. 188.
39. Watson, *Chuang Tzu*, p. 134.

40. *Wei-chih* (Kaiming ed.), 24.0987.4.

41. *Lieh-tzu* (*SPPY* ed.), 2.13a.

42. Ku K'uei-kuang, *Yüan-shih hsüan*, 6.7b.

43. *Ch'üan T'ang-shih* (Peking, 1960), 372.6.4179.

44. See above, pp. 30–31.

45. See Lu Chi (261–303), "In Imitation of 'Today Is a Fine Feast' " (*Ni chin-jih liang yen-hui*), *Ch'üan Chin-shih* (*CHNPCS* ed.), 3.15a.

46. *Li Ch'ang-chi ko-shih*, p. 122.

47. See above, Chapter One, p.48, and the commentary to Lyric 79 in Chapter Five. A brief biographical notice on A-li hsi-ying appears in *CYSC*, I, p. 631.

48. See Wang Chih-chien, *Piao-i lu* (*TSCC* ed.), 1.7.

49. See *Shih-chi*, 123.0267.1.

50. *Chiu-chia chi-chu Tu-shih*, 472.34.3–4.

51. The "Nirvana Perfected One" (*Ni-wan chen-jen*) is a title appropriate to some Taoist adept. *Ni-wan*, a term obviously borrowed from Buddhism, in Taoism refers to the *tan-t'ien* (field of cinnabar) in the brain, one of three such fields in the body where the so-called "internal pill of immortality" can supposedly be formed. See Henri Maspero, *Le Taoism*, Vol. II (Paris, 1950), p. 19. As such, *Ni-wan chen-jen* is a term anachronistic to the setting of this poem in the third century B.C. "Crimson Palace" (*chiang-kung*) is a Taoist term for the mind; this line therefore seems to mean that the "Perfected One" has taken leave of his senses!

52. Yen-chih was a Hsiung-nu term for the wife of a noble, especially in the case of the Khan or the Heir-Apparent; see *Shih-chi*, 110.0242.1–4.

53. In the Hsiung-nu tribal hierarchy there were a number of *wang* (princes); for instance, there were Hsien wang of the Left and the Right and Lu-li wang of the Left and the Right; see *Shih-chi*, 110.0244.4.

54. "Sprinkle grievances in the heart" translates *chiao lin-hsü*, which literally means "sprinkling the rugged mountain peaks," or perhaps "pouring libations to the rugged mountain peaks." However, this seems reminiscent of a statement in the *Shih-shuo hsin-yu*, CA.48a: "Wang Fu said, 'Since there was *lei-k'uai* in Juan Ch'i's [210–268] breast, he had to sprinkle [*chiao*] wine on them.'" This is apparently the origin of the expression, common still in modern Chinese, *hsiung-chung lei-k'uai* (grievances in the heart). *Lei-k'uai* or *k'uai-lei* literally means "piles and clods," the irregular, upset feeling in the heart. It is likely that the expression *lin-hsün* (craggy, jagged [peaks]) means the same thing.

55. This is an allusion to the story of the guest of Lo Kuang (d.304) who saw a reflection of a bow, which was hanging on the wall, in his winecup and thought it to be a snake. See *Chin-shu* (Kaiming ed.), 43.1202.1.

56. Chih Yao was a man of the state of Chin of the Warring States era (403–221 B.C.). He is supposed to have ignored his father's warning that, if not diligent, he would lose his territory. He lost it as predicted. This

allusion to him here seems inappropriate. Chu Fan seems to have borrowed the name Chih Yao to identify Lo Kuang's guest, whose name is not mentioned in the records.

57. Mao-tun succeeded his father, T'ou-man, as Khan after he had him assassinated. Mao-tun trained his cavalry to shoot, under penalty of death, at what he shot at with a special arrow fitted with a "singing arrowhead." When he shot at his father, the Khan, his men dispatched him in a volley of arrows. See *Shih-chi*, 110.0244.4. Since Mao-tun could have his own father murdered, how could the Yüeh-chih king expect any mercy from him!

58. Chu Fan, *tzu* Fan-yüan, was a native of Yü-shan in Kiangsi. This poem is preserved in *Yüan-shih t'i-yao*, 5.6a–6b.

59. *Chiu-chia chi-chu Tu-shih*, 542.4.3–4.

60. Chou Mi, *Ch'i-tung yeh-yü* (*TSCC* ed.), 10.119–20.

61. K'ang Hsi, nominal ed., *Yü-ting li-tai t'i-hua shih lei* (woodblock ed. of 1677), 32.11b.

62. See the biography of *Huang T'ing-chien* in *Sung-shih* (Kaiming ed.), 444.5619.1.

63. See Chapter One, p. 40.

64. See above, pp. 39–40.

65. *Lieh-tzu*, 7.3b.

66. Juan Yüan, *Liang-che chin-shih chih* (*Shih-k'o shih-liao ts'ung-shu* ed.), 18.57a.

67. Yang Yü, *Shan-chü hsin-hua* (*Pi-chi hsiao-shuo ta-kuan* ed.), 23a. See also Herbert Franke's translation of Yang's work, *Beiträge zur Kulturgeschichte Chinas unter der Mongolenherrschaft: Das Shan-kü sin-hua des Yang Yü* (Wiesbaden, 1956), pp. 128–30.

68. Ku Ssu-li, *YSH, fan-li*, 1b.

69. See Ku Ssu-li, *Lü-ch'iu hsien-sheng tzu-ting nien-p'u* (*Ping-tzu ts'ung-pien* ed.), 10a. John D. Langlois mentions this fact in "Ku Ssu-li, the *Yüan-shih hsüan*, and Loyalism in Late Seventeenth-Century China."

70. Huang Yü-chi, *Ch'ien-ch'ing t'ang shu-mu* (*Liao Chin Yüan i-wen chih* ed.), p. 280.

71. See *KCWC*, 9.21b, and Appendix I.11.

72. Lang Ying, *Ch'i-hsiu lei-kao* (Shanghai, 1961), p. 494.

73. Huang Yü-chi's activities in this project are described in the *ch'u-pan shu-ming* (Explanation Concerning the Publication) to the Commercial Press edition of the *Ming i-wen chih* (Peking, 1959), pp. 2 ff.

74. *KCWC*, 9.22a, and Appendix I.12.

75. Ou-yang Hsüan notes the various kinds of prose writings that Kuan composed in *KCWC*, 9.23a, and Appendix I.12.

76. *Ch'eng Hsüeh-lou wen-chi*, 25.7b, and Appendix IV.

77. The editors of the *Ssu-k'u ch'üan-shu*, in their *t'i-yao* (résumé of annotations) to the *T'an ching-chün*, suggest that Hsü was active during

the *Ch'eng-hua* era of the Ming (1465–1487). See this notice which heads the edition included in the *SKCSCP*, second series.

78. Hsü Po-ling, *T'an ching-chün*, 11.15b.

79. This collection of short stories in the T'ang *ch'uan-ch'i* style is a sequel to a similar collection entitled *Chien teng hsin-hua* (New Stories to Tell after Trimming the Lamp) by Ch'ü Yu (1341–1427).

80. The story of Liu Ying and Chao Luan-luan apparently inspired a *nan-hsi* (Southern Drama) of the late Yüan or early Ming entitled *Liu Ying* which is now lost. See Feng Yüan-chün, ed., *Nan-hsi shih-i* (Taipei, reprint of the Harvard–Yenching Institute ed., 1969), 2.207–208.

81. Fan Su was the beautiful singing girl whom Po Chü-i had taken as a concubine; see Arthur Waley, *The Life and Times of Po Chü-i* (New York, 1949), p. 196.

82. Li Chen, *Chien teng yü-hua* (Shanghai, 1957), pp. 207–208.

83. Two of the anthologies which contain *shih* by Kuan, the *Sung Yüan ssu-shih-san chia chi* (F in the Finding List) and the *Yüan-shih hsüan* (G in the Finding List) attribute poetry to him which is actually by his contemporary, Yüan Chüeh. The former, compiled by P'an Shih-jen, includes eight *lü-shih* which can be found in Yüan's collected works, the *Ch'ing-jung chü-shih chi*: two poems entitled *Sung Wang Chi-hsüeh*, 10.8b; *Kuan-wu*, 11.2a–2b; *Chi K'ai-yüan K'uei lü-shih*, 12.13b; *Wu-t'i tz'u Ma Po-yung yün ssu-shou*, 10.14b–15a. The latter, compiled by Ts'ao Hsüeh-ch'üan, contains four of these eight: *Chi Wang Chi-hsüeh* and three of the four *Wu-t'i tz'u Ma Po-yung yün* poems. Since Ts'ao's anthology appeared fifteen years later than P'an's, Ts'ao probably copied his selection from P'an, thus repeating his error. P'an and Ts'ao also both refer to Kuan as having the *tzu* (personal name) of Fu-ts'en (Ephemeral Mountain[s]). There is no other corroborating source, nor has it been possible to determine whose personal name this might have been, since it does not appear to have anything to do with Kuan.

Chapter Four

1. See *CYSC*, I, pp. 208–16.

2. See *CYSC*, I, pp. 154–91, 230–77.

3. The only other sources of Yüan date which deal with the general nature and function of the *san-ch'ü* are: Teng Tzu-chin's preface to *Ch'ao-yeh hsin-sheng t'ai-p'ing yüeh-fu* (1351), certain parts of Chou Te-ch'ing's (fl. c. 1300–1325) *Tso tz'u shih-fa* (Ten Sets of Rules for Composing Lyrics) (*SKTK* ed.), and the various prefaces to Chou Te-ch'ing's *Chung-yüan yin-yün* (A Rhyme Book in the Pronunciation of the Central Plain), with a preface dated 1324, *CKKT* ed., especially those by Yü Chi, Ou-yang Hsüan, and by Chou himself. A complete translation of the Teng Tzu-chin preface

appears in my "Some Attitudes of Yüan Critics toward the *San-ch'ü*," *Literature East and West* 16, No. 3 (1974), pp. 951–55.

4. *Yang-ch'un pai-hsüeh* (White Snow of Sunny Spring) was originally the title of a melody popular in the ancient state of *Ch'u*. It is mentioned, for instance, in the *Tui Ch'u-wang wen* (In Reply to a Question from the King of Ch'u) by Sung Yü (fl. late third century B.C.); see *Wen-hsüan*, 45.1b–2a.

5. Preface to *Yang-ch'un pai-hsüeh*, 1a–1b.

6. See Wayne Schlepp, *San-ch'ü: Its Technique and Imagery* (Madison, Wisconsin, 1970), p. 3, n. 1, and my "Some Yüan Critics," p. 950.

7. Preface to *T'ai-p'ing yüeh-fu*, p. 3.

8. Chu Tung-jun, *Chung-kuo wen-hsüeh p'i-p'ing shih ta kang* (Taipei, 1968), p. 215.

9. See Schlepp, *San-ch'ü*, pp. 10–11; the translations of *hao-fang* and *ch'ing-li* are my own.

10. See Chapter One, pp. 41–42 and pp. 44–46.

11. For example, Ou-yang Hsiu's (1007–1072) lyrics *(tz'u)* were appended in three *chüan* as *Chin-t'i yüeh-fu* (Modern Ballads) to his collected works, the *Ou-yang Wen-kung ch'üan-chi* (*SPTK* ed.).

12. See Chapter One, pp. 49–50.

13. Chu Ch'üan, *T'ai-ho cheng-yin p'u* (*CKKT* ed.), p. 18.

14. See Chapter One, p. 50. Teng Wen-yüan praised Kuan in similar terms in his preface to Kuan's collected works; see Appendix III.3 at the end of Chapter One.

15. Chu Ch'üan, *T'ai-ho cheng-yin p'u*, pp. 146–47.

16. *Ibid.*, pp. 167–68.

17. *Ibid.*, p. 168.

18. *Ibid.*

19. *Ibid.*, p. 172.

20. *Ibid.*, pp. 16–18. The twelve writers are: Ma Chih-yüan, Chang K'o-chiu, Pai P'u, Li Shou-ch'ing, Ch'iao Chi, Fei T'ang-ch'en, Kung T'ien-t'ing, Wang Shih-fu, Chang Ming-shan, Kuan Han-ch'ing, Cheng Kuang-tsu, and Pai Pi (in that order).

21. Wang Shih-chen (1526–1590), *Ch'ü-tsao* (*CKKT* ed.), p. 25.

22. Li Tiao-yüan, *Yü-ts'un ch'ü-hua* (*CCKT* ed.), p. 7.

23. Two of these have survived: *Fan Chang chi shu* (Mr. Chang has a Chicken and Millet Meal Prepared for Mr. Fan, *YCH*, No. 55) and *Ch'i-li t'an* (Seven Mile Beach, *YCHWP*, No. 127).

24. Wang Shih-chen (1634–1711), *Ts'an-wei hsü-wen* (A Supplementary Collection of Writings from the Silkworm's Tail, *Tai-ching t'ang chi* ed.), 14.6a.

25. See Chapter One, pp. 49–50.

26. Jen Na, *Ch'ü-hsieh* (*SCTK* ed.), 1.4a.

27. *Ibid.*, 1.4b.

28. *Ibid.* Chou's criticism of Lyric 1 appears in *Tso tz'u shih-fa*, 4.16a–16b.

29. Jen Na, *Ch'ü-hsieh*, 1.5a.

30. Cheng Chen-to, *Ch'a-t'u-pen Chung-kuo wen-hsüeh shih*, Vol. 4 (Hong Kong, 1965), p. 736.

31. Liu Ta-chieh, *Chung-kuo wen-hsüeh fa-chan shih* (Taipei, 1968), pp. 773–74.

32. *Ibid.*, p. 774. Lo Chin-t'ang's critical survey of Kuan's lyrics in *Chung-kuo san-ch'ü shih*, Vol. 1 (Taipei, 1956), pp. 773–74, is so much derived from the remarks of Liu Ta-chieh that it does not warrant separate attention here.

33. Place names have not been included in this count unless they seem to have some functional significance. The many references to places in the Hangchow–West Lake region are so numerous that to include them, for example, would have been to distort the real amount of allusion involved.

34. Almost all the allusions in Kuan's lyrics can be found indexed in the *Chūgoku koten gikyoku goshaku sakuin* (An Index to Explanations of Terms which Appear in Chinese Classical Drama, Nagoya, 1970).

35. See Chapter Two, p. 80.

36. See James R. Hightower, *The Poetry of T'ao Ch'ien* (Oxford, 1970), pp. 124–63.

37. An analysis of the *san-ch'ü* from the point of view of the difference between its use of Literary Chinese and Vernacular Chinese has been pioneered by Tanaka Kenji in "Gendai *sankyoku* no kenkyū" (Study of Yüan Dynasty *San-ch'ü*), *Tōhōgaku* 15 (1969), pp. 1–114.

38. James I. Crump, "The Ch'ü and Its Critics," *Literature East and West* 16, No. 3 (1974), pp. 968–69.

39. Tanaka Kenji argues this point most convincingly in "Sankyoku 'Ko-so kan kyō' kō' " (A study of the *San-ch'ü* "Kao-tsu Returns to His Village"), *Yoshikawa haku-shi taikyū kinen Chūgoku bungaku ronshū* (Tokyo, 1968), pp. 569–87; see also Crump, "The Ch'ü and Its Critics," pp. 967 ff.

Chapter Five

1. Chang Hsiang, *Shih tz'u ch'ü yü tz'u-hui shih* (A Glossary of Terms Found in *Shih*, *Tz'u*, and *Ch'ü*, Taipei, 1968), p. 722.

2. Hsü Chia-jui, *Chin Yüan hsi-ch'ü fang-yen k'ao* (A Study of Dialect Terms in Dramas of the Chin and the Yüan, Shanghai, 1956), p. 36, and supplement, p. 19. *I-fu*, in this context, is explained by Chiang Hsiang as "a fellow brothel patron who shares the same prostitute, equivalent to the modern facetious term *t'ung-hsüeh* (boot-sharer); see *Shih tz'u ch'ü yü tz'u-hui shih*, p. 722. *I-fu* literally means "auntie's husband."

3. *Ch'üan Sung-tz'u*, Vol. 1, T'ang Kuei-chang, comp. (Shanghai, 1965), p. 278.

4. *Chiu-chia chi-chu Tu-shih*, 397.23.4.

5. Su Shih, *Tung-p'o chi* (*Tung-p'o chi ch'i-chung* [*SPPY* ed.]), 4.7a.
6. *Ch'üan Han-shih* (*CHNPCS* ed.), 2.13a.
7. *Han-shu* (Kaiming ed.), 54.0492.2.
8. *Wen-hsüan*, 19.1a.
9. For a thorough treatment of this motif, see Schafer, *The Divine Woman*, pp. 73–88.
10. *Shih tz'u ch'ü yü tz'u-hui shih*, pp. 719–22.
11. *I-ching: Chou I yin-te* (A Concordance to Yi Ching), Harvard–Yenching Institute Sinological Index Series Supplement No. 10), 1.1 *ch'u, hsiang, yen*.
12. *Shih-chi*, 71.0194.4.
13. *Shih-chi*, 32.0123.3.
14. See the commentary to Lyric 3.
15. *K'ai-yüan T'ien-pao i-shih*, Wang Jen-yü, comp. (*Hsü pai-ch'uan hsüeh-hai* ed.), 2b.
16. For an annotated translation of these two lyrics, see Irving Lo, *Hsin Ch'i-chi* (New York, 1971), pp. 90–92.
17. *Ch'üan Sung-tz'u*, Vol. 1., p. 225.
18. *Li Chang-chi ko-shih*, p. 46.
19. The play is now lost, but it may have inspired the vernacular short story, *Ch'ien-t'ang meng* (author unknown), which is prefaced to the 1498 edition of *Hsi-hsiang chi* (The Western Chamber) by Wang Shih-fu (included in the *Ku-pen hsi-ch'ü ts'ung-k'an*, first series).
20. See *CYSC*, I, 366.
21. For a treatment of how this motif figures in the poetry of Li Shang-yin, see *The Poetry of Li Shang-yin*, pp. 45, 51.
22. See Chapter One, p. 44.
23. Wang Wei, *Wang Yu-ch'eng chi chien-chu* (*SPPY* ed.), 7.12a.
24. *Chin-shu* (Kaiming ed.), 81.1293.3.
25. *Li Ch'ang-chi ko-shih*, pp. 164–65.
26. Translation by James R. Hightower, *The Poetry of T'ao Ch'ien*, p. 79.
27. *Ch'üan Sung-tz'u*, Vol. 1, p. 228.
28. *The Poetry of Li Shang-yin*, p.78.
29. Translation by James Legge, *Confucian Analects, The Chinese Classics*, Vol. 1., p. 212.
30. *Chin Yüan hsi-ch'ü fang-yen k'ao*, p. 23.
31. *CYSC*, I, p. 812.
32. Han Yü, *Ch'ang-li hsien-sheng chi* (*SPPY* ed.), 3.7a.
33. Chou Tzu-chih (b. 1082), *Chu-p'o shih-hua* (Talks on Poetry from the Bamboo Slope, *Li-tai shih-hua* ed.), 14b–15a.
34. *CYSC*, I, pp. 787–88.
35. See Wang I's preface to the *Li-sao* in his *Ch'u-tz'u chang-chü* (*SPTK* ed.), 1.1b.
36. See *The Songs of the South*, p. 91.

37. See James Legge, *The She King or Book of Poetry, The Chinese Classics*, Vol. 4., p. 61.

38. *CYSC*, I, 338–39.

39. Quoted in *CYSC*, I, 631.

40. Meng Ch'i, *Pen shih-shih* (*Li-tai shih-hua hsü-pien* ed.), 1a.

41. Cheng Ch'ien, *Ch'ü-hsüan* (Taipei, 1967), p. 66.

42. See *CYSC*, I, 379.

43. *Ch'üan Chin-wen* (*Ch'üan shang-ku-tai Ch'in Han San-kuo Liu-ch'ao wen* ed.), 26.10a.

44. *T'ai-p'ing yü-lan* (*SPTK* ed.), 41.2b–3a.

45. Richard Wilhelm, trans., *The I Ching, or Book of Changes* (English translation by Cary F. Baynes), Vol. 2 (New York, 1950), p. 15.

46. See *CYSC*, II, 1645.

47. Jen Na, comp., *Suan-t'ien yüeh-fu* (*SCTK* ed.), 1.14a–15a.

48. Liu Fu, *Ch'ing-so kao-i* (Shanghai, 1958), pp. 46–49.

49. *Chin-shu*, 96.1335.2.

Selected Bibliography

ABBREVIATIONS

CHNPCS = *Ch'uan Han San-kuo Chin Nan-pei-ch'ao shih.* Edited by Ting-fu-pao. Taipei: Shih-chieh shu-chü, 1962. 3 vols.

CKKT = *Chung-kuo ku-tien hsi-ch'ü lun-chu chi-ch'eng.* Peking: Chung-kuo hsi-chü ch'u-pan she, 1959. 10 vols.

CYSC = *Ch'uan Yüan san-ch'ü.* Edited by Sui Shu-sen. Peking: Chung-hua shu-chü, 1964. 2 vols.

HJAS = *Harvard Journal of Asiatic Studies.*

HYS = *Hsin Yüan-shih.* Kaiming.

JNCBRAS = *Journal of the North China Branch of the Royal Asiatic Society.*

Kaiming = K'ai-ming Book Company edition of the *Erh-shih-wu shih* and the *Erh-shih-wu shih pu-pien.*

KCWC = *Kuei-chai wen-chi* (see under Ou-yang Hsüan below).

KHCPTS = *Kuo-hsüeh chi-pen ts'ung-shu.*

MAC = *Mu-an chi* (see under Yao Sui below).

MS = *Monumenta Serica.*

MWESC = *Meng-wu-erh shih-chi* (see under title below).

SCTK = *San-ch'ü ts'ung-k'an.* Edited by Jen Na. Taipei: Chung-hua shu-chü, 1964. 4 vols.

SKCSCP = *Ssu-k'u ch'üan-shu chen-pen.*

SPPY = *Ssu-pu pei-yao.*

SPTK = *Ssu-pu ts'ung-k'an.*

SSCCS = *Shih-san ching chu-shu.* Notes by Juan Yüan. Shanghai: Chin-chang t'u-shu chü, 1932.

TP = *T'oung-pao.*

TSCC = *Ts'ung-shu chi-ch'eng ch'u-pien.*

WLCKTP = *Wu-lin chang-ku ts'ung-pien.*

YCH = *Yüan-ch'ü hsüan.* Edited by Tsang Mao-hsün. Peking: Chung-hua shu-chü, 1958. 4 vols.

YCHNP = *Yüan hsing-sheng ch'eng-hsiang p'ing-chang cheng-shih nien-piao.* Kaiming.

223

YCHWP = *Yüan-ch'ü hsüan wai-pien.* Edited by Sui Shu-sen. Peking: Chung-hua shu-chü, 1961. 3 vols.
YS = *Yüan-shih. Po-na-pen* ed.
YSH = *Yüan-shih hsüan* (see under Ku Ssu-li below).
YSSTP = *Yüan-shih shih-tsu piao.* Kaiming.

1. Pre-Modern Chinese Works

Ch'ao-yeh hsin-sheng t'ai-p'ing yüeh-fu. Edited by Yang Chao-ying. Peking: Hsin-hua shu-chü, 1955.
CHENG CHÜ-FU. *Ch'eng-hsüeh lou wen-chi. Yüan-tai chen-pen chi-hui* ed.
CHU CH'ÜAN. *T'ai-ho cheng-yin p'u. CKKT* ed.
Huang Yüan feng-ya. See item A in the Finding List at the end of Chapter Three.
KU SSU-LI. *Yüan-shih hsüan.* Woodblock ed. of 1694, 1702 and 1720.
KUAN YÜN-SHIH. *Hsin-k'an ch'üan-hsiang Ch'eng-chai Hsiao-ching chih-chieh.* Peking: Lai-hsün-ko, 1938 photolithographic reprint of the Yüan woodblock ed.
————. *Suan-chai-chi. YSH* ed.
Meng-wu-erh shih-chi. Edited by T'u Chi. Woodblock ed. of 1934.
OU-YANG HSÜAN. *Kuei-chai wen-chi. SPTK* ed.
Sung Yüan ssu-shih-san chia chi. See item F in the Finding List at the end of Chapter Three.
T'ai-p'ing yüeh-fu. See *Ch'ao-yeh hsin-sheng t'ai-p'ing yüeh-fu.*
Yang Ch'un pai-hsüeh. Edited by Yang Chao-ying. *SCTK* ed.
Yü-ting t'i-hua shih-lei. See item L in the Finding List at the end of Chapter Three.
Yüan-shih hsüan. See under Ku Ssu-li.
Yüan-shih hsüan. Edited by Ku K'uei-kuang. See item N in the Finding List at the end of Chapter Three.
Yüan-shih t'i-yao. See item C in the Finding List at the end of Chapter Three.
Yüan tien-chang. Kōteibon Gentenshō keibu, Vol. 2. Kyoto: Research Institute of Humanistic Studies, 1970.

2. Modern Works in Chinese and Japanese

CHIANG HSIANG. *Shih tz'u ch'ü yü hui-shih.* Taipei: Chung-hua shu-chü, 1968.
CHENG CHEN-TO. *Ch'a-t'u-pen Chung-kuo wen-hsüeh shih.* Hong Kong: Commercial Press, 1965. 4 vols.
CHENG CHIEN. *Ch'ü-hsüan.* Taipei: Hua-kang, 1967.
CHU TUNG-JUN. *Chung-kuo wen-hsüeh p'i-p'ing shih ta-kang.* Taipei: Kaiming shu-tien, 1968.

Chūgoku koten gikyoku goshaku sakuin. Nagoya: Saika shorin, 1970.
Ch'üan Yüan san-ch'ü. Edited by Sui Shu-sen. Shanghai: Chung-hua shu-chü, 1964. 2 vols.
Hsü Chia-jui. *Chin Yüan hsi-ch'ü fang-yen k'ao.* Shanghai: Commercial Press, 1956.
Jen Na. *Ch'ü-hsieh. SCTK* ed.
Liu Ta-chieh. *Chung-kuo wen-hsüeh fa-chan shih.* Taipei: Chung-hua shu-chü, 1968.

3. Works in Western Languages

Chen Yüan. *Westerners and Central Asians in Yüan China under the Mongols; their Transformation into Chinese.* Translated by Ch'ien Hsing-hai and L. C. Goodrich. Los Angeles: University of California Press, 1966.
Crump, James I. "The *Ch'ü* and Its Critics," *Literature East and West* 16, No. 3 (1974), pp. 961–79.
Dardess, John W. *Conquerors and Confucians.* New York: Columbia University Press, 1973.
Lynn, Richard J. "Some Attitudes of Yüan Critics toward the *San-ch'ü,*" *Literature East and West* 16, No. 3 (1974), pp. 950–60.
Schlepp, Wayne. *San-Ch'ü: Its Imagery and Technique.* Madison: University of Wisconsin Press, 1970.
Yang Tsung-han. "Hsiao-Yün-Shih Khaya (1286–1324)," *MS* 9 (1944), pp. 92–100.

Index